The last two decades have witnessed 'the return of the peasant' to South Asian history. New empirical research and innovative methodologies have enabled this historical reconstruction of agrarian economies, politics and society in colonial and post-colonial India. In this key volume in the *New Cambridge History of India*, Professor Sugata Bose presents a critical synthesis of existing scholarship and offers a new interpretation of agrarian continuity and change from 1770 to the present.

The author examines the related themes of demography, commodity production, agrarian social structure, and changing forms of peasant resistance. Agrarian relations are addressed along lines of gender and generation as well as class and community. By focussing on 'peasant labour', Bose integrates the histories of land and capital. He also explores the relationship between capitalist development of the economy under colonial rule and elements of both change and continuity at the point of primary production and appropriation.

Although the author draws most of his empirical material from rural Bengal, he makes important comparisons with regional agrarian histories across India and beyond. *Peasant Labour and Colonial Capital: Rural Bengal Since 1770* is essential reading for the understanding of rural India's colonial and post-colonial experience. It is also of relevance to all those interested in agrarian societies in the developing world and debates about the origins and character of agrarian capitalism.

# THE NEW CAMBRIDGE HISTORY OF INDIA

*General editor* GORDON JOHNSON

Director, Centre of South Asian Studies, University of
Cambridge, and Fellow of Selwyn College

*Associate editors* C. A. BAYLY

*and* JOHN F. RICHARDS

Professor of History, Duke University

Although the original *Cambridge History of India*, published between 1922
and 1937, did much to formulate a chronology for Indian history and
describe the administrative structures of government in India, it has
inevitably been overtaken by the mass of new research published over the
last fifty years.

Designed to take full account of recent scholarship and changing conceptions of South Asia's historical development, *The New Cambridge History
of India* will be published as a series of short, self-contained volumes, each
dealing with a separate theme and written by a single person, within an
overall four-part structure. As before, each will conclude with a substantial
bibliographical essay designed to lead non-specialists further into the
literature.

The four parts are as follows:

I The Mughals and their Contemporaries.

II Indian States and the Transition to Colonialism.

III The Indian Empire and the Beginnings of Modern Society.

IV The Evolution of Contemporary India.

A list of individual titles already published and in preparation will be found at the end
of the volume.

# THE NEW CAMBRIDGE HISTORY
# OF INDIA

*Peasant Labour and Colonial Capital:*
*Rural Bengal Since 1770*

Bengal landscapes, Gopal Ghosh

# THE NEW CAMBRIDGE HISTORY OF INDIA

III:2

*Peasant Labour and Colonial Capital:*
*Rural Bengal Since 1770*

SUGATA BOSE

ASSOCIATE PROFESSOR OF HISTORY, TUFTS UNIVERSITY

CAMBRIDGE
UNIVERSITY PRESS

Published by the Press Syndicate of the University of Cambridge
The Pitt Building, Trumpington Street, Cambridge CB2 1RP
40 West 20th Street, New York, NY 10011–4211, USA
10 Stamford Road, Oakleigh, Victoria 3166, Australia

First published 1993

Printed in Great Britain at the University Press, Cambridge

*A catalogue record for this book is available from the British Library*

*Library of Congress cataloguing in publication data*

Bose, Sugata.
Peasant labour and colonial capital: rural Bengal since 1770 /
Sugata Bose.
p.   cm. – (The New Cambridge History of India: III.2)
Includes bibliographical references and index.
ISBN 0 521 26694 7
1. Peasantry – India – Bengal – History. 2. Bengal (India) –
Colonization – History. 3. Bengal (India) – Industries – History.
4. Bengal (India) – Rural conditions. I. Title. II. Series.
DS436.N47   1987
[HD1537.I4]
954 s–dc20
[305.5′633′095414]   92–12666   CIP

ISBN 0 521 26694 7 hardback

TO MY PARENTS
SISIR KUMAR BOSE
AND
KRISHNA BOSE

# CONTENTS

# ILLUSTRATIONS

## MAPS

## FIGURES

# TABLES

# GENERAL EDITOR'S PREFACE

*The New Cambridge History of India* covers the period from the beginning of the sixteenth century. In some respects it marks a radical change in the style of Cambridge Histories, but in others the editors feel that they are working firmly within an established academic tradition.

During the summer of 1896, F. W. Maitland and Lord Acton between them evolved the idea of a comprehensive modern history. By the end of the year the Syndics of the University Press had committed themselves to the *Cambridge Modern History*, and Lord Acton had been put in charge of it. It was hoped that publication would begin in 1899 and be completed by 1904, but the first volume in fact came out in 1902 and the last in 1910, with additional volumes of tables and maps in 1911 and 1912.

The *History* was a great success, and it was followed by a whole series of distinctive Cambridge Histories covering English Literature, the Ancient World, India, British Foreign Policy, Economic History, Medieval History, the British Empire, Africa, China and Latin America; and even now other new series are being prepared. Indeed, the various Histories have given the Press notable strength in the publication of general reference books in the arts and social sciences.

What has made the Cambridge Histories so distinctive is that they have never been simply dictionaries or encyclopedias. The Histories have, in H. A. L. Fisher's words, always been 'written by an army of specialists concentrating the latest results of special study'. Yet as Acton agreed with the Syndics in 1896, they have not been mere compilations of existing material but original works. Undoubtedly many of the Histories are uneven in quality, some have become out of date very rapidly, but their virtue has been that they have consistently done more than simply record an existing state of knowledge: they have tended to focus interest on research and they have provided a massive stimulus to further work. This has made their publication doubly worthwhile and has distinguished them intellectually from other sorts of reference book. The editors of the *New Cambridge History of India* have acknowledged this in their work.

The original *Cambridge History of India* was published between 1922 and 1937. It was planned in six volumes, but of these, volume 2 dealing with the period between the first century AD and the Muslim invasion of India never appeared. Some of the material is still of value, but in many respects it is now out of date. The last fifty years have seen a great deal of new research on India, and a striking feature of recent work has been to cast doubt on the validity of the quite arbitrary chronological and categorical way in which Indian history has been conventionally divided.

The editors decided that it would not be academically desirable to prepare a new *History of India* using the traditional format. The selective nature of research on Indian history over the past half-century would doom such a project from the start and the whole of Indian history would not be covered in an even or comprehensive manner. They concluded that the best scheme would be to have a *History* divided into four overlapping chronological volumes, each containing about eight short books on individual themes or subjects. Although in extent the work will therefore be equivalent to a dozen massive tomes of the traditional sort, in form the *New Cambridge History of India* will appear as a shelf full of separate but complementary parts. Accordingly, the main divisions are between I. *The Mughals and their Contemporaries*, II. *Indian States and the Transition to Colonialism*, III. *The Indian Empire and the Beginnings of Modern Society*, and IV. *The Evolution of Contemporary India*.

Just as the books within these volumes are complementary so too do they intersect with each other, both thematically and chronologically. As the books appear they are intended to give a view of the subject as it now stands and to act as a stimulus to further research. We do not expect the *New Cambridge History of India* to be the last word on the subject but an essential voice in the continuing debate about it.

# PREFACE

In writing this work of synthesis and interpretation I have felt indebted to several recent generations of at least two unorganized academic collectivities – agrarian historians of India spread out across at least three continents and, more parochially, Bengali scholars and the intellectual tradition they have sustained despite the tribulations of the twentieth century. Most of these debts are explicitly or implicitly acknowledged in the text of this volume. But I would like to mention especially the late Eric Stokes, who taught me in Cambridge. Among the many people from whom I have learnt much over the years from personal exchanges the works of the following have had a direct bearing on the arguments of this book: Shapan Adnan, Partha Chatterjee, Binay Bhusan Chaudhuri, Rajat Kanta Ray, the late Ratnalekha Ray, Tapan Raychaudhuri and Amartya Sen.

I have greatly benefited from comments made on the drafts of this book by C. A. Bayly, David Ludden and David Washbrook. Chris Bayly has helped not only with his criticism and encouragement but also by setting the standards for this series as well as the field in general. I would also like to thank Chris and Susan Bayly for their hospitality during my visits to Cambridge. I am sure that ideas generated during my many conversations with David Washbrook in Cambridge, Massachusetts, have found their way into this book. I am grateful to Gordon Johnson and John Richards for their interest in this work.

Grants from the Social Science Research Council of the USA and the Faculty Research Awards Committee of Tufts University have helped fund research for this project. I have drawn on the resources and goodwill of many libraries and archives in South Asia, the UK and the USA, especially the India Office Records and Library in London. I wish to thank Gill Thomas of Cambridge University Press for overseeing the publication process and Janet Hall for her meticulous copy-editing.

Among my many helpful friends and colleagues at Tufts University Leila Fawaz and Sol Gittleman must be specially mentioned for their enthusiastic support. My sister Sarmila and brother Sumantra have

xv

provided intellectual stimulation and warm affection. Ayesha Jalal has contributed much to this volume while at the same time reminding me that there is more to life than agrarian history. My parents Sisir Kumar Bose and Krishna Bose have provided unstinted intellectual and emotional support. It is to them I dedicate this book.

# INTRODUCTION

In 1978 Eric Stokes, the doyen of agrarian historians at Cambridge, welcomed 'the return of the peasant to South Asian history'. He berated historians and political scientists for their 'laggardliness' in recognizing that 'the balance of destiny in South Asia rests in peasant hands' but expressed satisfaction that 'among the students of the colonial revolution in South Asia the city slickers [we]re at last quitting town'.[1] The difficulties in achieving a meaningful intellectual engagement with peasant history stemmed partly from the misperception of a discontinuity between state structures and politics on the one hand and agrarian economies and societies on the other that had been one of the most lasting legacies of nineteenth-century theorists and comparative sociologists. Besides, there was the vexing problem of sources associated with studying social groups who left few written records of their own and were mere objects in the enquiries of external observers, especially colonial officialdom. During the 1970s and 1980s new empirical research and innovative methodologies enabled not only an historical reconstruction of agrarian economy, society and politics and their interrelations in various regions of colonial India but, through a critical evaluation if not deconstruction of colonial texts, restored to the peasantry their subjecthood in the making of history.

A study of the historical experience of the labouring classes in the Indian countryside during colonial rule is of vital importance and general relevance to historians in two ways. First, the nature and extent of the 'colonial revolution' in South Asia cannot be grasped without addressing the question of agrarian transformation. Second, the evidence from colonial India could form the basis of a scholarly intervention in broader debates providing insights into contemporary agrarian societies in the developing world and leading to a more balanced understanding of the origins and character of agrarian capitalism than is afforded by the literature with its deeply ingrained European emphasis.

The notion of dramatic and far-reaching change in South Asian

[1] Eric Stokes, *The Peasant and the Raj* (Cambridge, 1978), pp. 265–6.

I

society under the impact of British colonialism has come under scrutiny and scepticism in a large body of historical writing over the past few decades. The issue of change versus continuity can be posed at three connected analytical levels: (1) the structure and character of the colonial state, (2) the intermediate layer consisting of merchants, bankers and gentry between the state and the largely agrarian society and (3) the social organization and reproduction of labour in the very substantial agrarian sector and the smaller but significant artisanal and industrial sectors. The 'threads of continuity' between pre-colonial and colonial India have been drawn together most skilfully in the work of C. A. Bayly with its main focus on the world of the intermediate social groups.[2] The argument about continuity of agrarian social formations advanced by a number of scholars in the 1970s has rested almost exclusively on descriptive criteria, such as the extent of landlessness and levels of differentiation at different moments in time. This volume deploys analytical categories in an attempt to ferret out the elements of qualitative change in an agrarian scenario where many social structural features appeared to remain unaltered. It does so by integrating the histories of land and capital in order to be better able to probe the dialectic between capitalist 'development' of the wider economy under colonialism and agrarian continuity or change at the point of production and primary appropriation. The coexistence of rapid commercialization of agriculture and resilient non-capitalist forms of agrarian relations is analysed within the context of the logic of colonial capitalism. Since the peasant family represented an important, perhaps the most important, component of the labour process underlying colonial capitalist development, peasant history is treated as an inextricable and crucial strand of labour history. The phrase 'peasant labour' in the title of this volume is intended to capture this thrust of the argument. The exploration of peasant labour's interaction with the forces of colonial capital and its legacy in the post-independence period forms a critical core of this book and explains the second half of the title.

There has been of late a marked shift of interest and emphasis among historians and economists which has led them to stress the social rather

[2] C. A. Bayly, *Indian Society and the Making of the British Empire (The New Cambridge History of India)* (Cambridge, 1988) p. 5. See also his classic study *Rulers, Townsmen and Bazaars: North Indian Society in the Age of British Expansion* (Cambridge, 1983). Bayly's *New Cambridge History* volume notes important changes at the level of the state, such as the creation of a large European-style standing army.

than the narrowly technological foundations of economic development. The historical debate in this regard is fully engaged with reference to pre-industrial Europe but there have been significant individual contributions by scholars of Asia, Africa and Latin America. The relative strength of the impact of demographic forces on agrarian economy and society is a question that for long has divided historians. Even those who treated pre-industrial peasant societies within the framework of demographic models were far from agreed on the issue of the peasant response to the market and the efficacy of the forces of commercialization in triggering social structural change and clearing the way for capitalist economic development. Some historians allowed a dynamic role to market forces while others tended to stress the precedence of the demographic factor in any causal sequence. A political Marxian critique of the late 1970s called into question all the variants of the demographically determined model and asserted the centrality of pre-existing class structures in shaping the nature of social and economic change. Another questioning view preferred to see the mode of production or the economic logic inherent in a feudal system rather than the political superstructure at the centre of analysis. The intellectual ferment achieved some important breakthroughs but left other aspects of agrarian change unaddressed or unresolved.[3]

To the extent that the conflicting interpretations stem from differences of emphasis and the choice of alternative frameworks for the analysis of related themes, the elucidation of the precise connections between these themes is a matter for empirical investigation and analysis. Colonial India, especially the Bengal region which was the earliest to come under British rule, affords some of the most fascinating evidence for this kind of investigation and analysis. But beyond the elucidation of connections between themes, the deployment of the historical method of investigative research in a time and place characterized by the articulation of non-capitalist social formations to wider economic systems based on capitalism can lay the groundwork for alternative global models of a transition whose nuances have been inadequately grasped by models resting for the most part on the European historical experience.

The history of rural Bengal from the early phase of colonial rule and

[3] See, for instance, T. H. Aston and C. H. E. Philpin, *The Brenner Debate: Agrarian Class Structure and Economic Development in Pre-Industrial Europe* (Cambridge, 1985), especially the contributions by M. M. Postan and John Hatcher, Emmanuel Le Roy Ladurie, Robert Brenner and Guy Bois.

the great famine of 1770 to the post-colonial conditions of widespread endemic malnutrition and hunger poses all the conceptual problems of an agrarian society resting on a subsistence base which over time increasingly became linked to wider economic systems including a capitalist world market. Under such circumstances how far was agrarian economic development constrained by the homeostasis of demographically determined ecosystems? To what extent did the links with wider economic systems possess transformative power? Or did the locus of historical initiative lie with the logic inherent in pre-existing social formations, specific cultures and the political balance of class forces? These are some of the questions addressed in this volume as it seeks to analyse and interpret the related themes of demography, commodity production and agrarian social structure unfolding over the long term in a colonial setting.

The choice of the Bengal region from which to draw substantive empirical information and 1770 as the starting-point of this study requires some explanation. It was partly a case of 'consenting to geographical sacrifices in order to maintain chronological ambitions'.[4] Colonial Bengal's agrarian history held out exceptional promise for the investigation of the key questions and themes over the long term. Throughout this volume, however, frequent comparisons are made with regional agrarian histories of other parts of South Asia. Existing research on rural Bengal and India in the modern period is brought under the light of critical synthesis and primary sources are used to fill in significant gaps in the secondary literature. The volume provides a thematic rather than an exhaustive treatment of complex economic, social and political phenomena and ultimately depends for a sense of unity and coherence on a set of arguments about historical change advanced by one scholar.

The date 1770 was selected as the point at which to begin the story after a deliberate rejection of 1793, the date of the Permanent Settlement of the land revenue with the zamindars of Bengal. The historiography of agrarian India has been hampered by a sterile engagement with formal, colonial land-revenue systems and a lopsided emphasis on landlords and rural elites. One of the purposes of this volume is to restore the perspective by shifting the spotlight away from the zamindari bhadralok and large landholding jotedars on to the vast majority of

---

[4] Labrousse offered this apology in a different context. See Peter Burke (ed.), *Economy and Society in Early Modern Europe: Essays from Annales* (New York, 1972), p. 6.

4

smallholding, land-poor and landless labour. Demographic movements since the great depopulation of 1770 had a bearing on changes in
the social organization of production and were influenced in turn by
the systems of production and appropriation. The choice of 1770 is not
meant to assign the demographic factor a priori causal primacy but to
serve as 'a partial control, or cross-check, for other kinds of long-term
movements'.[5] Chapter 1 tracks the demographic cycles and the significant shifts that occurred in the domain of ecology over the two
centuries of colonial rule and its aftermath.

From about 1820 rural India became subject to the influence of the
rhythms and fluctuations of a wider capitalist economy. Chapter 2
looks at the process of agricultural commercialization and commodity
production for a capitalist world market as simultaneously an
economic and political phenomenon. It examines the extent to which
the colonial state set rules and restrictions in the marketplace and how
the state–market nexus affected the subsistence needs of peasant
labour. Particular attention is paid to the ways in which the state's
financial policies moulded the social impact of the vicissitudes of the
world market. The case studies of the indigo economy of the nineteenth century and the jute economy of the twentieth century are
designed to lend substantiation to the argument about styles and
phases of commercialization and the experience of the primary producers who engaged in the process.

The broader demographic and market trends interacted with an
agrarian social structure characterized by a colonial rule of property
and different types of relations of production. Chapter 3 explores the
property–production dialectic in agrarian society and advances a
typology of the main forms of material production and social reproduction of labour. It documents the strands of continuity in the social
organization of production and establishes what it was that changed
under colonial rule in apparently enduring social structures. Since the
labour process in agriculture was predominantly familial in character,
the issue of change is addressed along lines of gender and generation as
well as those of class and community.

While the social organization of production exhibited important
features of continuity, the relations of surplus-appropriation went

---

[5] The phrase is borrowed from Le Roy Ladurie, but not his broader formulation and
methodology. Emmanuel Le Roy Ladurie, *The Peasants of Languedoc* (Urbana, Illinois,
1973), p. 6.

through a clearer series of mutations over time. Chapter 4 explains the major transitions and offers a periodicization by predominant modes of appropriation. The successive pre-eminence of the rent, credit, lease, land and capital markets defined the principal axis of exploitation at different historical moments and had a close bearing on the history of agrarian resistance.

The structures and trends of demography, commercialization, production and appropriation were fashioned by the contest between the forces of domination and resistance. Chapter 5 explicitly addresses the topic of changing forms of agrarian resistance and probes the inner recesses of the mentalities of peasant labour. Understanding new states of peasant consciousness is by far the most delicate task faced by agrarian historians. It is attempted in this volume by unravelling the interplay of thoughts and ideological struggles with the relations of production and distribution.

This interpretative work seeks to avoid two potential false dichotomies between, first, the status of the 'economic' and the 'political' and, second, 'material conditions' and 'culture/consciousness' in agrarian and labour history. Social relations of production and exploitation explored in this book were simultaneously economic and political realities. Thinly veiled charges of 'economism' and 'politicism' notwithstanding, the more subtle and nuanced studies of agrarian economy and politics contain sufficient insights into the intertwining of economic and political forces.[6]

Agrarian and labour historians with a staunch materialist orientation may have overstated the case for economic determination. But in deriding the cruder forms of matter-over-mind reductionism, the new historiographical emphasis on culture is in danger of divorcing mind from matter, and consciousness from the dialectic of material production and social reproduction.[7] In order to avoid the pitfalls of economic determinism, it is hardly necessary to abandon the domain of material life and the economy. To do so would mean leaving the entire

[6] On differences of emphasis on the economic and the political see, for instance, Sugata Bose, *Agrarian Bengal: Economy, Social Structure and Politics, 1919–1947* (Cambridge, 1986) and Partha Chatterjee, *Bengal 1920–1947: the Land Question* (Calcutta, 1984). Also Bose's review of Chatterjee in *Indian Economic and Social History Review*, 24, 3 (1987), 336–9, and Chatterjee's review of Bose in *Journal of Asian Studies* (Autumn, 1988), pp. 670–2.

[7] For sophisticated versions of the argument against 'economism' in labour and agrarian history see, for instance, Dipesh Chakrabarty, *Rethinking Working-Class History: Bengal 1890–1940* (Princeton, 1989) and Gyan Prakash, *Bonded Histories: Genealogies of Labour Servitude in Colonial India* (Cambridge, 1990).

field of agrarian and labour history uncontested to those who see peasant labour as an objectified entity moulded by 'impersonal' demographic and commercial processes. This volume attempts to show how structures and processes of demography, commercialization, production and appropriation represented a combination of economic, political and cultural phenomena and were shaped by the tussle between domination and resistance. If, as the votaries of the importance of culture rightly claim, economic and political factors do not operate outside culture, they must also be viewed as key constitutive elements in the formation of culture and not merely as matters of detail in an historically given cultural context.

Since economic, political and cultural forces interact in complex ways in agrarian history, it is best not to be too overconfident while expounding on the subject of peasant consciousness. The present author sees the Indian peasant, despite having to contend with an array of exploiters, as a free spirit, who demands understanding but is best allowed to evade the bondage of the academic interpreter.

# CHAPTER 1

# ECOLOGY AND DEMOGRAPHY

Agrarian history at its most elementary level is the story of the interaction between land and people. The changing relationship between varying numbers of human beings and a fixed quantity of land has been from time immemorial a simple but crucial dynamic in agrarian developments. Historical reality has rarely been quite so simple as to be captured within a single relationship of a variable and a constant. Too many things other than population change, and land, despite its appearance, does not lack movement. Besides, the power of simplicity often misleads; it is all too easy to overemphasize the demographic factor in agrarian history.

Demography nevertheless is important, not necessarily as a causal determinant of the nature and course of agrarian developments but as a defining principle of parameters within which rural production occurs. Putting demography in its place is a daunting task. To the extent that historians have made contributions to grand theory in the twentieth century, studies of the long-term in pre-industrial history in which demographic cycles loom large have been, more often than not, the empirical vehicle for theoretical interjection.[1] The *Annales* school of historians in particular has lent this genre both sophistication and the status of orthodoxy. What is more, the part of the world that is the subject of this book is precisely one of those many regions in the 'developing' world where the 'problem' of population is especially acute. In 1770, the starting-point of this study, the agrarian scene in Bengal was marked by the scarcity of people and vast stretches of uncultivated fertile land. Two centuries later, land in the two Bengals has some of the highest densities of population and some of the lowest yields of production in the world. In 1981, 625 people crowded into a single square kilometre of space in Bangladesh, just eleven fewer, 614, in West Bengal.[2]

[1] Quentin Skinner (ed.), *The Return of Grand Theory to the Human Sciences* (Cambridge, 1985), pp. 19, 177–98.
[2] Government of Bangladesh, *The Preliminary Report on Bangladesh Population Census 1981* (Dacca, 1981), p. 1; Government of India, *Census of India 1981, Series 23, West Bengal: Provisional Population Totals* (Calcutta, 1981), p. v.

Popular views of population increases and densities tend to diverge remarkably from scholarly perspectives. In the popular perception, unbridled demographic growth creates an awesome burden on the land which contributes in no uncertain way to widespread mal-nutrition and hunger, not only in the two Bengals but in South Asia generally. An influential scholarly school, on the other hand, regards population pressure as a potential stimulus which, other things being equal, should induce innovation in agricultural techniques and in so doing enhance productivity. The specialist literature, however, is far from being unanimous on the question of population as a positive or negative trigger. It is even more divided on the direction of causality between population and production in agriculture and occasionally quite arbitrary in defining surfeits and deficits. An historical perspective over the *longue durée* can help untangle the intricate twists of the causal chain, while the context of the social relations of production and appropriation can provide a reliable gauge to measure surpluses and shortfalls of labour in relation to land.

Population, whether seen as independent or dependent on other factors, is a variable. Land, that classic 'non-producible' means of production, is after all supposed to be the constant in this abiding relationship. So it is best to begin by surveying the lie of the land.

## THE ECOLOGY OF RURAL BENGAL

In any discussion of the geographic structures of the Bengal country-side, rivers come first. This immediately qualifies the common notion of historians of the *longue durée* that geographic structures are constants.[3] Nothing is really permanent in the deltas of great rivers; there is little that endures. In rural Bengal – a land of torrential monsoon rains, warm and humid air, catastrophic cyclones and tumultuous earthquakes – the mighty distributaries of the Ganga carried away vast tracts in their sweep until they themselves were obliterated and lost their identities in newer, stronger currents. It was probably the transparent transience of their physical environment that inculcated in the peasants of Bengal a spirit of resignation and renunciation. The popular song – 'The day is done and the evening

---

[3] Fernand Braudel, *Mediterranean and the Mediterranean World in the Age of Philip II*, Vol. I (London, 1972), ch. 1; Emmanuel Le Roy Ladurie, *The Peasants of Languedoc* (Urbana, Illinois, 1974), p. 7.

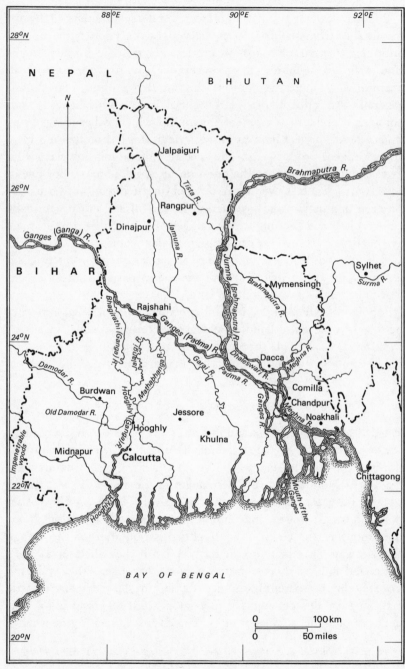

1. The rivers of Bengal

come, pray my God, take me over the ferry' – poignantly expresses the wistful longing to cross the river and go home.[4]

The turbulent hydrography of its great rivers has had a close bearing on the agrarian economy of Bengal. Over the centuries the main river has repeatedly changed course, altering the balance of the river system as a whole. The periodic breakouts were brought on by a process of gradual levelling of the land and silting up of the old river beds.[5] The Bhagirathi flowing through the heart of western Bengal or Rarh had risen to pre-eminence during the Mughal era upon the dwindling fortunes of the Bhairab and Saraswati. Its decline paralleled that of the Mughals and its fate was finally sealed once its distributary, the Damodar, awkwardly lurched southward in 1770. Since the early seventeenth century the Ganga had pressed for outlets further east and found them in the Gorai in Faridpur and, more importantly, the Padma which wove a wide swathe through much of east Bengal including Dhaka, Faridpur and Bakarganj. The general eastward swing of the river system was in part accentuated by catalytic events in the later eighteenth century as environmental upheavals matched political ones. The earthquake of 1762 and the floods of 1769–70 and 1786–8 spawned the creation of half a dozen new rivers or at least presented old rivers in completely new incarnations – the Tista, Jamuna, Jelanghi, Mathabhanga, Kirtinasa and Naya Bhangini.[6] The glory of the Jelanghi and Mathabhanga, which gave the eastern parts of Murshidabad, Nadia and Jessore a new lease of life in the nineteenth century, proved to be shortlived, a consequence of the bridging role played by the Jamuna between the Ganga and the Brahmaputra. Following the great inundation of 1787 the Tista, formerly a tributary of the Ganga, linked up with the Brahmaputra, which moved west to meet the Ganga near Goalundo in Dacca via the much enlarged channel of the Jamuna. The merged waters of the two mighty Himalayan rivers, the Ganga and the Brahmaputra, poured into the Meghna near Chandpur in Tippera.[7] Padma and Meghna henceforth became two names etched deeply into east Bengali rural identity.

The strides taken eastward by the Ganga, assisted by a westerly

[4] 'Hari din to gelo, shondhe holo, par karo amare' goes the Bengali refrain.
[5] Birendra Nath Ganguli, *Trends of Population and Agriculture in the Ganges Valley* (London, 1938), p. 205.
[6] Radha Kamal Mukerjee, *The Changing Face of Bengal: a Study in Riverine Economy* (Calcutta, 1938), p. 9.
[7] Ganguli, *Trends of Population*, p. 206.

push of the Brahmaputra, moulded the differentiated ecological contexts within which agriculture and agrarian society developed. The most striking contrast to emerge was the one between the active delta in the east and the moribund delta in west Bengal. The former became the full beneficiary of the fertilizing, flooding action of the overflowing rivers and came to be known as the land of the new alluvium. The latter suffered through the process of slow decay of its rivers and found its soil relegated to the status of the old alluvium. The divergence came to be reflected in the cropping patterns and ultimately in the demographic capacities of the two regions. Both were primarily areas of wet rice cultivation, but the silt-laden earth of the east yielded more. Parts of west central Bengal produced some sugar-cane and indigo in the early nineteenth century, especially during the brief revival of the streams passing through Murshidabad and Nadia. Later in the century cash crops shrank to insignificance in terms of acreage and there was even a marked shift from the superior winter (aman) rice to the inferior autumn (aus) variety. Meanwhile it was the November spectacle in east Bengal of rich, golden-green sheafs of winter paddy waving gently in the breeze that so stirred the sensibilities of Bengali poets.[8] From the 1870s a golden fibre, jute, began to take on importance as a cash crop, more so in the inland districts of the delta – Mymensingh, Dhaka, Faridpur and Tippera – than in the littoral districts such as Bakarganj. The possibility of intensive double cropping helped sustain high densities of population.

Two other ecological zones, though smaller in extent than the active and the moribund deltas, deserve to be mentioned. First, a narrow strip of raised ground on the western fringes of Bengal formed a sort of halfway house on the way to the Chhotanagpur plateau. This was an area of less secure rice cultivation acutely susceptible to the vagaries of rainfall. Second, rising up from the northern edges of the deltaic plains were the Himalayan foothills. At a time when the plant producing the dye in west Bengal was being resented as an unwarranted imposition and the fibre of east Bengal had yet to reveal its magic, colonial capital discovered that a precious leaf grew in Jalpaiguri and Darjeeling. Once labour could be set to work on tea plantations in this terrain, the scope for both exploitation and profits proved to be immense.

---

[8] Rabindranath Tagore in his famous song Sonar Bangla (Golden Bengal) sees the mother's honeyed (indulgent) smile in the laden fields in November ('O ma, aghrane tor bhara khete ki dekhechhi modhur hashi').

It has become increasingly evident in recent years that durability and change in the environment can hardly be regarded as purely natural phenomena. There is, of course, an element of helplessness against the fury of nature as when powerful cyclones and tidal surges have swept everything in their path in littoral Bengal. Yet human agency appears to have shown a little less ability in harnessing the forces of geography than in aggravating their destructive consequences. There is not much doubt that the building of road and railway embankments in the mid nineteenth century dislocated drainage patterns and hastened the process of atrophy of rivers of the moribund delta. Stagnant pools became the breeding-ground of anopheles mosquitoes, the carrier of waves of malaria epidemics in the second half of the nineteenth century. The areas with the most extended railway and road networks were the ones that showed the highest incidence of malaria.[9] It was recognized in the early twentieth century that controlled river irrigation in the decaying west would not be feasible without constructing 'a barrage across the Ganges'.[10] A barrage was built at high cost in the 1960s but politics, among other factors, ensured that it had little positive impact on west Bengal agriculture.

Meanwhile, Bangladesh has remained vulnerable to devastating floods such as the ones in 1974 and 1988. In the aftermath of the 1988 floods, the military government of Bangladesh has been seeking funds to implement an ambitious plan mooted by French engineers to construct hundreds of miles of tall embankments that will contain the mighty rivers of the Bengal delta. On a conservative estimate this 'development' project, which would be the biggest ever in Bengal's history and has received qualified backing from the World Bank, would cost $6 billion to build and $165 million in annual maintenance. This venture aiming at flood prevention rather than flood control would stop the natural beneficial flooding action by which the rivers have from time immemorial deposited fertile sediments along their banks. Drawn up without any reference to the peasants who are supposed to benefit from it, the plan is being seen by environmentally conscious critics to be fundamentally flawed on technical, economic and political grounds. If allowed to go ahead without consideration of more suitable alternatives or serious amendment, it may well turn

[9] C. A. Bentley, *Malaria and Agriculture in Bengal* (Calcutta, 1925), pp. 27–32.
[10] S. C. Majumdar, *The Rivers of the Bengal Delta* (Calcutta, 1942), p. 82.

out to be the most disastrous human interference yet in the ecology of rural Bengal.[11]

Nature, it is true, is not always bountiful, but nor does it entirely of its own accord exhaust the earth. On a long historical view it has displayed enduring nurturing qualities in rural Bengal. Yet even the best of these have proved increasingly insufficient since the 1930s in the struggle to carry the human burden.

## DEMOGRAPHIC CYCLES

The impression of rural Bangladesh and west Bengal apparently sinking under the weight of overpopulation in the 1990s is a far cry from the demographic 'low-water mark' that characterized the eastern Indian countryside in 1770. The great famine of that year had wreaked massive depopulation – anywhere between one third and one fifth of the population of Bengal and neighbouring Bihar were thought to have died.[12] Nearly a century later, W. W. Hunter placed an absolute figure choosing quite arbitrarily the highest of the impressionistic ratios of contemporries. His conjecture, probably an overestimate, suggested a death toll of 10 million out of 30 million inhabitants of Bengal and Bihar.[13] Although no systematic count was taken of India's population until the first decennial census of 1872, it is not impossible on the basis of scattered evidence prior to that date and more informed enumeration since then to establish the broad trends in population movements as well as the key points of inflection. Three distinct phases can be staked out within which to study the relationship between population and agricultural production: 1770–1860, 1860–1920 and 1920–90.

From 1770 to about the mid-point of the nineteenth century, all parts of Bengal shared in a secular all-India trend of population increase which was more marked in some regions than others. It was in this phase that the agrarian economy of colonial Bengal showed the high concordance between population and production that has been found to be such a notable feature of agrarian economies of ancien régime Europe. The demographic behaviour of west and east Bengal diverged sharply from the middle of the nineteenth century to about 1920. The decay of the rivers and a high mortality rate owing to malaria

[11] See James K. Boyce, 'The Political Economy of Flood Control in Bangladesh' in Sugata Bose and Ayesha Jalal (eds.), *Democracy and Development in South Asia* (forthcoming).
[12] John Shore, Minute of June 1789, *Parliamentary Papers*, 1812, 7, 182.
[13] W. W. Hunter, *Annals of Rural Bengal* (reprint, Calcutta, 1975), p. 45.

epidemics resulted in a demographic arrest and a reduction in the area under cultivation and output in west Bengal. During the first half of this period, c. 1860–90, east Bengal witnessed a secular rise in population and rapid expansion of cultivation and total output through the extensive proliferation of peasant smallholdings. Between 1890 and 1920, although the extensive margins were reached in many parts, population growth induced new intensive techniques, which more than offset the diminishing returns from new lands in terms of productivity. The overall picture, however, during these three decades shows stagnation in agricultural production.[14] From the 1920s, better control of disease brought about a sharp fall in the death rate in west Bengal, so that the population graph once again swung upwards but failed on this occasion to have any commensurate impact on production. In east Bengal, too, demographic growth appeared to acquire an autonomous, self-sustaining character while output stagnated. Between 1920 and 1990 population rose almost inexorably, barring the setback during the great famine of 1943, spurred along by a high fertility regime. On the production side of the equation, cultivated area displayed 'near-constancy' and yield per acre 'a near-zero trend' between 1920 and 1946.[15] In the period 1949–80 the performance of total output improved, but figures of per capita growth indicated that production was trailing way behind population in both west and east Bengal.[16]

Noting the points of inflection and demarcating demographic cycles still does not allow a consideration of the vexed question of 'under'- and 'over'-population in relation to resources, especially land. In each of the phases was population or labour in surplus or deficit? The neo-Malthusian[17] approach to the question within the framework of population–resources scissors does not seem to be very helpful for a number of reasons. For one, subsistence crises in Bengal with dire demographic consequences, whether in 1770 or later, were not, as will be shown, Malthusian disasters in any sense. For another, contrary to

[14] George Blyn, *Agricultural Trends in India, 1891–1947: Output, Availability and Productivity* (Philadelphia, 1966), pp. 102–7.

[15] M. M. Islam, *Bengal Agriculture 1920–1946: a Quantitative Study* (Cambridge, 1979), p. 203.

[16] James K. Boyce, *Agrarian Impasse in Bengal: Institutional Constraints to Technological Change* (Oxford, 1987), chs. 3, 4 and 5.

[17] The term is used in the sense familiar to historians of agrarian change in Europe. For a range of other connotations in the work of economists and demographers, see Boyce, *Agrarian Impasse*, pp. 30–3.

the neo-Malthusian view that the population–resources scissors cannot go on widening, evidence from Bengal after 1920 and from other Asian and African societies suggests that the axis of these scissors can break open. The irrelevance of Malthus cannot be disguised either by declaring him a prophet of the past or by exiling him from Europe to the Third World. While the need for an alternative perspective could not be greater, Marxian positions on historical demography are not particularly well developed. A starting-point, however, for drawing a conceptual outline is available in the acknowledgement that 'what may be overpopulation in one stage of social production may not be so in another, and their effects may be different'.[18]

The aspect of the Marxian angle on overpopulation that is clearly enunciated is the unique tendency within the capitalist mode of production to create relative surplus labour emphasizing productivity rather than actual numbers. Yet this is the one condition lacking in agrarian social formations not characterized by capitalist relations of production though they might be tied to wider capitalistic economic systems including a capitalist world market. Three antecedent analytical phases, however, can be defined and, despite partial overlapping, can be seen in broad terms to correspond to the demographic cycles in Bengal stretching from 1770 to 1860, 1860 to 1920 and 1920 to 1990. The first phase of absolute deficit population is one in which contiguous cultivable lands would remain uncultivated even if there were no constraints on extensive cultivation other than those of a natural-demographic kind. The next phase of relative deficit population is one in which the extents of the arable have been reached but labour may still be seen to be in deficit in relation to the opportunities and demands of intensive cultivation. The final phase of absolute surplus population arises when the intensive margins of labour productivity circumscribed by resource limitations and current technology have been reached. It is generally characterized by a process of pauperization and growth of landlessness.[19] The transformation of absolute surplus labour to relative surplus labour under full-blown capitalist agriculture is a

---

[18] Karl Marx, *Grundrisse: Foundations of the Critique of Political Economy* (Harmondsworth, 1973), p. 604; for an attempt to reconcile classical Marxism with historical demography see W. Seccombe, 'Marxism and Demography' in *New Left Review*, 137 (1983).

[19] The concepts of absolute deficit, relative deficit and absolute surplus labour have been elucidated in their theoretical aspect by Shapan Adnan, 'Conceptualising Fertility Trends in Peripheral Formations' in *Determinants of Fertility Trends: Theories Re-examined* (Liege, Belgium, 1983).

teleological assumption made by many Marxian theoreticians. It is important not to invest a matter of historical possibility with overtones of inevitability. The schematic outline drawn here is a heuristic device which can aid in a closer analysis of the demographic parameters of agrarian production while at the same time showing up the limits of the role of the demographic factor.

## 1770–1860

Ten years after the famine of 1770 the jungles of Birbhum had spread so far and become so overgrown that the English East India Company offered a reward for each tiger's head sufficient to meet a peasant family's subsistence needs for three months.[20] The famine clearly resulted in drastic depopulation and loss of cultivation. Yet the famine itself was no Malthusian event; it had occurred within a pre-existing context of at least a relative deficit of labour. In the western districts the 'bargi' or Maratha raids of 1740–51 had contributed to this scarcity; but even in the easternmost district of Chittagong (which escaped the famine) population was sparse and a mere 25% of the district was cultivated in 1761.[21] Labour scarcity was only one of the factors constraining the extent of cultivation. Sluggish grain prices during the 1760s, caused at least in part by a reduced money supply consequent on the sharp drop in the import of bullion, may have been another. Besides, the zamindars faced financial problems as the English factors and the Company's military servants displaced the indigenous shroffs as creditors in the late 1750s and early 1760s, a situation only partly rectified after the Company's assumption of the Diwani in 1765.

So rural Bengal in 1770 did not suddenly face a natural calamity which dramatically, if cruelly, relieved its overburden of population. Labour was clearly not overabundant and the crop failures of 1768 and 1769 provide at best an insufficient explanation of the catastrophe. It would be appropriate to see the apparent decline in food availability as creating very adverse conditions within which failures in exchange entitlements occurred.[22] The 'violent upswing' in prices was much greater than the shortfall in production would have 'normally

---

[20] Hunter, *Annals*, p. 41.
[21] W. W. Firminger (ed.), *Midnapur District Records, 1763–67* (Calcutta, 1926), Vol. I, 53; A. M. Serajuddin, *The Revenue Administration of the East India Company in Chittagong, 1761–85* (Chittagong, 1971), ch. 5.
[22] On the theory of exchange entitlements, see Amartya Sen, *Poverty and Famines: an Essay on Entitlement and Deprivation* (Oxford, 1981).

justified'.[23] Even in the outskirts of the capital Murshidabad, where a rupee had bought ten to twenty seers of rice in previous years, it fetched only three seers in July of 1770. The entry of the Company's government as a buyer in the grain market contributed to the inflationary spiral. Some 120,000 maunds of grain were bought up in Bengal and Bihar for use by the Company's army.[24] The credit market in grain ceased to operate as grain dealers stopped lending. On the contrary, the Company's servants and their Indian gomastas cornered local supplies. Mohammad Reza Khan, naib diwan, and Richard Becher, resident at Murshidabad, complained bitterly about these grain monopolies but did little themselves either to ease the revenue demand or to provide relief. While the early colonial state netted some £8,000 more in 1770–1 than in 1768–9 (over £1.5 million a year) in revenue collections, it provided a paltry 40,000 rupees towards relieving distress.[25]

It was the role of the state and the economically powerful in effecting declines in entitlements to food of vulnerable social groups that turned the 'dearth into a famine'.[26] Already in May 1770 the government expressed fears that one third of the population had been decimated. Richard Becher suggested in June 1770 that the number to have perished was 'as six to sixteen of the whole inhabitants'. Warren Hastings, after undertaking extensive tours in 1772, largely corroborated the impressions of witnesses to the tragedy. The most conservative estimates in the later eighteenth century placed the mortality ratio at one fifth.[27] Given the nature of agricultural techniques and the absence of any labour reserve in the pre-famine period, the extent of cultivation and consequently of production was also reported by observers to have declined proportionately.

The western and central Bengal districts of Nadia, Murshidabad, Midnapur, Birbhum, and Burdwan, Rajshahi and Dinajpur further north and most districts in adjoining Bihar were hardest hit by the famine. Dhaka escaped lightly although many weavers in the city died;

[23] Binay Bhushan Chaudhuri, 'Agricultural Growth in Bengal and Bihar: Growth of Cultivation since the Famine of 1770' in *Bengal Past and Present*, 95 (1976), p. 294.

[24] *Ibid.*, p. 295; see also Nikhil Sur, *Chhiattarer Manwantar o Sannyasi Fakir Bidroha* [The Famine of 1770 and the Sannyasi Fakir Rebellion] (Calcutta, 1982), pp. 16–22.

[25] G. Campbell (ed.), *Extract from the Records in the India Office relating to Famines in India, 1769, 1788* (Calcutta, 1868), pp. 36, 60.

[26] The phrase is Adam Smith's in *The Wealth of Nations* cited in N. K. Sinha, *The Economic History of Bengal: From Plassey to the Permanent Settlement*, Vol. II (Calcutta, 1970), p. 58.

[27] Letter to the Court of Directors, 3 November 1772, cited in *ibid.*, p. 54; also, John Shore, Minute of June 1789, *PP*, 1812, 7, 182.

rice surpluses from Chittagong and Bakarganj provisioned Calcutta; and Rangpur was something of a haven for refugees in search of food and employment. The report of the Amini Commission published in 1778 presented some graphic details of the famine's impact on population and production in west Bengal districts.[28] In Birbhum, the worst affected, vast tracts lay deserted in 1771–2; according to the Amini statistics the percentage of the revenue assessment on palataka or deserted lands to the total revenue assessment was as much as 36%. The number of village settlements in the district had shrunk from 6,000 in 1765 to 4,500 in 1770–1.[29] In Nadia the deserted lands accounted for 15% of the total revenue assessment. Laments about depopulation caused by death and desertion could be heard from Burdwan. Some peasants from Midnapur had actually sought refuge in Maratha-controlled districts to the west.[30] An investigation in four villages in Rajshahi tracked a grim story of dwindling resident families: 1,076 in 1768–9 to 1,033 in 1769–70 to just 373 in 1770–1. Of the 660 families lost in the famine year only 153 had deserted; the rest had fallen victim to starvation and famine-related disease. The uncultivated fields bore testimony to the devastating impact of the famine on the smallholding peasantry. Yet some other social groups fared even worse; these were the families of boatmen, fishermen, weavers, silk-winders and other workers who had wholly lacked any direct entitlement to grain. The evidence for this is provided partly by contemporary observers and partly by price statistics which record the dearness of manufactures and the cheapness of agricultural products in the aftermath of the famine.

Population and agricultural production recuperated fairly rapidly in the decades after 1770 despite a number of constraints and brief interruptions. The accelerator effect of the disaster early in the process of recovery was probably negated by the setback caused by the smaller famine of 1787. This one, unlike the 1770 catastrophe, did not spare east Bengal.[31] The pace of demographic recovery in the late eighteenth

[28] Report of the Amini Commission, 25 March 1778, Home Miscellaneous Series, Vol. 206 (IOR), printed in R. B. Ramsbotham, *Studies in the Land Revenue History of Bengal, 1769–1787* (Calcutta, 1926) cited in B. B. Chaudhuri, 'Agricultural Growth', p. 336 and Aditi Nag Chowdhury-Zilli, *The Vagrant Peasant: Agrarian Distress and Desertion in Bengal, 1770 to 1830* (Wiesbaden, 1984), pp. 22–5.
[29] Campbell (ed.), *Extracts from Records relating to Famines*, p. 79.
[30] Firminger (ed.), *Midnapur District Records*, Vol. IV, 15.
[31] J. Taylor, *A Sketch of the Topography and Statistics of Dacca*, p. 304 cited in P. J. Marshall, *The New Cambridge History of India. Bengal: The British Bridgehead, Eastern India 1740–1820* (Cambridge, 1988), II, 2, 25.

and early nineteenth centuries is difficult to ascertain since quantitative estimates of population prior to the taking of censuses are neither very reliable nor comparable. But observations of knowledgeable contemporaries and comparison with demographic evidence from other parts of India suggest growth at a faster rate than backward extrapolation from late nineteenth-century census evidence would indicate. In 1789 a total figure of 22 million people was suggested for the Bengal presidency based on district collectors' reports. At the turn of the century the number probably stood at around 27 million. By 1822 another enquiry using the services of district officers suggested that the total population had risen to 37.6 million. Close observers of the Bengal rural scene like H. T. Colebrooke and Francis Buchanan-Hamilton clearly believed that population had built up steadily during this period despite a high death rate, although the latter probably exaggerated the size of cultivation on which he based his population estimates.[32] These views were in consonance with broader trends elsewhere in India, especially the United Provinces, the Bombay Deccan and the Madras presidency. In U.P. a rapid upward climb of the population curve from 1800 to 1855 was halted briefly only during the famine of 1837–8. The rate of growth slowed perceptibly in the latter half of the nineteenth century. In the Bombay Deccan population moved along at a fair trot between 1820 and 1850 and continued to advance though at a more moderate pace between 1850 and 1875. There was a fourfold increase in the population of the Madras presidency during the nineteenth century, the fastest rates being recorded before 1870.[33]

A close parallel can be noticed between movements of population and agricultural production in Bengal. This accords well with the evidence from U.P. and south India but not with findings in the Bombay Deccan. The demographic increase was clearly a major influence on production in this phase of mostly extensive growth. According to one estimate, the acreage under cultivation in the Bengal presidency rose from 30 million in 1793 to 70 million in

[32] The various population estimates are critically evaluated in Chaudhuri, 'Agricultural Growth', pp. 323–30.

[33] Cf. Simon Commander, 'The Agrarian Economy of Northern India, 1800–80' (unpublished Ph.D. dissertation, Cambridge, 1980); Sumit Guha, *The Agrarian Economy of the Bombay Deccan, 1818–1941* (Oxford, 1985), esp. ch. 6; Dharma Kumar, *Land and Caste in South India* (Cambridge, 1965), esp. pp. 105–6.

1857.[34] In the decades immediately following the famine of 1770, however, a number of constraints ensured that output did not increase with the same buoyancy as population. One was the high revenue demand of the early colonial state, especially the pernicious tax called najai which sat most heavily on the surviving neighbours of those who had died or deserted. Another was the general malaise in the grain market and periodic phases of acute depression like the one between 1794 and 1798. These negative impulses were countered, however, by a rising demographic trend in a context of absolute deficit labour which enabled the negotiation of advantageous rental rates for reclamation of fallow land. In west Bengal districts, which had reached a more advanced stage of cultivation in 1770 than the eastern ones, short-distance migration by paikasht (temporary and migratory) raiyats played an important part in the process of recovery until about 1820. It was once believed by some historians upon the examination of local evidence that these paikasht peasants were none other than well-off and enterprising khudkasht (settled or permanent) raiyats who collected a band of poorer dependants and settled where they could extract better terms from the zamindars.[35] A more complete and balanced sifting of the evidence now suggests that in addition to these 'entrepreneurs' there was another sizeable class of atomistic small peasants who were able to 'desert' with their agricultural implements and expand cultivation where the logic of the person–land ratio put them in a good bargaining position.[36] In the western districts of Birbhum and Midnapur, tribal migrants were often the paikasht raiyats. Elsewhere, middling caste Hindu and Muslim peasants were full participants in the processes of recovery and reclamation.

In the mature parts of west and central Bengal, peasants were probably already nibbling away at the extensive margins by the 1820s. An estimate of the population of Burdwan in 1816 gave a count of one and a half million people with a very high density of more than 600 persons per square mile.[37] By the mid-thirties it was being reported

---

[34] W. N. Lees, *The Land and Labour of India* (London, 1867) cited in Asok Sen, 'Agrarian Structure and Tenancy Laws in Bengal 1850–1900' in Partha Chatterjee, Saugata Mukherjee and Asok Sen, *Perspectives in Social Sciences* II (Calcutta, 1982), p. 6.

[35] Ratnalekha Ray, *Change in Bengal Agrarian Society c. 1760–1850* (Delhi, 1979); R. K. Gupta, *The Economic Life of a Bengal District: Birbhum 1770–1856* (Burdwan, 1984).

[36] Chowdhury-Zilly, *The Vagrant Peasant*, ch. 3.

[37] W. B. Bayley, 'Statistical View of the Population of Burdwan', *Asiatick Researches*, 12 (1816), 551.

that west and central Bengal was 'far too populous to admit to tracts of land remaining uncultivated'.[38] The first census report of 1872 was quite categorical about the steady increase of the population in the western parts of Burdwan division during the course of the century. The levelling noticed in the eastern parts was probably of very recent origin. The tightening of the land–person ratio in much of west Bengal is quite evident from the 1828 report of collector Halhead.[39] So it would be incorrect to emphasize only the extensive nature of growth in west Bengal between 1830 and 1860. As one scholar has noted, districts such as Burdwan and Hooghly had reached densities of more than 700 per square mile by the mid nineteenth century, which was nearly twice that of urbanized, industrial Belgium, the world's most heavily populated country at the time.[40] These densities could only be sustained through some resort to intensive techniques including limited switching to cash-crops like sugar-cane, cotton and mulberry. But it would be a mistake to assume that the move to cash-cropping in this period was mainly demographically driven. Indigo, the most important cash-crop of this period, was largely a forced cultivation. It is noteworthy, however, that the compulsion occurred within and may have been facilitated by an emerging framework of demographic pressures.

In the more expansive delta of east Bengal, laterally proliferating small peasant cultivation provided the main impetus to increased agricultural production. Early evidence of the spread of cultivation came in the replies of judges and district collectors to the enquiry initiated by Wellesley in 1801. In the southern parganas of Dhaka, for instance, cultivation was said to have increased by some 12.5% since the Permanent Settlement. The extension of the arable, even accounting for the district collector's obvious over-optimism, was striking in Chittagong.[41] In Tippera, where in the 1760s hills and jungles predominated over cultivated land, Buchanan-Hamilton saw in 1798 'one continuous field yielding the richest crops'; in 1801 seven-ninths of the district was reported to be under the plough. The proportion might

[38] N. Alexander, 'On the Cultivation of Indigo' in *Transactions of the Agricultural and Horticultural Society of India*, 2 (1836), 35.

[39] Report No. 46 by collector Halhead, March 1828, Bengal Revenue Proceedings, Range 50, Vol. 54 (IOR).

[40] Ira Klein, 'Malaria and Mortality in Bengal, 1840–1921' in *Indian Economic and Social History Review*, 9, 2 (1972), p. 156.

[41] Bengal Judicial Civil Proceedings, 8 July 1802 and *PP* (1812–13), 9, cited in Chaudhuri, 'Agricultural Growth', p. 305.

well have been an overestimate but the district settlement officer in the 1910s, after weighing the available evidence, suggested almost a doubling of the cultivated area between 1793 and the revenue survey of 1860–4.[42] In Faridpur and Mymensingh the scale of the new cultivation was far greater than the pockets of decline. Rennell's survey of 1770–8 had revealed 1,128 square miles of unoccupied waste in Bakarganj; that was down to 925 square miles in 1793 and to 526 square miles by the time of the Revenue Survey of 1859–65.[43] The ecology of this littoral district cut across by numerous streams gave rise to an extraordinary pattern of subinfeudation under substantial farmers known as haoladars to facilitate the work of reclamation.

In the northern tracts of jungle in Rangpur and Dinajpur, population and production increased moderately in this period. It would appear that the cultivated area in Rangpur in the early 1870s was about 15% greater than in 1809 and much of the reclamation by rich farmers known as jotedars was recent.[44]

Overall, a high birth rate outdistanced a high death rate between 1770 and 1860. Except in years of exceptional dearth fertility rates appeared to remain unaffected by the apparent fragility of life. Demographic growth was a strong, but not the sole, factor in the spread of cultivation and rising gross output. Prices, with a possible exception in the period 1800–20, showed no secular fluctuations with population and production. There is little firm data on wage levels. The agricultural surplus was mainly appropriated through the mechanisms of revenue and rent, both depending for their enhancement primarily on the expansion of acreage. So the colonial state, the recipient of land revenue, and the zamindars, collectors of rent, benefited from a high fertility regime. It has been speculated that the logic of the predominant relations of surplus-appropriation through revenue and rent may have had some bearing on the rising demographic trend. By the middle of the nineteenth century peasants in west Bengal had exhausted the extensive margins at the current low level of technology and had begun to exploit new intensive strategies. Some open spaces still remained in

[42] Notes by G. Ironside, Orme Manuscripts, 'India', 17, 4950 (IOR); F. Buchanan-Hamilton, 'Account of a Journey through the Provinces of Chittagong and Tipperah', Add. Ms. 19286, folio 3 (IOR); PP (1812–13), 9, 416; W. H. Thompson, Report on the Survey and Settlement of Tippera District, 1915–19 (Calcutta, 1919).

[43] J. C. Jack, Report on the Survey and Settlement of Bakarganj District, 1900–08 (Calcutta, 1915).

[44] E. G. Glazier, A Report on the District of Rangpur (Calcutta, 1873); A. C. Hartley, Report on the Survey and Settlement of Rangpur District, 1931–38 (Calcutta, 1941).

east Bengal which both invited and challenged hardy Muslim and Namasudra peasants.

*1860–1920*

The census of 1921 showed that the population of Bengal increased by 28.6% over its level in 1881, at an annual incremental rate of 0.7% which was slightly ahead of the all-India increase of just under 20% over the forty-year period at nearly 0.5% per annum. Rural population in Bengal, a more relevant variable and accounting for 94% of the total population in 1891 and 93% in 1921, had risen by 27.6% from 34.77 million to 44.38 million.[45] These aggregate figures, however, mask a striking discrepancy between the demographic movements in west and east Bengal. It was the east that was primarily responsible for the rising trend. The west, reeling under the impact of a series of malaria epidemics, had suffered a demographic arrest.

In west Bengal, C. A. Bentley reported in 1916, 'outbursts of epidemic fever ... from 1860 onwards marked the transition from a formerly comparatively salubrious state, similar to that still observable in parts of Eastern Bengal, to one of widespread prevalence of malaria'.[46] Burdwan, once renowned as a sanatorium, lent its name to this strange fever which enervated its victims as much as it baffled medical experts. It had made its first appearance, however, in Jessore in 1836. During the latter half of the nineteenth century it traversed every district of the old alluvium in the course of its menacing rural itinerary. Serious epidemics occurred in Jessore in 1847–8 and 1854–6, Nadia in 1857–64 and 1880–1, Hooghly and the 24-Parganas in 1857–64 and 1878, Burdwan in 1868–72, and Birbhum, Midnapur and Howrah in 1870–2. Even after the disease became endemic, it flared up periodically in epidemic form in the late nineteenth and early twentieth centuries. Consequently, although Bengal did not share with the rest of India the high famine mortality of the 1890s or even the worst ravages of the influenza epidemic of 1918–19, the recurring pattern of malaria epidemics in west Bengal ensured that population growth in the province was firmly held down.

Local officials believed in the early 1870s that they were witnessing a Malthusian phenomenon of population having pressed up against a

[45] Government of India, *Census of India 1921*, Vol. V: *Bengal*, Pt 2, Tables; R. H. Cassen, *India: Population, Economy and Society* (London, 1978), ch. 1.
[46] C. A. Bentley, *Report on Malaria in Bengal* (Calcutta, 1916), pp. 30–8.

ceiling of foodgrains output.[47] These Malthusian bureaucrats did not, however, present any clear argument emphasizing the role of demographic growth in a process of causal determination. The result of the epidemics, however, was clear enough – the pressure of population on land of declining fertility was dramatically relieved. Population density in Burdwan fell back from over 700 to under 550 per square mile during the 1860s and 1870s. The population of Hooghly was said to have been halved between the late 1850s and the late 1870s. In the malaria-infected parts of Midnapur population declined by nearly a third in the latter half of the nineteenth century. Local investigations in selected villages of Nadia, Jessore, Burdwan, Birbhum and Hooghly confirmed the impression of large-scale depopulation in epidemic years. Looking back from 1921 over a 50-year time-span, it appeared that rural population had remained more or less stagnant in most west and central Bengal districts while it had actually declined by nearly 10% in Nadia and Jessore.[48]

If the incidence of malaria was influenced by ecological decay hastened by human interference, its detrimental effects were differentiated through the mediation of the agrarian social structure. It was discovered in 1875, for instance, that mortality was highest among the poorer classes of day-labourers, settled peasants and artisans in that order. An enquiry in Birbhum in 1874 revealed the distribution of malaria-induced mortality among different social classes: 37% among 'daily labourers and beggars', 31% among 'cultivating ryots', 19% among 'artisans such as smiths, potters, washermen and goldsmiths' and 12% among 'upper non-labouring classes, such as zamindars, merchants, priests and farmers'.[49] As the decline of labour–land ratios grew common at the level of family holdings, a necessary though unequal combination of middling-caste peasants and low-caste and tribal landless labourers steadily lost ground in their battle against the encroaching jungle at the level of agrarian society.

The performance of agriculture was adversely affected in west

---

[47] Burdwan Magistrate to Burdwan Commissioner, 7 March 1874, Bengal Gen. (Statistics, Head No. 1) Progs., September 1875, Collection 4–7/8 cited in Binay Chaudhuri, 'Agricultural Production in Bengal: Co-existence of Decline and Growth', *Bengal Past and Present*, 88, 2 (166) (July–December 1969), 152–206.

[48] Chaudhuri, 'Agricultural Production', p. 160; GOI, *Census of India 1921*, Vol. V: *Bengal*, Pt 1, 48–55.

[49] GOB to GOI, 15 September 1875, and Birbhum Collector to Burdwan Commissioner, 8 January 1874, Bengal Gen. (Statistics, Head No. 1) Progs., September 1875, Collection, 4–13 cited in Chaudhuri, 'Agricultural Production', p. 163.

Bengal both by the exhaustion of the land of the moribund delta and by the mortality as well as morbidity of labour as a consequence of malarial infection. In the Magura and Jhenida subdivisions of Jessore, for instance, a survey in 1876 had reported 75% of the gross area to be under cultivation; by 1920 the proportion had shrunk to under 40%. In addition to the 'dearth of labour', 'the agricultural population stricken by malaria [had] lost their physical vigour and energy' and became 'incapable of hard work in the field'.[50] With depopulation reducing acreage and debilitation affecting yields, it is likely that gross output in west Bengal declined between 1860 and 1920 in a context of stagnant population. The monotony of this bleak picture was broken only by some small pockets of growth. One was provided by the slow but steady retreat of the Sunderbans in the 24-Parganas, Khulna and parts of Midnapur effected by the money and supervision of enterprising farmers and the labour of small peasants. Another was opened up by the withdrawal of the government's salt monopoly in the 1860s in the Contai and Tamluk subdivisions of Midnapur which became a safe haven for Mahishya peasants fleeing from the scourge of malaria.

In east Bengal, by contrast, growth was the norm and decline the exception. The secular trend of expanding population and cultivation of the pre-1860 period was maintained in the sixty years that followed with only a slight slackening of the pace towards the end of the period and brief interruptions caused by a major cyclone in 1876 and an earthquake in 1897. While population had remained stationary in the moribund delta, it increased by some 60% in the active delta. Despite a limited amount of inter-regional and inter-district migration, this was almost entirely a natural increase caused by a high birth rate outstripping the death rate. By 1921 Dhaka, Tippera, Noakhali and Faridpur reached densities of over 1000 persons per square mile with Bakarganj, Mymensingh, Pabna and Bogra following close behind. During the later nineteenth century, much of the region made the transition from the state of absolute deficit labour to relative deficit labour. The gradual emergence of high densities notwithstanding, labour may still be seen to have been in a state of relative deficit between 1860 and 1900 in the context of possibilities for resort to intensive techniques.

The extension of cultivation by Muslim and Namasudra peasants in the active delta was by and large atomistic and not communal in nature. In Bakarganj, where peasants had settled 'wholly without any refer-

[50] M. A. Momen, *Jessore Settlement Report, 1920–24* (Calcutta, 1925), p. 20.

ence to any future village community',[51] the 'unoccupied waste' shrank from 526 square miles in the early 1860s to 184 square miles in 1905, despite the accretion of 180 square miles of new alluvial land. Cultivation in the 'occupied area' posted a 23% increase.[52] In Mymensingh the cultivated area increased from 3,562 square miles to 4,292 square miles between 1872 and 1910, which included 470 square miles of stiff clay in the Madhupur jungle on the Dhaka border. Extensive cultivation had 'almost reached its full limits'. By the second decade of the twentieth century nearly all land cultivable at the current level of technology was being cultivated in most east Bengal districts. In Noakhali 'every inch of land ... fit for cultivation' was reportedly growing crops or fruit-bearing trees. The settlement officers of Dacca wondered 'to what extent the land [could] be induced to provide the rapidly increasing numbers with employment'.[53]

The crunch would have been felt sooner had it not been for two developments: first, the exploitation of the intensive margins partly through a switch to a high-value and labour-intensive cash-crop, and second, the utilization of the escape-hatch of migration particularly to the flood plains of the Brahmaputra in neighbouring Assam. Around 1920 double-cropping accounted for 34% of the net cropped area in east Bengal; the corresponding figure for west Bengal was a mere 18%. Moreover, the value of the second crop was generally much greater in the east. Jute had assumed importance as a cash-crop from the early 1870s onwards and experienced a major spurt in its acreage in 1906–7. From then on between 10% and 22% of the acreage under cultivation was devoted to jute in the seven major jute-producing districts of east Bengal.[54] Unlike forced commodity production in west Bengal in the second quarter of the nineteenth century, the pace and character of the commercialization process in east Bengal at the turn of the century were set and shaped to a significant extent by the demographic context.

[51] J. E. Gastrell, *Geographical and Statistical Report on the Districts of Jessore, Fureedpore and Backergunje* (Calcutta, 1868) cited in Ralph Nicholas, 'Villages of the Bengal Delta' (Unpublished D.Phil. dissertation, Chicago, 1962), p. 67.
[52] J. C. Jack, *Bakarganj Settlement Report, 1900–08* (Calcutta, 1915), pp. 10–11; on expansion of cultivation in Faridpur, see J. C. Jack, *Faridpur Settlement Report, 1904–14* (Calcutta, 1916), p. 5.
[53] *Mymensingh District Gazetteer* (1919), p, 48; F. A. Sachse, *Mymensingh Settlement Report, 1908–19* (Calcutta, 1919), p. 29; W. H. Thompson, *Noakhali Settlement Report, 1915–19* (1919) cited in Ganguli, *Trends of Population*, p. 239; F. D. Ascoli, *Dacca Settlement Report, 1910–17* (Calcutta, 1917), p. 50.
[54] Ganguli, *Trends of Population*, p. 244; M. Azizul Huque, *The Man behind the Plough* (Calcutta, 1939), p. 59.

The migration of nearly a million peasants, often in search of jute lands, from overcrowded east Bengal districts to Assam during the first three decades of the twentieth century was an indication that even the intensive margins were being exhausted.[55] Somewhat analogous to the migratory movements from Java to Sumatra or from northern to southern Vietnam, it was usually an arduous trek for those who were edged out of the scramble for a plot along the banks of the Padma, Meghna and Jamuna.

The frontiers of north Bengal developed social relations of production so markedly different from both west and east Bengal that the broad contours of demographic movements need to be sketched separately for this region. The behaviour of birth and death rates in the western fringe of the old alluvium (in western Dinajpur, for instance) roughly paralleled that of west and central Bengal. A similar concordance held true for demographic trends in eastern parts of the active delta of north Bengal formed by the Tista and Jamuna (in eastern Rangpur, for instance) and those typical in east Bengal. However, the immigration of mostly Santal, Oraon and Munda tribal labour from Bihar boosted population in the western parts of north Bengal between 1860 and 1920. Starting soon after the repression of the tribal insurrection of 1855 in Bihar, the process gathered strong momentum very late in the nineteenth century.[56] Immigrant labour played a crucial role in the clearance of jungle in these parts. The tea gardens in Jalpaiguri and Darjeeling also recruited immigrant labour on a large scale, enough to offset the depletion caused by malaria. The 1901 census reported a sharp rise in the number of immigrants in Jalpaiguri in one decade from 143,922 to 188,223, about half of whom were tea plantation coolies from Chhotanagpur and the Santhal Parganas. In 1911 as many as 126,214 residents of Jalpaiguri were found to have been born in Ranchi district of Bihar, while in 1921 the 'most numerous' people among the labour force were reported to be Oraons and Mundas.[57]

On a broad view, an accelerated mortality rate can be seen in west Bengal to have brought about a demographic retreat. The large quantities of fallow land in west Bengal around 1920 owed their existence, however, to a combination of unfertile land and scarce

[55] GOI, *Census of India 1921*, Vol. V: *Bengal*, Pt 1, pp. 32–3; Md. Abdul Hamid, *Pater Kabita (Verses on Jute*, Juriya, Assam, 1930).
[56] Chaudhuri, 'Agricultural Production', pp. 172–3.
[57] C. A. Bentley and S. R. Christophers, *The Causes of Blackwater Fever in the Duars* (Simla, 1908), pp. 22–5; GOI, *Census of India 1921*, Vol. V: *Bengal*, Pt 1, p. 389.

Table 1. *Inter-censal annual rates of growth of rural population (by per cent)*[58]

|  | 1921–31 | 1931–41 | 1941–51 | 1951–61 | 1961–71 | 1971–81 |
|---|---|---|---|---|---|---|
| West Bengal | 0.72 | 1.47 | 0.79 | 2.76 | 2.34 | 1.83 |
| Bangladesh | 0.54 | 1.57 | −0.07 | 1.84 | 2.81 | 1.76 |

labour. In east Bengal the birth rate continued to be marginally higher than in west Bengal and the death rate considerably lower. Settlement of unoccupied waste did not present the same physical or financial obstacles to reclamation as the jungles of the frontiers, and proceeded apace. The phase of relative deficit labour was associated with the resort to more intensive methods and crops. By now the labour process resting on increasing exploitation of peasant family labour tended towards the perpetuation of a high rate of fertility. Proliferating population in east Bengal was mostly a natural increase based on a large surplus of births over deaths. This was not so in north Bengal where immigrant labour was unhinged from its original tribal habitat in Bihar to be set to work as sharecroppers and plantation labourers.

*1920–90*

This final phase of demographic cycles in Bengal has been characterized by declining per capita output in a context of the generation of absolute surplus labour. The continuation of the rising demographic trend in east Bengal provides a remarkable example of population growth over the course of more than two centuries. A dramatic decline in mortality rates in west Bengal after 1920 brought that region more in line with the increase in numbers in the rest of the province. Inter-censal rates of growth of rural population of what are now Bangladesh and West Bengal provide a rough indication of the similarity of the trends. If the population–resources scissors had been widening, its axis now broke open. Put another way, if a technologically determined ceiling on output existed, population appeared to have no difficulty in shooting through it.

The upswing in population all across Bengal began in the early 1920s, acquired momentum in the 1930s, and then received a sharp jolt

[58] Boyce, *Agrarian Impasse*, pp. 139–40.

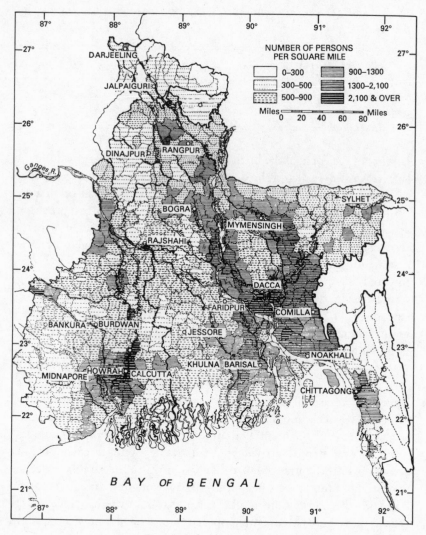

2. Density of population, 1941

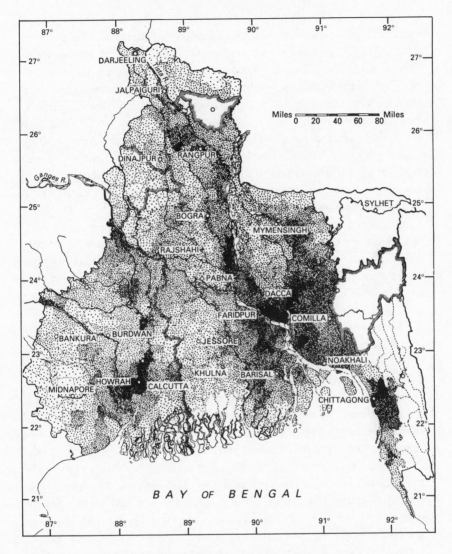

3. Regional spread of Famine-year mortality, 1943.
Each dot represents 100 deaths

in the 1940s as a result of the high mortality induced by the famine of 1943. The famine, which was precipitated by entitlement failures rather than any aggregate decline in food availability, was responsible for an excess mortality between 1943 and 1946 of at least 2.7 to 3 million people.[59] If the average mortality of 1941–2 rather than the figure given in the 1931 census is accepted as normal mortality, the number of famine-related deaths rises to betwen 3.5 and 3.8 million.[60] The high mortality inflicted by the famine was, of course, differentiated by region and class, with the landless poor taking the brunt of the disaster. Ironically, the Bengal countryside produced a record harvest during the famine year. The rates of population growth peaked in the 1950s and 1960s and appear to have climbed more slowly since the early 1970s. Bangladesh experienced another major famine in 1974. Although the official figure of famine mortality was given as 26,000, one estimate suggests as many as one million excess deaths between August 1974 and January 1975 and another half million during 1975.[61] Yet population increased in Bangladesh at 1.76% per annum between 1971 and 1981, a decade torn by war and famine.

Demographic pressure clearly failed in this phase to operate as a force adequate to induce technological innovations which would have enhanced productivity. Between 1920 and 1946, according to the best available estimate, total agricultural output grew at a mere 0.3% per annum and food crops output stagnated, while population increased at an annual rate of 0.8%. Burdwan division, the heart of rural west Bengal, actually showed a negative output growth rate of −1.08%. The relatively high growth rate in agricultural output of 1.1% in the Presidency division can probably be explained by reclamation in the Sunderbans tracts in Khulna and the 24-Parganas. In east Bengal output rose at 0.4% per annum in Dacca division and declined at the rate of −0.7% in Chittagong division. Output in the Rajshahi division, which included the north Bengal districts, grew at an annual rate of 0.5%.[62] So even in the areas of aggregate agricultural growth, per capita output declined.

In the post-independence period, the growth performance of agri-

[59] Sen, *Poverty and Famines*, pp. 195–216.
[60] Paul Greenough, *Prosperity and Misery in Modern Bengal: the Famine of 1943–44* (New York, 1982), pp. 299–315.
[61] M. Alamgir, *Famine in South Asia: Political Economy of Mass Starvation in Bangladesh* (Cambridge, MA, 1980) discussed in Sen, *Poverty and Famines*, p. 134.
[62] Islam, *Bengal Agriculture*, pp. 50–6.

Table 2. *Per capita agricultural output, 1949–80*[63]

|  | 1949–64 | 1965–80 | 1949–80 |
|---|---|---|---|
| West Bengal | −1.42 | 0.27 | −0.57 |
|  | (−1.49) | (0.10) | (−0.69) |
| Bangladesh | −0.59 | 0.38 | −0.11 |
|  | (−0.76) | (−0.27) | (−0.51) |

culture improved but still lagged behind population. Between 1949 and 1980, total agricultural output grew at an estimated rate of 2.03% in Bangladesh and 1.74% in West Bengal. A positive break in the trend was noticeable in the mid 1960s. Output grew in Bangladesh at the rates of 1.57% and 2.49% during the subperiods 1949–64 and 1965–80, respectively; a similar acceleration occurred in West Bengal from 1.20% to 2.27%. The northern districts of both Bangladesh and West Bengal put in a relatively strong showing based mainly on area growth in the first subperiod but fell back, particularly in West Bengal, in the second, performing relatively poorly on the productivity front. Five core districts of West Bengal and the southeastern and northwestern districts in Bangladesh have displayed the fastest growth rates based on yields and cropping pattern in the west and yields alone in the east. The painfully slow growth in the yield of aman rice, which accounted for about 50% of gross acreage in both east and west, acted as a principal constraint on any better performance of output. It was the higher growth rates of secondary crops, namely aus (autumn) and boro (summer) rice, wheat and potato, which enabled production to stay at all in the race with population. As for jute, since partition output has increased in the west but stagnated in its natural habitat in the east.

Careful sifting of the data relating to the 1949–80 period has revealed that the process of induced innovation stemming from rural population growth was by no means absent even though it failed to make itself felt forcefully on agricultural performance. A static analysis of the linkage between population density and agricultural productivity in 1971 showed positive results. A dynamic analysis also suggested that population growth has had positive associations with subsequent

[63] Boyce, *Agrarian Impasse*, pp. 141–2. The main figures denote rates of growth of output per capita of rural population; the rates of growth per capita of total population are given in parentheses.

performance of agricultural output. Given a context of absolute surplus labour, it can be surmised that this could not have occurred simply as a function of labour intensity without innovative labour-utilizing and land-saving techniques. The existence of reverse connections between agricultural growth and demographic growth countering positive impulses provided by population pressure threatens to undermine or offset the benefits of innovation in the long run. Yet a close examination of the population–production linkage in all its ramifications makes it amply clear that population growth in Bengal, contrary to the alarms raised by Malthusian doomsayers, is 'not an unmitigated evil'.[64]

Nevertheless, a high fertility regime in the context of absolute surplus labour since 1920 is an intriguing phenomenon. High fertility rates appear to have enjoyed a relative autonomy from the productive and exploitative processes at the level of the agrarian social structure. They were not unrelated, however, to the requirements of the material reproduction of peasant family labour caught in a downward spiral of pauperization and increasingly seeking employment outside the sphere of land in order to survive. Before 1920 high fertility was a strategy of survival for peasant families as production–consumption units; after 1920 it was still a desperate means of trying to subsist as income–consumption units. In that sense, the continued generation of elaborate surplus labour has been a 'dialectical response' to the agrarian structure though not a 'functional consequence' or 'operational precondition' of the rural economy.[65]

### The role and limits of the demographic parameters

The concordance between population and production, characteristic of pre-industrial Europe, was observed in colonial Bengal only in the early phase of absolute deficit labour between 1770 and 1860. The relationship held fast regardless of variations in different regions in the character of the social relations of production which are fully elucidated later in this study. But one must be careful even in the analysis of this phase to avoid the implicit, and occasionally surreptitious, elevation of correlations to the status of causal relationships that is the wont of the neo-Malthusians. One powerful interpretation of the *longue durée* in French agrarian history, for instance, explains the launching of the expansive phase of a grand agrarian cycle primarily in terms of

[64] *Ibid.*, p. 159.   [65] Adnan, 'Conceptualising Fertility Trends', p. 220.

demographic growth. The conclusion of the cycle, however, is seen to be brought about by the inability to break through a ceiling of growth imposed mainly by a technological impasse which is reinforced by the rigid and unimaginative mentalities of the age.[66] The strength as well as the direction of causality remains hidden behind impressive parallelisms. The aspect of technological determination in this line of argument has found some resonances in South Asian historiography. A 'ceiling to the gross product' set by 'available land and technique' has been discovered in nineteenth-century western India and sought to be generalized for 'tropical countries from 1880 to 1913'.[67] The evidence from colonial and post-independence Bengal cautions against this sort of demographic and techno-economic determinism.

Firstly, while an investigation of the relationship between population and production is indispensable for defining an important set of parameters, it is almost meaningless to attempt to discern neat, secular rhythms of population, production, prices and wages within a demographic conjuncture since these were muddied, as chapter 2 will demonstrate, by the disrupting influences of wider economic trends from at least the 1820s. Agrarian crises were shaped from then on not principally by population and output but by changes in prices and the availability of credit emanating from supra-regional economic systems based on capitalism. Secondly, the evidence from Bengal suggests that the process of induced innovation in the realm of technology triggered by population growth was certainly not non-existent but was rather blocked or aborted by other forces. The blockage to induced innovation in post-partition Bengal, especially in the field of water-control development which is the leading input, has lain in the character of social and political institutions.[68] The forces of production were fettered more effectively by the relations of production, which are analysed in chapter 3, rather than by any preordained technological barrier.

Taking close cognizance of the demographic parameters impels one to place the problem of technological constraints, in the sense of the relative stagnation of the average range of techniques in use in Bengal's agrarian economy, in its larger economic and social contexts. These include the capitalist world market and the colonial political economy

---

[66] Ladurie, *Peasants of Languedoc*, pp. 289–311.
[67] Guha, *Agrarian Economy of the Bombay Deccan*, p. 198.
[68] Boyce, *Agrarian Impasse*, chs. 6 and 7.

as well as the social relations of production and appropriation. Demography then, instead of being assigned causal primacy, might be seen to a large extent as a variable dependent on the logic of material and social reproduction. This chapter has hinted at how surplus-appropriation through rent extraction, a topic to be discussed in more detail in chapter 4, gained from high fertility rates in a phase of absolute deficit labour. Of course, the thrust of rent maximization was constrained in this phase by the imperative of ensuring the material reproduction of the working peasantry and the social reproduction of labour relations, the latter vulnerable to the possibility of migration. Once the intensive margins came to be utilized in a phase of relative deficit labour, the production process based on increasing exploitation of family labour, especially of women and children, contributed to the maintenance of high fertility rates. The continued generation of absolute surplus labour after 1920 is a more puzzling phenomenon but still explicable in terms of the severely limited options for material reproduction of a peasantry in the process of pauperization.

Unrestrained fertility in colonial Bengal has been seen aptly as one of the chief survival strategies of the rural poor.[69] Adopted initially as a poverty-combating mechanism which appeared to make perfect economic sense to male heads of family households, it eventually backfired once both extensive and intensive margins at a relatively low and stagnant level of technology were exhausted. Yet even if unrestrained fertility had now played as never before into the hands of the appropriators of the agrarian surplus, there were few obvious alternative strategies for a vast proportion of pauperized peasant families which operated both as production–consumption units and income–consumption units. The premium on family labour capacity meant relentless exploitation of women's reproductive capacities and largely unremunerated productive capacities as an expenditure-saving device, and of children's labour capacities as both an expenditure-saving and an income-earning mechanism. Among families of landless labourers at the bottom of the agrarian hierarchy, women, relatively unconstrained by cultural norms of segregation, also joined in the ranks of income-

[69] Willem van Schendel and Aminul Haque Faraizi, *Rural Labourers in Bengal, 1880–1980* (Rotterdam, 1984), pp. 108–14; Mead Cain, 'The Economic Activities of Children in a Village in Bangladesh', *Population and Development Review*, 3, 3 (1977), 201–27; Mead Cain et al., 'Class, Patriarchy and Women's Work in Bangladesh', *Ibid.*, 5, 3 (1979), 405–38; Naila Kabir, 'Gender Dimensions of Rural Poverty: Analysis from Bangladesh' in *Journal of Peasant Studies*, 18, 2 (January 1991), 241–62.

augmenters. Survival resting solely on family labour power has been achieved largely at the cost of exploitation within the family.

Beyond the family, at the level of agrarian society, the extensive margins of cultivation were not defined except in the broadest sense in natural-demographic terms. This brought about considerable overlap in the utilization of extensive and intensive margins. Price movements of land and its products, as well as flows of credit for financing cultivation, interacted with the parameters set by demography. Access to ownership and use of the land was restricted through the deployment of economic and social power and an elaborate system of layered rights to the land including the property right in revenue collection granted by the colonial state. Agrarian change over the long term can only be fully apprehended by considering the context of political economy within which commodity production took place and the complex of property and possessory rights which underpinned the exercise of power in the Bengal countryside.

CHAPTER 2

# COMMERCIALIZATION AND COLONIALISM

The response of agrarian society to demographic constraints and pressures to which it was subject was shaped, to a large extent, by the context of opportunities and risks emanating from wider economic systems increasingly based on capitalism and a colonial political order possessing its own agenda of economic priorities. The theme of 'commercialization', which has been such a favourite among agrarian historians of colonial India, must be recognized as simultaneously an economic and political process. The story that is to be told in this chapter is not simply one of expanding market forces which through dynamics of their own surely and steadily engulfed rural Bengal and redirected the thrust of its people's productive activities. It is equally a story of imperatives of states and political cultures which behind the facade of a rhetoric of free trade from the early nineteenth century onwards sought to impose and extend sets of monopolies. State-supported restriction and regulation of primary producers' options moulded the nature of their involvement in the marketplace. Politics did not, however, succeed in wholly reining in the laws of motion of economic arrangements over which it presided. Ever since the 1820s colonial and post-colonial states as much as peasants and agricultural labourers have been susceptible to the rhythms and fluctuations of wider economic trends.

These economic cycles and movements operating on a scale beyond the strict borders of agrarian society had significant income effects, both inflationary and deflationary, on the working peasantry. This alone makes it important to track the direction and strength of these trends as they bore down on the Bengal countryside. Moreover, the vulnerability to downturns generally proved greater than the capacity to ride the upswings. This suggests the need to analyse the structures of articulation of the region's economy and society to broader-based socio-economic entities, especially a well-integrated capitalist world market which emerged during the nineteenth century and the state's fiscal and financial policies as they deflected or magnified market trends before they had their full social impact.

38

COMMERCIALIZATION AND COLONIALISM

## THE LOGIC OF COMMERCIALIZATION

A number of contending perspectives have differed in pointing to the primary locus of historical initiative behind the process of commercialization of agriculture in colonial India. An early view emphasized the key link between the colonial systems of land revenue and increased agricultural production for the market. The role of the imposition of inflexible revenue demands in cash in powering the engines of monetization and commercialization seemed palpable enough.[1] Although the revenue–money–commerce nexus is undeniable, the levels of monetization and commercialization reached in the immediate pre-colonial era should caution against acceptance of any notion of an inexorable sequence set in train by the cash-hunger of the colonial revenue establishment. The particular kind of land revenue settlement made in eastern India has been seen more recently as having constituted a bourgeois revolution in land. The creation of zamindari 'property' facilitated, in this view, the task of bringing land and its products under the sway of capital. The 'formal' if not 'real' subsumption of labour under capital then gave rise to a distinctive 'colonial' mode of production.[2] An ingenious twist to 'transitions of modes of production' models, the semantic distinctions made from this theoretical standpoint, nevertheless, seem insufficient to take account of the complexities and varieties of both agrarian production and capitalist markets and serve to obliterate the intricate modes of articulation between the two.

Another forceful model postulates the 'incorporation' of agrarian zones, including regions of India, into a capitalist world-economy. The stimulus for expansion comes from the European 'core', which imposes an international division of labour ensuring its dominance over the 'periphery'. The question from the world-systems perspective is why the process of 'incorporation' took the form of colonial conquest in India.[3] From the South Asian angle of vision it is clear that

---

[1] See Daniel and Alice Thorner, *Land and Labour in India* (Delhi, 1965). For a more recent qualified reiteration see K. N. Raj, 'Introduction' in K. N. Raj (ed.), *Essays on the Commercialization of Indian Agriculture* (Delhi, 1985), pp. vii–xx.

[2] Hamza Alavi, 'India and the Colonial Mode of Production' in *Economic and Political Weekly*, 10 (1975), 1236–62; 'India: Transition from Feudalism to Colonial Capitalism' in *Journal of Contemporary Asia*, 10, 4 (1980), 359–98; Jairus Banaji, 'Capitalist Domination and the Small Peasantry' in *Economic and Political Weekly*, 12, 33 and 34 (1977), 1375–404.

[3] Immanuel Wallerstein, 'The Incorporation of the Indian Subcontinent into the Capitalist World-Economy', mimeo. (Delhi, 1985); 'World-Systems Analysis and Historical

pre-existing inter-regional linkages and regional structures, as well as the social organization of intermediate groups and subaltern working classes, were only partially reordered during the transition to colonialism. The dynamics of indigenous identities and institutions have been shown to have determined the pace of European 'expansion' and shaped the character of the colonial relationship, certainly in the period prior to industrialization in Europe.[4] The two perspectives provide a different periodicization of the connection forged between agrarian India and a worldwide capitalist economic system or systems. One emphasizes the expansionary logic of a Europe-based system from 1750 onwards; the other stresses the primacy of internal contradictions and developments in the late eighteenth century and observes fluctuations in a capitalist world economy casting their influence only after South Asia lost its ability to export its artisanal products around 1820. One of the most recent interventions in this debate has located the transition to colonial capitalism even later – between 1840 and 1880 – when expanded production of commodities in rural India was geared emphatically for a capitalist world market. This interpretation is premised on the existence of disparate commodity economies in separate agrarian regions of the subcontinent which were eventually merged by widening networks of proliferating commodity production.[5]

Any synthesis of or new departure from the present state of the debate must integrate the economic and political dimensions of commodity production. While recognizing the importance of agrarian commerce in pre-colonial regional economies, it is important not to lose sight of the colonial state as a key factor in bringing about major shifts in the scale and character of commodity production. An over-emphasis on the prior existence of commodity economies in agrarian regions of South Asia might result in missing the dimension of extra-economic coercion deployed by capitalism through institutions of state to make regional agrarian economies serve its requirements of expanded commodity production. While some of the impetus in this

Particularity: Some Comments' in Sugata Bose (ed.), *South Asia and World Capitalism* (Delhi, 1990). For a critique see David Washbrook, 'South Asia, the World System and World Capitalism', in *ibid*.

[4] C. A. Bayly, *Rulers, Townsmen and Bazaars: North Indian Society in the Age of British Expansion, 1770–1870* (Cambridge, 1983), especially ch. 6; 'Beating the Boundaries: South Asian History, c. 1700–1850' in Sugata Bose (ed.), *South Asia and World Capitalism*.

[5] David Ludden, 'World Economy and Village India, 1600–1900: Exploring the Agrarian History of Capitalism' in Sugata Bose (ed.), *South Asia and World Capitalism*.

process came from the centre of an emerging capitalist world economy based in Europe, indigenous arrangements and organizations of society and political economy were by no means passive elements. These not only moulded the impact of colonial capitalism, but compelled a significant degree of adaptation to pre-existing networks and patterns in an era of qualitative change. Colonial capitalists engaged in both contest and compromise with intermediate social groups of merchants and service gentry; even as subaltern classes of artisans, peasants and labourers were constrained to reorder their priorities in production and consumption, aspects of their social organization remained fundamentally unaltered. After all, the power of capitalism lay in its being *sufficiently informed* and *materially able* to choose the sphere of its action'.[6] The sectors and degrees of intervention in agrarian economy and society varied considerably. The discontinuities between market economy and capitalism were sharp and serious.

## TYPES AND PHASES OF COMMERCIALIZATION

Identifying the forces that propelled the process of agricultural commercialization does not necessarily unravel its meanings from the angle of vision of a commodity-producing working peasantry. A threefold characterization of types of commercialization, employed in a study of peasant economy in China, might be helpful in an understanding of the process in colonial India.[7] First, there is the kind of commercialization closely associated with increased accumulation, giving rise to expansion of productive scale based on managerial farming or plantation agriculture. In eastern India, although entrepreneurial farmers played a role in reclaiming waste lands, commodity production did not typically develop under their supervision. Plantations tended to be the preferred area of investment and operation of European capital, the tea plantations of the northern districts of Darjeeling and Jalpaiguri using large-scale migrant labour being the most prominent example. The second major type has been dubbed 'subsistence commercialization', where poor peasants driven by their concerns of securing basic subsistence in a context of demographic and social pressures turned to the cultivation of high-value and labour-

[6] Fernand Braudel, *Civilization and Capitalism, 1500–1800*, Vol. II: *The Wheels of Commerce* (New York, 1981–4), p. 400.

[7] Cf. Philip C. Huang, *The Peasant Economy and Social Change in North China* (Stanford, 1985), pp. 121–37, 299.

intensive cash-crops in an attempt to eke out a larger gross income from their diminishing smallholdings. The prime example of this sort of agricultural 'involution' based on a strategy of subsistence via the market is the smallholding production of jute in east Bengal in the late nineteenth and early twentieth centuries. A third major form has been labelled 'dependent commercialization', characterized by intrusive foreign merchant capital which brings the agricultural production process firmly under its sway but stops short of capitalist accumulation and consolidation of land. The common usage of the phrase 'indigo plantations' with its capitalistic connotations notwithstanding, production of indigo in west Bengal in the first half of the nineteenth century comes closest to this style of agricultural commercialization.

There can be no easy equation between a typology of agricultural commercialization and a periodicization of the process, although an analysis of the typology–periodicization dialectic provides insights which may be of some theoretical importance. Teleological assumptions underlying a large corpus of studies of capitalist development in agriculture have led scholars to discern movements along a pre-ordained path towards full-blown capitalism. Yet historical evidence from colonial India belies any notion of unilinear progression, or even drift, towards the quintessence of agrarian capitalism derived from the European historical experience. It is not that a capitalist world market merely 'skimmed cash-crops off a stagnant agrarian base';[8] yet nor did commercialization lead inexorably, if slowly, towards a capitalist transformation of production relations in agriculture. A number of significant and durable forms of the relationship between production and the market emerged, which lay along the spectrum encompassed by the two poles. Between these there were historically specific movements of both 'progression' and 'retrogression'. A capitalist economic system had made, for instance, much deeper inroads into the social organization of production of indigo in the early nineteenth century than into that of jute in the early twentieth. This apparent instance of 'retrogression' is an important problematic in any analysis of socio-economic development by historical stages, but not a 'problem' once the teleology of capitalist development is rejected. It is explicable in terms of socio-political

[8] The phrase is Eric Stokes' in *The Peasant and the Raj* (Cambridge, 1978), p. 270, commenting on Clifford Geertz, *Agricultural Involution* (Berkeley, 1963).

variables, including the balance of forces within the agrarian social structure in particular conjunctures, a theme addressed more fully later in this study.

While no neat sequencing over time of the main types of agricultural commercialization is discernible, it is nevertheless possible and important to note the phases of agrarian commerce according to its direction, commodity composition and state initiatives and restrictions. During the years between 1770 and 1813, commonly referred to as a period of mercantilism, the Bengal countryside principally placed fine artisanal products, especially textiles, at the disposal of the English East India Company for sale on the world market. This was a phase of 'plunder' by the state because political ascendancy had obviated the need to import silver and made it possible to plough back revenues into 'investment' in export goods. At the same time there is evidence of the emergence of an integrated regional grain market during the late eighteenth century in response to the rising demand for food in the province.[9] From 1813 to the 1860s, although the ideological currents of free trade were in full flow in the wake of industrialization in Europe, the process of agricultural commercialization in India's colonial setting was in an interesting transitional stage. The opening up of India's external trade by the Charter Act of 1813 gave a clear edge to free-trader industrial capitalists over their rival Company monopolists and marked a dramatic turnaround in the composition of imports and exports. The Company managed, however, to help finance its lucrative China tea trade through profits made on exports of commodities such as indigo and opium from eastern India. Opium was a government monopoly and formed a direct link in the Britain–India–China triad of international trade. State sponsorship of the production and trade in indigo, although in the hands of private capitalists, was complex and indirect but by no means insignificant. The period from the 1860s to 1914 is marked by the classic colonial form of unequal exchange of India's agricultural commodities for British manufactured goods, notably textiles, and the generation of an export surplus through the sale of raw materials to the rest of the world which through an intricate mechanism of payments offset Britain's deficits.[10] Raw cotton, raw

---

[9] Rajat Datta, 'Merchants and Peasants: a Study of the Structure of Local Trade in Grain in Late Eighteenth Century Bengal' in *Indian Economic and Social History Review*, 23, 4 (1986); cf. D. L. Curley, 'Rulers and Merchants in Late Eighteenth-Century Bengal', unpublished Ph.D. dissertation (Chicago University, 1978).
[10] See S. B. Saul, *Studies in British Overseas Trade* (London, 1967), pp. 55–63.

jute, tea, coffee, wheat, oilseeds and hides figured prominently on India's export list, jute and tea being the substantial contributions of the primary producers of Bengal. The classic colonial pattern of trade and payments was disrupted by economic crises and political convulsions in the era of war and depression stretching from 1914 to the mid 1940s. The vulnerability of those who had resorted to 'subsistence commercialization' was fully exposed during this time as the colonial political economy geared itself to a rearguard defence of the interests of the metropolis and the colonial state within a context of severe market fluctuations. Independence and partition represented a partial disjuncture in the relationship between the state and commodity production. Import-substituting industrialization became one of the chief concerns of the Indian and Pakistani states, although the relative emphasis on capital goods rather than consumer goods was greater in India. Reorientation of exports was not easy to organize, nor did it receive the same priority. Partition placed an artificial barrier between the jute-growing eastern districts and the jute mills that had come up in the west around Calcutta. Tea remained the single important primary product export of post-independence West Bengal, a sector which saw the slow retreat of European capital and the tightening of Indian capitalist control of the plantations. Between 1947 and 1971 east Bengal found itself cast into the role of an internal colony, its export earnings from raw jute being siphoned off by dominant social groups and the central state apparatus located in the western wing of Pakistan.[11] Faced with all the weaknesses inherent in being dependent on a single export crop, Bangladesh since 1971 has been making tentative attempts to reduce the reliance of its political economy on agrarian commerce and to create a viable, if small, industrial base.

On a long historical view, two types of agricultural commercialization have been most pervasive in moulding the productive activities of the working peasantry of eastern India. These were dependent commercialization of the late eighteenth and the nineteenth centuries, during which indigo was the leading commodity, and subsistence commercialization of the late nineteenth and the twentieth centuries, during which jute was the leading commodity. A close analysis of these styles of commercialization in the early nineteenth and the early twentieth century respectively can add substance and nuance to the

[11] See Ayesha Jalal, *The State of Martial Rule: the Origins of Pakistan's Political Economy of Defence* (Cambridge, 1990), chs. 3–5.

conceptual arguments advanced so far in this chapter. The structures of articulation and trends within the markets for these commodities cannot, however, be divorced from the production and marketing of the chief subsistence-cum-commercial crop, rice, throughout this period. Not only was some part of the rice crop put on the market alongside non-food commercial crops to generate much-needed money income, but the balance of acreage, relative costs and prices and connected credit networks ensured that the issues of subsistence and the market were inextricably intertwined. The rest of the chapter deploys the method of case studies to unearth the motives and meanings underlying dependent commercialization and subsistence commercialization for those who engaged in these processes.

### DEPENDENT COMMERCIALIZATION: THE 'INDIGO' PHASE

In 1788 indigo was identified by the Company's Directors as 'an article which, considered in a political point of view, ha[d] every claim to ... attention, as having a tendency to render the Company's possession in Bengal more valuable by creating from the soil and labour of the natives an export commerce, capable of being carried to a very great extent'.[12] Some of the stimulus for increased production of indigo no doubt came from increased demand in Europe in the late eighteenth and early nineteenth centuries – a 'blue phase' in dressing for European war and fashion. The eyes of British entrepreneurs turned to India because of the loss of supplies consequent on American independence and the shift to more lucrative coffee production in the Caribbean, developments which threatened to leave Britain at the mercy of erratic supplies from French and Spanish colonies. The beginnings of industrialization in Britain also sharply undermined the export of valuable textiles from India as the basis of profits and remittances. Indigo was already an established crop in northern India. The Company's state made sure, however, that the cultivation and manufacture of this 'object of national importance' was promoted and extended 'within [their] immediate possessions', that is, Bengal.[13] Despite expectations that the cheapness of labour would ensure good profits, indigo

[12] Letter from Court of Directors, 28 March 1788, cited in Benoy Chowdhury, *The Growth of Commercial Agriculture in Bengal* (Calcutta, 1967), p. 75.
[13] Letters from Court of Directors, 12 April 1786, 3 February 1796, and 27 July 1796 cited in *ibid.*, pp. 75, 77.

as a relatively new major export crop experienced some early teething problems in establishing itself as a viable medium of remittances.[14] Between the mid 1780s and 1810 Bengal's exports, including indigo, showed a gentle rising trend but were still subject to considerable short-term fluctuations. By 1810, however, indigo appeared to have been entrenched as 'a great staple of Bengal'.[15]

The state's role in consolidating indigo production for export was significant but not as direct as in the case of two other important commodities in the same period. Opium cultivation was a state monopoly and mulberry production was almost entirely state-financed. The Company did make limited advances to contractors operating in the indigo sector until 1802. Subsequently, indigo production and trade was financed with capital borrowed from Agency Houses (until their collapse in 1833), chartered banks, Managing Agencies (after the fall of the Agency Houses) and a government-sponsored system of hypothecation. The indigo 'planters' were predominantly British, although a few Indian zamindars made tentative forays into this field when the market looked buoyant. The import of capital being as yet insignificant, the planters borrowed extensively from trading and financial institutions which raised capital locally. Much of this was invested as fixed capital in indigo factories which produced the dye, and the rest formed the circulating capital, some of which was passed on through contractors to reach the peasants who tended the plant. Although the evidence on the structure and trends in agrarian commerce is much fuller on the planters and their financiers during the period from 1800 to 1860, scattered information from the early nineteenth century and the detailed depositions before the Indigo Commission in 1860 make possible an attempt to view the problem from the primary producers' perspective as well.

In the early nineteenth century indigo was the main area of operation of capital supplied by the Agency Houses, the typical multi-faceted institutions of trade and finance formed by ex-servants of the Company and free merchants. The volume of indigo exports from Calcutta to London rose from 40,000 maunds in 1800 to 120,000 maunds in 1815, and between 1826 and 1830, the beginning of a period

[14] Letter from Court of Directors, 28 March 1788, cited in *ibid.*, p. 78; Report on the External Commerce of Bengal (R. 174, 13), India Office Records.
[15] Letter from Court of Directors, 20 June 1810, cited in Chowdhury, *Growth of Commercial Agriculture*, p. 80.

COMMERCIALIZATION AND COLONIALISM

of severe instability, averaged 118,000 maunds.[16] According to a petition of the Agency Houses in 1827, 'nearly the whole of indigo cultivation, absorbing for mere annual outlay a capital exceeding two crores of rupees, depend[ed] upon advances' made by them.[17] This process of financing, dominated by a few firms, paved the way for monopsonistic control of indigo production. Of the estimated annual outlay of Rs 20 million, as much as 80% came from the six giant houses of Alexander, Colvin, Cruttenden Mckillop, Fergusson, Mackintosh and Palmer.[18]

Of the two main forms of indigo cultivation on raiyati or peasant lands and nij or demesne lands (where the planter had bought into a superior tenurial right), the former was much more widely prevalent. For instance, as much as 61,000 bighas out of 75,000 cultivated under the Bengal Indigo Company in 1860 was found to be of the raiyati variety.[19] Compared to the mass of information collected in 1859–60, there is little firm evidence on the ways in which the system of advances affected raiyats in the initial stages. It is possible that in the first quarter of the nineteenth century indigo was not quite the kind of forced cultivation that it became after 1825. Faced with a build-up of population pressure on land as well as a revenue and rent offensive, peasants in west Bengal districts may well have opted for what looked like a higher-value and more labour-intensive cash-crop which not only promised a larger income but came with cash advances which could be used to pay the rent. Rammohan Roy's observation in 1829 that indigo-growing peasants looked 'better clothed and better con- ditioned' than their neighbours might well have referred to a carry- over from the era of relative well-being.[20] In 1830 the magistrate of Dhaka referred to the 'misfortune' of receiving indigo advances which reduced the raiyat to 'little better than a bond-slave to the factory'.[21]

It can be extrapolated from evidence garnered much later that a peasant would typically receive an advance of Rs 2 per bigha of indigo cultivation. The terms between the planter and the peasant were

[16] Ibid., p. 83; cf. Parliamentary Papers, 10 (1831–2), Part 2, Appendix 14.
[17] Petition of Six Agency Houses, 6 March 1827, cited in Chowdhury, Growth of Commercial Agriculture, p. 83.
[18] Ibid.
[19] Evidence of R. L. Larmour, General Mofussil Manager of the Bengal Indigo Company, Answer No. 1939, Report of the Indigo Commission (Calcutta, 1860).
[20] Raja Rammohan Roy, English Works, eds. K. Nag and D. Burman (Calcutta, 1947), Vol. IV, 83.
[21] Chowdhury, Growth of Commercial Agriculture, p. 133.

engraved in black and white on a duly stamped official contract enforceable in a court of law. The peasant was paid at a rate which generally varied, being a rupee for anything from six to eight 'bundles' held together by a six-foot chain strung around the centre of the plant. The amount advanced, the value of the stamp, the cost of seed and transportation costs were carefully deducted from the price paid to the peasant. Most knowledgeable accounts of the cost of production and the product price suggested that between 1830 and 1860 indigo cultivation was generally unremunerative for the peasant. The most optimistic estimate given to the Indigo Commission tallied the cost of cultivation including stamp paper, seed, ploughs, sowing, weeding, cutting and rent at Rs 3 annas 3 per bigha while the very best plant yielding 20 bundles at 5 bundles a rupee would fetch Rs 4.[22] Realistically, however, profit-making for the peasant was out of the question. One Murshidabad planter candidly reported that 'not even a rupee a bundle would pay the raiyat in some places'.[23] Apart from outright coercion, the only reason for wanting to cultivate indigo was the money advance which came with it. The planters were not minded to get indebted peasants to pay off their balances and hardly ever took a defaulting peasant to court. 'Every planter', as one among them conceded, 'endeavours to persuade them to retain their advances and work them out'.[24] Debts were reckoned to pass from father to son. In the Nischindapur concern in Nadia, out of 864 peasants planting 3,300 acres with indigo, a mere 110 had no outstanding balances, while in the Mulnath concern the lucky number was 237 out of 1,378. Unpaid balances mounted over the generations to astronomical figures which no indigo peasant could hope to redeem. Here was a marketing and production mechanism that efficiently and relentlessly attached unpaid labour to indigo cultivation.

If the planters had fashioned the interlinked product and credit markets to suit their purposes, they themselves were vulnerable to the vicissitudes in wider markets which they could only in part pass on to the primary producers. As it was, the Agency Houses were hampered in the process of capital formation as a result of the periodic withdrawals by partners. Further, the government tended to intervene as a

[22] This was the estimate of J. Cockburn, Deputy Magistrate of Jessore, in December 1959. See papers relating to Indigo Cultivation in Bengal, Vol. I, Section 10.
[23] Evidence of W. G. Rose, planter of Murshidabad, Answer No. 398, *Report of the Indigo Commission.*
[24] Evidence of R. P. Sage, Answer No. 596, *ibid.*

competitor in the money-market. Floating loans to meet its own pressing requirements, the government often had the effect of drawing off funds from agrarian production and trade. Most important, the qualitative change in the character of India's external trade around 1813, sparked by the dramatic decline in the exports of manufactures, resulted in a steady drop in the import of bullion. Having reached its peak value of Rs 47.5 million in 1818–19, the value of bullion imports dwindled to Rs 5.4 million in 1832–3.[25] For the first time in centuries India ceased to be a metropolitan magnet that attracted precious metals. The sparse character of bullion imports contributed to recurring liquidity problems in the Indian economy until the mid 1850s.

The susceptibility of eastern India's regional agrarian economy to crises at the centre of the capitalist world economy in Britain was manifest in the late 1820s, early 1830s and late 1840s. The state of demand in remote European markets increasingly determined price levels and the volume of credit in Bengal. The peak of a boom in the indigo market was reached in 1823. As signals of the trade depression in Britain reached Indian shores, the market in indigo began to wobble in 1825–6 and collapsed with the leading Agency Houses between 1830 and 1833. The fall of the house of Palmer in January 1830 was a major turning-point which shattered the confidence of nearly all, Europeans and Indians alike, who had deposited with the Agency Houses. Agricultural prices in Bengal went into a steep decline although volumes marketed and exported did not contract sharply.[26] The 'want of capital, the loss of credit, the destruction of trade and the contraction of currency' were identified as the key features of a bleak scenario.[27] The Agency Houses had the sympathy of Governor-General Bentinck, but little financial assistance from the government, which was increasingly reluctant to bale out a system that it believed was not only 'hollow' but 'rotten' to the core. The Bank of Bengal, a semi-government institution which had received a charter in 1809, offered help at the height of the crisis but ended up burdened with unprofitable indigo estates. The best that government could do was to arm the planters with a legal weapon, Regulation 5 of 1830, enabling

[25] Letters from the Court of Directors, 17 April 1833 and 15 April 1835, cited in Chowdhury, *Growth of Commercial Agriculture*, pp. 88–9; cf. *Ninth Report of the Select Committee*, 1783, 14.
[26] See K. N. Chaudhuri, 'Foreign Trade and Balance of Payments' in Dharma Kumar (ed.), *The Cambridge Economic History of India*, Vol. II (Cambridge, 1983), pp. 829–31.
[27] B. B. Chaudhuri, 'Agrarian Relations: Eastern India' in *ibid.*, p. 103.

49

them to use powers of distraint to enforce indigo contracts on an already emaciated peasantry. Nothing, however, could revive the ailing Agency Houses as the financiers of indigo cultivation.

While it is an exaggeration to claim that the system of production in Bengal was now 'completely geared' to the needs of industrialized Britain, it is nevertheless arguable that to a large extent the region's 'economy prospered or decayed according to fluctuations in the London market'.[28] The rhythms of a capitalist world economy cast a broad influence on economic trends interacting with other factors, notably high revenue demand, decline in elite consumption and the closure of mints (an erstwhile mechanism of drawing hoards into circulation). Local conditions were also important and help explain the variations in the precise timing and the degree of impact of wider fluctuations on the regional economies in the hinterlands of Calcutta, Bombay and Madras in the 1830s and 1840s.[29]

The Agency Houses gave way to a type of trading organization which came to be known as the Managing Agency system. These commercial agents relied on two important sources of finance – the Company's scheme of hypothecation and the Union Bank of Calcutta. The former preceded the fall of the Agency Houses as another mechanism since 1829 to facilitate remittances from India to Britain. The latter emerged as the financial plank on which the indigo system of eastern India rested. Having had a small beginning in 1829 with a capital of Rs 1.2 million, it expanded phenomenally during 1835–40 by which time it boasted a paid-up capital of Rs 10 million. A large proportion of these funds was given out in loans to indigo planters despite legal questions about its propriety. With the weakening of demand for indigo in the London-based market from the early 1840s, the Bank, operating virtually as an indigo agency, found itself in deep trouble. Between 1841 and 1843 several indigo concerns, including Ferguson, Gilmore and others, failed, leaving behind debts amounting to nearly Rs 6 million.[30] As indigo prices tumbled, suggestions were made to cut back supplies by burning agreed quantities of indigo plants. The severe depression in the British economy in 1847–8 proved to be the last straw for the acutely strained indigo-based commercial

[28] Amales Tripathi, *Trade and Finance in the Bengal Presidency, 1793–1833* (Calcutta, 1979), p. 155.
[29] C. A. Bayly, *The New Cambridge History of India: Indian Society and the Making of the British Empire* (Cambridge, 1988), pp. 123–8.
[30] Chowdhury, *Growth of Commercial Agriculture*, p. 113.

economy of Bengal. From September 1847 one indigo concern after another went bankrupt. Already in the first week of October the liabilities of these failed houses were estimated at £20 million sterling. The Calcutta newspaper *The Bengal Harkaru* carried reports from London describing the 'total disruption of the whole fabric of commerce' as 'an earthquake'.[31] The regional economy of eastern India felt the tremors in the form of a general crisis of confidence in credit transactions which practically paralysed internal trade. The Union Bank, deeply enmeshed in the indigo mess, shut its doors in December 1847. If there were structural weaknesses inherent in financing the indigo operations with borrowed capital, these were exposed and exacerbated by the downward fluctuations emanating from the centre of the larger economic system to which the region was now closely tied.

The drying up of capital and credit following the collapse of the Union Bank made the planters, who retained their factories or bought new ones at distress sales, increasingly reliant on coercive powers partly sanctioned by the state, and a rent offensive in their capacity as holders of tenurial rights, to maintain indigo production. Once the planters had become wary of making new advances to the peasants, the only rationale for wishing to cultivate indigo disappeared. Some further changes in the economic context between 1854 and 1860 set the stage for the 'blue mutiny' of 1859–60.

The beginnings of British capital investment in railways in 1854 exerted upward pressures on prices and wages in India. Since wage labour formed a small part of the agrarian economy of eastern India, it was the dramatic movement in prices which had the greatest bearing on the mostly smallholding peasantry. The outbreak of the Crimean War (1854–6) cut off the supplies of flax and hemp from Russia and created a new demand for Bengal jute. The volume and value of Bengal jute exports jumped from 111,218 maunds and Rs 152,924 in 1839–40 to 1,194,470 maunds and Rs 3,274,768 in 1855–6.[32] Demand for rice in the markets of Europe and China, as well as a diversion of some rice lands to jute and oil-seeds, set an inflationary trend in the rice price beginning in 1855. The price of rice rose steadily in Bengal districts between 1855 and 1860 (see Table 3). While the inflow of foreign capital and the tug of demand in foreign markets had pushed prices up

[31] *The Bengal Harkaru*, 8 December 1847.
[32] *The Hindoo Patriot*, 25 December 1857.

Table 3. Dhan *(paddy) prices per maund in Bengal districts*

| District | 1855 | 1860 |
|---|---|---|
| Jessore | Rs o As 10 Ps o | Rs 1 As  4 Ps o |
| Burdwan | Rs o As 10 Ps o | Rs 1 As  7 Ps 6 |
| Nadia (Santipur) | Rs o As 10 Ps o | Rs 1 As  6 Ps o |
| Nadia (Krishnanagar) | Rs o As 10 Ps 6 | Rs 1 As  4 Ps 6 |
| 24-Parganas (Barasat) | Rs o As 12 Ps o | Rs 1 As 10 Ps o |
| Hooghly | Rs 1 As  o Ps o | Rs 2 As  2 Ps o |

Source: *Report of the Indigo Commission*, Appendix 3.

between 1854 and 1857, the dislocations and scarcities after the onset of the 1857 revolt took over as the leading factors in the inflationary process.

In a context of general increase in the prices of commodities and foodgrains, the forced cultivation of a wholly unremunerative crop like indigo came to be resented by the peasantry as never before. They received key tactical support from indigenous moneylending landlords who now saw better prospects in the rice sector. The European indigo planters had long been objects of scorn in the peasant mind: 'they entered like needles and went out as ploughshares' as a folk ditty in idiomatic Bengali put it. But now a conjuncture had arrived when they could actually mount a frontal assault on the entire process of dependent commercialization to which they had been subject for so long. The planters were defeated in Bengal but regrouped to fight another day in neighbouring Bihar. The dismantling of an exploitative system of production for the market did not of itself resolve the problems of subsistence of peasant labour. The crucial link between subsistence and the market ensured that moneylending landlords and traders within a reordered context of colonial political economy were to emerge as major claimants of the peasants' surplus in a phase of subsistence commercialization from the later nineteenth century.

## SUBSISTENCE COMMERCIALIZATION: THE 'JUTE' PHASE

Time was when fibres sold on European markets were 'warranted free from Indian jute'. Although the decision of the Netherlands government in 1838 to use jute for coffee sacks elevated this commodity to a higher caste status, it was really the loss of flax and hemp supplies during the Crimean War that made the older prejudice against jute unaffordable. From a very low base, the volume of jute exports jumped fortyfold between 1838–43 and 1868–73. During the decade of the 1860s, the value of raw jute exports increased from Rs 4.1 million to Rs 20.5 million, before encountering the first of the major recurring downward fluctuations in its world market during the depression of 1872–3, which saw prices cut by nearly half in some places.[33] Famine conditions in Bengal in 1873–4 also induced a switch back from jute to rice by primary producers. During the final quarter of the nineteenth century the rapid expansion in international grain trade provided the stimulus for the growth of the acreage under raw jute as well as the establishment of a jute manufacturing industry in eastern India. The demand closer at home for container bags to export grain from Bengal to the famine-afflicted regions of Bombay and Madras presidencies in the mid 1870s helped pull the jute sector out of the slump of 1873–4.

For the next three decades the jute economy of Bengal followed a pattern of short periods of buoyant prices and expanding acreage culminating in sharp setbacks. A brief era of high incomes and optimism for jute cultivators ended in dramatic losses and gloom in the downturn of 1882–3 when demand in Western markets shrank unexpectedly. Another expansionary phase reached its peak in the late 1880s. The acreage expanded in districts where the fibre was already established, while its cultivation spread to new districts like Noakhali where it had previously been unknown. But in the crisis of 1890–1 the price again fell nearly by half and, consequently, in districts as diverse as Dinajpur, Tippera and Purnea a good part of the crop was left to rot in the fields.[34] Bengal jute entered its most vigorous and sustained period of boom in 1906, one which lasted until the outbreak of the First World War. In 1907 jute cultivation reached its high point of 3.88 million acres.[35] After that date, although peasants engaged in short-term switching between jute and autumn rice in response to relative

[33] See Hem Chandra Kar, *Report on the Cultivation of and Trade in Jute* (Calcutta, 1877); Binay Bhushan Chaudhuri, 'Growth of Commercial Agriculture in Bengal: 1859–1885' in *Indian Economic and Social History Review* (hereafter *IESHR*), 7, 2 (1970), pp. 240–1; Chaudhuri, 'Foreign Trade' in Kumar (ed.), *Cambridge Economic History*, Vol. II, pp. 851–2.

[34] Chaudhuri, 'Commercial Agriculture: 1859–85', *IESHR*, 7, 2 (1970), 244.

[35] Rajat Ray, 'The Crisis of Bengal Agriculture – Dynamics of Immobility' in *IESHR*, 10, 3 (1973), 261–2.

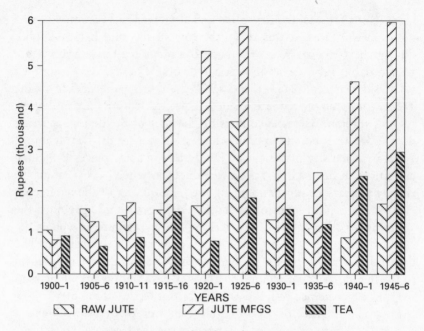

Figure 1. Bengal: value of major exports

prices, no long-term upward trend in its acreage was discernible. The total value of Bengal's jute, however, rode a long-term upward trend until the worldwide depression struck in 1930.

In an altogether different social setting, the expansion of tea as a major commercial crop on the slopes of the hills of north Bengal was roughly coterminous with the spread of jute in the river basins of east Bengal. Inaugurated in the hill district of Darjeeling in 1850, the first tea garden in the submontane tract known as the Western Duars of Jalpaiguri district was opened in 1874. Although the number of gardens fell back after reaching a peak of 235 in the Duars at the turn of the century, the acreage under tea and the size of the labour force rose steadily until 1930 (see Table 4). The colonial state facilitated the initial expansion by making 'tea grant' land available on favourable terms to European planters. The value of tea exports eventually overtook the value of raw jute exports in the 1930s and 1940s (see Fig. 1). But in terms of the sheer numbers of primary producers dependent for their livelihood on the state of agrarian commerce, jute remained by far the more important cash crop affecting the subsistence needs of the region.

Table 4. *Tea cultivation in the Jalpaiguri Duars*[36]

| Year | Gardens | Acreage | Permanent labour | Temporary labour | Total labour |
|---|---|---|---|---|---|
| 1901 | 235 | 76,403 | 47,365 | 21,254 | 68,619 |
| 1911 | 191 | 90,859 | 56,693 | 18,622 | 75,315 |
| 1921 | 131 | 112,688 | 86,693 | 1,871 | 88,564 |
| 1931 | 151 | 132,074 | 112,591 | 4,262 | 116,853 |

The imperative of peasant subsistence was closely related to the process of commercialization of both the plantation and smallholding sorts. It was desperate rural poverty that had unhinged tribal labour from their original habitats and placed them at the mercy of sardars who recruited for the tea plantations.[37] Raising a cash-crop which promised a higher gross income seemed to the mass of smallholders the better bet for assuring subsistence in the early twentieth century than growing insufficient quantities of rice.[38] According to one impression, some half of the population of the jute-growing districts 'live[d] on holdings of an acre in area or less' in 1930, relying on jute for the 'wherewithal to supplement their food and pay their rents'.[39] It is clear from the findings of the Indian Central Jute Committee in 1937 that nearly 80% of jute-growing families produced less than 30 maunds of jute each, the approximate yield of 2 acres of land.[40] In pursuing this strategy of subsistence through the route of the jute market the smallholding peasants had to contend with the inequities of the marketing structure and the uncertainties of world market trends.

The mechanism that extracted jute from the villages to the docks and mills near Calcutta was designed and refined by the exporting and manufacturing interests through a process of trial and error, and was periodically reordered according to the exigencies of world market fluctuations. The degree of linkage between the product and credit markets consequently altered in different phases. Beginning with the

[36] A. Mitra, Census of India 1951, Vol. VI, Part 1A (Calcutta, 1953), p. 263 cited in Sharit Bhowmick, *Class Formation in the Plantation System* (Delhi, 1981), p. 53.

[37] Bhowmick, *Class Formation*, pp. 43–52.

[38] See Sugata Bose, *Agrarian Bengal: Economy, Social Structure and Politics, 1919–1947* (Cambridge, 1986), pp. 46–58.

[39] *Report of the Land Revenue Administration in Bengal, 1930–31* (Calcutta, annual), p. 5.

[40] Cited in Omkar Goswami, 'The Peasant Economy of East and North Bengal in the 1930s' in *IESHR*, 21, 3 (1984), 337–8.

first jute mills on the banks of the Hooghly in 1855, the manufacturing interest gradually expanded until it started to take a larger share of the jute crop than the exporters during the First World War. Figures from the late 1920s and early 1930s show that just over 50% of the raw product went to the mills.[41] European dominance in the jute manufacturing sector, by contrast with cotton in western India, was pervasive, abetted if not directly aided by British officialdom, but Indian capitalists prised open a few points of entry in the inter-war period. Besides, despite the existence of branches of some European firms in mofussil marketing towns, it was mostly a chain of Indian intermediaries, Bengalis as well as Marwaris, which connected the ultimate buyers to the primary producers.

Most studies of the structure of the jute market suggest that atomistic peasant producers stood at a position of disadvantage in relation to traders and manufacturers better organized to act in concert to secure their interests. It is useful, however, to distinguish here the adversities stemming from the nature of the articulation to the product market from those inherent in the structure and processes of production and reproduction in the agrarian economy which are analysed in the next two chapters. In the late nineteenth century, the practice of handing down advances to obtain the crop at a lower price did not seem very common. The Bengal Jute Commission of 1873 reported on the basis of evidence given by jute cultivators and traders that there was generally 'no demand for advances'. This was so, according to the enquiry, because the numbers of jute cultivators were relatively sparse, the initial 'out-of-pocket expenses' modest and 'the labour, seed and manure ... the cultivators' own'.[42] When prices slumped unexpectedly, peasants often left the jute uncut in the fields. The purchasers of jute in this early phase were hampered in their operations by uncertain control over supply and inaccurate forecasting of demand. Although the Indian Jute Mills Association, established in 1884, had some early success in protecting themselves by resort to short-time working, their price-fixing schemes attempted in 1895 and 1901 turned out to be unqualified failures.

The quantitative leap in the jute acreage in 1906 also represented a qualitative transformation in its marketing pattern and hierarchy. As

[41] *Report of the Bengal Provincial Banking Enquiry Committee 1929–30*, vol. I, 104–5; *Report of the Bengal Jute Enquiry (Finlow) Committee 1934*, p. 157.
[42] Cited in Chaudhuri, 'Commercial Agriculture: 1859–85', 228.

COMMERCIALIZATION AND COLONIALISM

the stakes were raised, manufacturers and exporters increasingly sought to maintain an assured supply of the raw product at much lower than the competitive price by getting more deeply involved in the financing of agrarian production and trade. The annual inflow of foreign finance and merchant capital became a crucial element, not only in the commercial agriculture of Bengal, but in the liquidity of the region's economy as a whole. Usury capital, which circulated within the countryside, now took its cues from the degrees of confidence displayed by the world of high finance. Although the usurer was often a rentier landlord not directly interested in the product market and distinct from the trader who provided dadans or advances, the product and credit markets were, between 1906 and 1929, effectively, albeit informally, integrated. The colonial government's interventions in currency and credit issues, either through manipulation of the pound–rupee exchange rate or its borrowing activities, provided the link between the market and the state.

The small traders, known as farias or beparis, who collected jute from the homes or villages of the cultivators, were in the early twentieth century more often than not commission agents of others higher up in the chain of middlemen, who in turn were recipients of funds from the ultimate purchasing companies. The dalal or broker of the baler and the aratdar or warehouseman were usually important intermediaries at trading centres in the districts. As a 1926 report from Tippera explained, '[v]ery large capital [was] required to finance the jute crop'; of this, the beparis, aratdars and dalals 'suppl[ied] some but the bulk [was] provided by the purchasing companies who borrow[ed] from banks'.[43] The interest rate on dadans ranged between 24% and 75%, and the debtor typically undertook to deliver the crop at 10% to 25% below the market price. In the mid 1920s, middlemen's commission was estimated to reduce by at least 20% what the primary producer might otherwise have received. Yet, as one historian has pointed out, 'the cultivators were denied fair prices, not primarily because of the intervention of too many middlemen, as alleged by British civilians', but 'mainly due to combination of European buyers of jute'.[44] The

[43] Collector of Tippera to Registrar of Cooperative Societies in *Report on the Marketing of Agricultural Produce in Bengal 1926* (Calcutta, 1928).

[44] Ray, 'Crisis of Bengal Agriculture', 261–2. For the estimate of middlemen's commission see Evidence of R. S. Finlow and K. Mclean, Director and Assistant Director of Agriculture Bengal in Evidence, *Report of the Royal Commission on Agriculture*, vol. IV, p. 13 and Appendix, vol. XIV, p. 70.

financial and organizational strength, despite some conflicts of interest, of the purchasers, and the lack of holding power, even if not tied to a dadandar, on the part of the producers, ensured a significant differential between average Calcutta prices and harvest prices in Bengal districts. For the 1910s, 1920s and 1930s these were reckoned to have been in the order of 32%, 31% and 33% respectively.[45] A wide array of methods of varying degrees of ingenuity was deployed to short-change the jute-growing peasant; one of the more effective means was the manipulation of grades by which different qualities of the fibre were ranked. During the 1930s depression the monopsonistically organized jute industry tightened its grip over the marketing mechanism at the expense of not only the primary producers but also the intermediaries. The middlemen's chain underwent a sharp contraction as the downstream flows of finance capital suddenly ceased. Peasant production, faced with severe structural constraints in finding alternatives to jute, did not adjust to the collapse in prices. Consequently, incidence of dadan, now largely unnecessary from the point of view of manufacturers and exporters, declined, enabling the industry to effect a painful 'rationalization' of what had been by all accounts an unwieldy marketing structure. Research on the Tamil Nadu countryside has suggested that the scything effect of the depression on elaborate commodity-extracting mechanisms was a widespread rural phenomenon and certainly not peculiar to Bengal.[46]

In the case of the other major commodity of export, tea, the relations of production based on wage-labour and the nexus between production and trade were qualitatively different. The fact of European dominance was not at any stage obscured by the cumbrous appearance of an elaborate marketing structure. Tea plantations, owned and managed by British-registered firms, despatched their tea to Calcutta and Chittagong to be shipped to London where auction sales were arranged. All other tea gardens engaged one of four European firms of brokers based in Calcutta who acted as auctioneers on their behalf. The lead-lined wooden chests of tea were stored in warehouses near the Kidderpore docks and sales were held usually once, and occasionally twice, a week. There was no intermediary between the tea-garden proprietors and the four brokerage firms.[47]

[45] Amiya Bagchi, *Private Investment in India, 1900–1939* (Cambridge, 1969), p. 287.
[46] See C. J. Baker, *An Indian Rural Economy: the Tamilnad Countryside, 1880–1955* (Delhi, 1984), ch. 4.
[47] *Report of the Bengal Provincial Banking Enquiry Committee 1929–30*, vol. I, 104.

Rice occupied for Bengal peasants the unique position of chief subsistence crop while at the same time being of considerble commercial importance. A 1930s enquiry revealed that relatively small proportions of rice were imported or exported into or out of the province relative to annual production, but the imports from Burma exercised a disproportionate impact on price.[48] As much as 44% of production may have entered the domain of exchange at least at the village level in 1941.[49] The bulk of the rice trade was inter-district in character. The marketing pattern bore some superficial resemblance to that of jute, although Europeans did not dominate at the top. The middlemen's chain was appreciably shorter in the 1920s and the practice of dadan was not as pervasive. The prices of these two commodities, the premier 'cash-crop' and 'food-crop', were organically linked and the relative trends in these two connected markets had the most critical bearing on the subsistence security of Bengal's peasantry.

A folk-poet of Bengal, Abed Ali Mian, once exclaimed in dismay that peasants who had abandoned rice to gamble on jute would one day have to eat the stem of the plant.[50] Yet it had not been an uncalculated risk taken by smallholders anxious to eke out yearly subsistence requirements in a difficult demographic and social environment. The Datta Committee's detailed investigation of prices between 1890 and 1912 had found that the growth of agricultural income had been sluggish compared to the rise in the cost of living. While 'agricultural income per head of population' was up 16% in 1909–13 over 1890–4, 'average retail prices' of an agriculturist's usual purchases had risen by 26%. However, peasants who had resorted to jute in east and north Bengal had made profits and were 'substantially better off than before'.[51] Folk ditties quite as much as price statistics recorded the

[48] *Report of the Bengal Paddy and Rice Enquiry Committee*, Vol. I (Alipur, 1940), pp. 33–9.
[49] *Report of the Marketing of Rice in India and Burma* (Delhi, 1941), p. 35.
[50] Bujhli na tui burar beta, Abeder katha noyko jhuta/Khete hope pater gora thik janish mor bhasha/Mone korechho nibo taka,/She asha tor jabe phanka/Panchisher poya habe tor, hrine porbi thasha/Nibi bate taka ghare/Peter daye jabe phure/Hisheb kore dekhish khata, jato kharacher pasha. (You did not heed Abed who never speaks false/You will have to eat the stem of your jute, mark my words/You think you will make money/That is but an empty dream/You will end up drowning in debt) (Abed Ali Mian, *Desh Shanti* (Gantipara, Rangpur, 1925).
[51] Cited in Chaudhuri, 'Agrarian Relations: Eastern India' in Kumar (ed.), *Cambridge Economic History*, vol. II, p. 147.

unique surge in prosperity which began in 1906.[52] Its foundation, however, was not quite as secure as the strong wooden posts on which the jute dealers had built their new four-roofed homesteads. The sharp drop in prices at the onset of the First World War quickly broke the idyll. The period of the war witnessed a 'naked confrontation of interests between the European business corporations and the British Government on the one hand and the native commercial classes and the peasantry on the other'.[53] The primary producers emerged from the conflict bruised and battered. The widening differential between the export price of gunny bags and cloth, and the import price of jute from the countryside into Calcutta between 1916 and 1921 showed the huge profits made by combinations of manufacturing and exporting firms at the expense of the peasantry.[54] The colonial government's exchange rate policy and public expenditure expansion had titled the terms of trade against the agrarian sector and fuelled inflation. After a brief recovery in 1919 and a setback during 1920–2, the jute economy of rural east Bengal appeared set to enter another extended era of prosperity.

The 1920s boom was, however, 'more apparent than real', with jute and rice prices consistently lagging behind the upswing in the all-commodities price index.[55] If augmentation of gross income was the chief rationale behind jute cultivation, the cash-crop option in this phase was earning diminishing dividends. On one calculation, the annual growth rate of real gross income from jute and aman rice in east and north Bengal districts was under 2% in the decade of the 1920s, which was about half the growth rate averaged in the fourteen years prior to the First World War.[56] If one factors in the growth of population during this decade, the picture of the 1920s as a boom period begins to look very doubtful indeed. Yet the bleakness of the 1930s casts the previous decade in much mellower light.

World market fluctuations by this time were not unexpected occur-

[52] One poem went: Nailya bepari, satkhanda bari/Joanshaiya thuni diya, banchhe choari (The jute dealer's seven huts in his homestead/The four roofs rest on posts of Joanshahi timber) (see Bose, *Agrarian Bengal*, p. 80).

[53] Ray, 'Crisis of Bengal Agriculture', p. 264.

[54] Saugata Mukherji, 'Imperialism in Action through a Mercantilist Function' in Barun De (ed.), *Essays in Honour of Professor Susobhan Sarkar* (Calcutta, 1974), p. 741; 'Some Aspects of Commercialisation of Agriculture in Eastern India, 1891–1938' in Asok Sen *et al.*, *Perspectives in Social Sciences 2: Three Studies in the Agrarian Structure in Bengal 1850–1947* (Calcutta, 1982), pp. 234–6.

[55] *Bengal Provincial Banking Enquiry Committee*, Vol. I (Delhi, 1931), p. 65.

[56] Goswami, 'Peasant Economy', p. 340.

rences in the lives of Bengal peasants. Yet past experience with periodic crises had not prepared them for the shock of the 1930s depression, which was unprecedented in terms of both intensity and duration. Having its origins in weakening demand for raw materials in the industrial West since 1926, the slump was accentuated in the agrarian world already overburdened with stocks once Western states put up tariff walls, deflated their economies and froze foreign lending in response to the 1929 crisis in the industrial economies. The value of Bengal's exports, which had peaked at Rs 1,460 million in 1925–6, was down to Rs 811 million in 1930–1 and had further declined to Rs 612 million by 1935–6, though export volumes fell temporarily by only about 15% between 1930 and 1933. Raw jute prices led the downslide but no export commodity avoided the tumble. The stoppage in the flow of finance capital triggered, through the closely wired circuits of credit, a generalized liquidity crisis which brought down domestic prices almost quite as much as export prices. Jute and rice prices dipped by more than 60% of their late 1920s level between 1932 and 1934 and did not really recover until 1938.[57] One estimate suggests that in east and north Bengal money income fell by over 50% from an annual average of Rs 978 million during 1926–9 to Rs 486 million during 1930–4, and real income shrank by at least 25%.[58]

It needs only to be added that between 1930–1 and 1934–5, when raw jute prices had reached the bottom of the trough, the differential between the harvest price and the prices of hessian and sacking manufactures widened to its largest recorded magnitude. Neither intermediary traders and financiers nor primary producers managed to escape the squeeze applied by the jute industry.[59] The colonial state contributed to the intensification of the crisis through a number of policy initiatives, mostly in the financial domain. Most importantly, the decision in London in September 1931 to take sterling off the gold standard and keep the rupee tied to the devalued pound signalled a large-scale dishoarding of gold from the Indian countryside. Rural Bengal's accumulated treasure, not for the first time, contributed handsomely to colonial India's payments to imperial Britain, but on this occasion in a new context of erosion of India's surpluses from exports of agricultural commodities.[60]

[57] See Sugata Bose, *Agrarian Bengal*, pp. 79–87.
[58] Goswami, 'Peasant Economy', p. 344.
[59] *Report of the Jute Enquiry (Finlow) Committee 1934*, p. 146.
[60] Bose, *Agrarian Bengal*, pp. 65–7; cf. Baker, *Indian Rural Economy*, ch. 2.

The primary rationale behind subsistence commercialization in the 'jute' phase had been the prospect of earning sufficient money income to pay for subsistence goods, rice in particular. The drop in rice prices during the depression prevented privation from turning into widespread starvation. The economic dislocations accompanying the Second World War confirmed the worst fears about the risks involved in the strategy of assuring subsistence via the jute market. The government's massive wartime expenditure fed an inflationary spiral while speculative buying and panic hoarding sent food prices soaring, especially from the autumn of 1942. Although after much dithering the provincial government had moved to regulate compulsorily the jute acreage, the relative price of this cash-crop remained weak compared to rice and other essential commodities. The result was a dramatic loss of exchange entitlements to rice of a mass of jute-dependent peasant smallholders. At the onset of the great Bengal famine in March 1943, the chief controller of jute regulation commented on conditions in the main jute-growing districts: '[m]ore jute means less paddy and the price of paddy at the moment is about one and a half times that of jute'.[61] The rustic poet's prophecy tragically had come true. One of the many ineffectual and contradictory measures taken by the government to pull the reins on galloping inflation was the imposition of maximum and minimum prices of jute in 1943. In the immediate post-war years the price ceiling played into the hands of manufacturers and exporters who in collusion with bureaucrats stubbornly opposed calls to decontrol jute prices during the harvest season of 1946.[62]

It took some time before the colonial legacy was shed in matters to do with the structure and trends in the jute market in independent India, Pakistan and, after 1971, Bangladesh. The partition of Bengal, of course, effected a sharp disjuncture by separating the industry from the hinterland that produced the raw product. The government of India restrained the managing agents within a web of regulatory measures from 1956 and, finally, through a piece of parliamentary legislation in 1967 abolished the age-old system altogether from 1970. The IJMA, however, lived on, though now a shadow of its former self. The government of Pakistan assisted West Pakistani capitalists to set up a jute manufacturing industry in the 1950s which kept going the time-honoured tradition of handing east Bengali peasants the prover-

61 'Note by Chief Controller Jute Regulation' cited in Bose, *Agrarian Bengal*, p. 91.
62 *Millat*, 12 July 1946.

bial raw deal.[63] If the structure of jute-based agrarian commerce exhibited a nagging habit of replicating itself in different contexts, the nature of trends in the marketplace underwent subtle but not insignificant alterations. In the pre-independence period harvest and terminal prices were often found to be moving in contrary directions. Since the early 1950s prices at the village, intermediary and terminal tiers have on the whole moved in the same direction, albeit by different orders of magnitude.[64] Intermediaries, partly due to inelastic transport costs reckoned by volume, and primary producers, mainly due to their economic weakness and lack of holding power, have continued to be relatively more vulnerable than the industry to the market's downward fluctuations.

## COLONIAL CAPITALISM AND COMMODITY PRODUCTION

In a sense, the peasants of eastern India lived in a 'global village' from at least the 1820s, occupying the lower rungs of an elaborate, inter-connected hierarchical structure based on an international division of labour. Yet, as commercialization of product and capital markets had advanced well ahead of the markets in land and labour, these rural producers of commodities continued to live in a very real sense in an agrarian society with its own distinctive tapestry of relations and culture. Of course, commodities like indigo and jute coloured their mental world just as they remoulded the landscape around them. Cash-cropping still was less of a 'romance', given the back-breaking labour that had to go into the pursuit of uncertain returns, than the venture of colonial capitalists in search of profits from manufacturing and export commerce. As Abdul Samed Mian put it in a folk poem:

*Pat ashia jakhan deshete pounchhilo*
*Pashchima eshe takhan dakhal karilo*
*Ekhon tader hate dekho paisa holio*
*Bangalire tara dekho kichhu na bujhilo*
*Na paito khaite jara chhatuar gura*

[63] See Jalal, *State of Martial Rule*, chs. 3, 4, and 5.

[64] On pre-independence movements, see Dharm Narain, *The Impact of Price Movements on Selected Crops in India* (London, 1965), Appendix Tables 1 and 14; on post-independence movements, see Shovan Ray, 'Modelling the World Jute Economy', unpublished Ph.D. dissertation (Cambridge University, 1986).

*Ballamer bhat khay bujhe dekho tara*
*Na mile Bangalire Rangooner bhat*
*Buba hoye gelo dekho Bangalir jat*
*(When jute reached our land*
*The Westerners came and took control*
*Now look how much money they have made*
*They can now be disdainful of the Bengalis*
*Those who could not get to eat crushed coarse grain*
*Today are consumers of good ballam rice*
*The Bengalis cannot even get rice from Rangoon*
*Look, the Bengali race is ruined.)*[65]

The pessimistic picture drawn by most agrarian historians of Bengal of the lack of any real developmental impact of the 'commercialization' of Bengal agriculture might be open to two sorts of scepticism. One stems from a view that eastern India represents one pole of the process of colonial development marked by sharp regional disparities. It is possible that more primary producers did better by playing the market in parts of Maharashtra, Gujarat and the Punjab.[66] Even in these regions, however, the evidence is mixed and the perspectives of different historians are quite divergent. The old nationalist positions on high colonial land revenue demand have been more surely undermined than the points about inequities flowing from the larger context of export trade in agricultural raw materials and the colonial political economy. Even in the showcase of Indian colonial development, the Punjab, serious distortions in the commercialization process have been recently noted.[67]

The second sort of sceptic might point to the undeniable differentiation within the peasantry. The motives and meanings underlying the commercialization process might consequently have varied for different strata of workers on the soil. This chapter has simply emphasized that in a scenario of predominantly smallholding cultivation, in both the 'indigo' and 'jute' phases, the overwhelming majority of primary

[65] Abdul Samed Mian, *Krishak Boka* (*The Foolish Peasant*, Ahara, Mymensingh, 1921), pp. 6–8.
[66] See Michelle McAlpin, *Subject to Famine* (Princeton, 1982); Donald R. Attwood, 'Capital and Transformation of Agrarian Systems: Sugar Production in India' in Meghnad Desai *et al.* (eds.), *Agrarian Power and Agricultural Productivity in South Asia* (Berkeley, 1984).
[67] Mridula Mukherjee, 'Commercialization and Agrarian Change in Pre-Independence Punjab' in K. N. Raj *et al.* (eds.), *Essays on the Commercialization of Indian Agriculture*, pp. 51–104; see also Imran Ali, *The Punjab under Imperialism* (Princeton, 1989).

producers cultivated cash-crops under compulsion. The subsistence-motivated commercialization of the 'jute' phase was not quite the forced cultivation of the latter part of the 'indigo' phase. The response to an externally provided market 'opportunity' was not a matter of unconstrained choice either, though a perfectly rational one. Peasant perceptions of the interlinked arenas of subsistence and the market have been unnecessarily confused by a false dichotomy between a subsistence ethic and rational economic behaviour which has crept into some of the peasant studies literature.[68] This is not to say that the making of monetary profit and the avoidance of starvation were not qualitatively different motives, but the problem of differentiation cannot be adequately tackled by simply looking at 'commercialized' output markets without a closer analysis of the related issues of property and production. From the early nineteenth century mostly smallholding Bengal peasants engaged in expanded commodity production for a capitalist world market. That did not necessarily entail capitalist transformation of the complex relations of property and production in agriculture.

[68] An example of this is Samuel L. Popkin, *The Rational Peasant: the Political Economy of Rural Society in Vietnam* (Berkeley, 1979), in large part intended as a critique of James C. Scott, *The Moral Economy of the Peasant* (New Haven, 1976).

CHAPTER 3

# PROPERTY AND PRODUCTION

Historians of colonial India have been puzzled lately by the mismatch between the rapid expansion of commodity production for a capitalist world market on the one hand, and low levels of productive investment in agriculture and an apparent continuity in non-capitalist agrarian social structures on the other. The sense of bewilderment is itself a scholarly advance from 'traditions' set in the later nineteenth century which saw markets, agricultural investment and agrarian relations as themes fit for separate enquiry. Needless to say, this led to 'debates' about the economic results of colonialism marked by a peculiar absence of dialogue.[1] Yet even the more perceptive scholars have continued to harbour teleological assumptions about capitalist trans-formation. This has led some to declare that the 'ultimate' dominance of capitalism denotes, willy-nilly, some form of capitalist mode of production in agriculture. Others, convinced that what they see in the rural areas is a 'semi-feudal' or simply a 'peasant' mode of production, have been concerned with identifying the 'obstacles' or 'impediments' in the way of capitalism bearing full sway.[2] Consequently, the much-needed probe into the analytics of the relationship between capitalist 'development' under colonialism and agrarian continuity or change has been almost always slightly off the mark.

Arguments about continuity in agrarian relations during colonial rule have rested generally, if not purely, on descriptive rather than analytical categories. It has been found acceptable to compare, for

---

[1] Reflections of some of these older debates can be found in Morris D. Morris *et al.*, *Indian Economy in the Nineteenth Century: a Symposium* (New Delhi, 1969) and also the more recent Dharma Kumar (ed.), *The Cambridge Economic History of India* (Cambridge, 1983). For an insightful critique of the 'traditional' historiography see D. A. Washbrook, 'Progress and Problems: South Asian Economic and Social History, c. 1720–1860' in *Modern Asian Studies*, 22 (1988), 57–96.

[2] J. Banaji, 'Capitalist Domination and the Small Peasantry: Deccan Districts in the Late Nineteenth Century' in *Economic and Political Weekly*, 12, 33 and 34 (1977), 1374–404; Amit Bhaduri, 'The Evolution of Land Relations in Eastern India under British Rule' in *Indian Economic and Social History Review*, 13, 1 (1976), 45–58; Abu Ahmed Abdullah, 'Landlord and Rich Peasant under the Permanent Settlement' in *Calcutta Historical Journal*, 4, 2 (1980), 89–154; Shapan Adnan, 'Peasant Production and Capitalist Development', unpublished Ph.D. dissertation (Cambridge, 1984).

instance, levels of peasant differentiation or landlessness at the beginning and at the end of the colonial era.[3] The descriptive approach has tended to obscure subtle but very real processes of change. Without developing well-defined analytical categories it is virtually impossible to identify, far less to pinpoint, the elements of change in agrarian structures which undeniably displayed a remarkable degree of resilience. For one thing, it is useful to make an analytic distinction between the relations of production and the relations of surplus-appropriation. The latter very clearly underwent a series of mutations over the two centuries following 1770. The successive rise to pre-eminence of the rent, credit, lease, land and capital markets as mechanisms of appropriating the surplus bears such an important relationship to the question of resistance by the working peasantry that it is being treated separately in chapter 4. The present chapter tracks the continuities and illuminates the nature of qualitative change by focusing upon 'the direct relationship of the owners of the conditions of production to the immediate producers'.[4]

Two key conditions of production were, of course, land and capital. Agrarian historians have displayed a general tendency to concentrate on land rather than on capital. Yet control over land did not make producers independent agents in the process of production if they were dependent on externally-supplied capital, often in the form of credit. The dominance of the owners of capital, especially in the lower echelons of its structure, had in turn occasionally to be substantiated by acquiring land. The issue of agrarian change can only be addressed by integrating the histories of land and capital. Neither land nor capital can be seen as a monolithic category. In speaking of land one is really referring to the multiple hierarchically-arranged layers of rights to it; the pyramidal structure of capital includes everything from high finance at the apex to petty usury in the countryside at the base. The counterpoint of land and capital is crucial to the history of labour in the agrarian context.

Within this context it is necessary to challenge the narrow definition of labour history which prevails in the field because it is more than just a matter of semantics. Labour, if it does not exclusively refer to the

[3] Rajat and Ratna Ray, 'The Dynamics of Continuity in Rural Bengal under the British Imperium' in *Indian Economic and Social History Review*, 10, 2 (1973), 103–28; Dharma Kumar, 'Land Ownership and Inequality in Madras Presidency, 1853–54 to 1946–47' in *IESHR*, 12, 3 (1975), 229–62.

[4] Karl Marx, *Capital: a Critique of Political Economy* Vol. III, (Harmondsworth, 1981), p. 927.

industrial working class, usually encompasses only that segment of the rural population which is unambiguously dependent on wages either as plantation workers or as landless or hopelessly land-poor labourers. Yet the success of capitalist development in colonial eastern India rested primarily on the exploitation of peasant family labour. Wage-labour was more often than not a mechanism to augment income to assure reproduction of peasant family labour, although a distinct wage-labouring class did exist in certain sectors. From this perspective the phenomenon of rapid market expansion and yet the persistence of non-capitalist forms of agrarian relations appears to be less a puzzling paradox than a logical relationship underpinning the intermeshing of economy and society. It is in this sense that peasant history establishes itself as one of the more important branches of labour history.

The typical unit of production, which was preserved rather than transformed during the colonial and immediate post-colonial periods, was the peasant smallholding. Who put in the labour on these units, and on what terms, was what defined and differentiated agrarian social structures. Large landholdings did exist, of course, and had an important dynamic relationship with the more common work-units of a predominantly small-scale agriculture. The chief contradiction to production and primary possessory rights based on peasant small-holding was provided, however, by (initially large-scale) property rights in revenue collection granted by the colonial state. So much of the social history of rural eastern India has been written around the dominance of zamindari bhadralok and the larger landholding 'jote-dari' peasantry that it is necessary to restore the perspective by investigating agrarian relations from the angle of vision of the small-holding, land-poor and landless working majority. This chapter engages in an exploration of the dialectic between property and production in the domain of agrarian society. Evolving within the framework of larger economic arenas based on capitalism, the property–production interaction deeply influenced social relations of entitlement to land, work and subsistence.

## SOCIAL RELATIONS OF PROPERTY AND PRODUCTION, C. 1770–1860

In the aftermath of the great famine of 1770, the English East India Company was deeply worried about the stability and certainty of the chief source of its revenues. In order to devise an effective and efficient land revenue system, it was necessary first to solve the vexed problem of the tenure of land. 'And so it happened', in the words of a late-nineteenth-century barrister of the Inner Temple,

that to English gentlemen – possessed of marvellous energy, great ability, the highest honesty of purpose, and spotless integrity, but destitute of that light which alone could have guided them to the truth – fell the task of solving this problem: and the solution appeared to them to depend upon the answer to this question – 'Who owned the land?' The missing ingredient in this otherwise blemishless English character was a knowledge of comparative jurisprudence, for regrettably 'law ... formed no part of the liberal education of an Englishman'.[5]

The flaw which went unacknowledged was the as yet incomplete education in local agrarian conditions, especially among those English gentlemen who wished to temper the cold calculations of revenue requirements with heady dreams of replicating capitalist estates in Bengal on the English model.

## Peasants' lands and landlords' demesnes

John Shore, who had taught himself more about the agrarian structures of Bengal than most of his contemporaries (especially Cornwallis), recognized that 'the land [was] divided into ryoty and khamar', adding not wholly accurately that 'the rents of the former [were] paid in money and the latter in kind'.[6] The direct control of zamindar overlords extended only over their demesnes. The possessory rights exercised by various strata of raiyats over their holdings were not seriously considered, however, to merit being dignified as a form of 'ownership' during the desperate search to find a peg on which to hang the concept of a private property right in land. The opposition in the debates leading to the Permanent Settlement with the zamindars in 1793 fought their case mainly on a theoretical plane, denying the existence of owners of land.[7] This happened despite the well-established and well-known, though not well-defined, terms on which raiyats wielded customary dominion over the soil in Mughal and nawabi Bengal.

A raiyat, the common Persian word for cultivator, was categorized

---

[5] C. D. Field, *Introduction to the Regulations of the Bengal Code* (Calcutta, 1912), p. 37.
[6] John Shore, Minute of June 1789, *Parliament Papers*, 1812, 7, 226.
[7] Ranajit Guha, *A Rule of Property for Bengal* (Paris, 1963); Ratnalekha Ray, *Change in Bengal Agrarian Society 1760–1850* (Delhi, 1980).

by state and society in late-eighteenth-century Bengal according to the rental and tenurial terms on which land was held. Raiyats, that 'numerous and inferior class of people, who held and cultivated small parts of land on their own account',[8] could be of the hari or mirasi, the fasli and the khamar types. The hari or mirasi raiyats were the most privileged and held permanent rights to land for which they paid fixed rents. The fasli raiyats, by far the largest category, paid variable rents depending on the kind and value of crops they produced on their lands. The khamar raiyats were those who did not actually hold raiyati land but worked the nij or khamar lands of zamindars and talukdars and generally shared the crop. If these were the categories based on rental terms, the duration of rights to a piece of land was of great importance in an era of labour scarcity and pervasive migrancy. This explains the near-obsession in the literature of the first century of colonial rule with khudkasht (permanent and resident) and paikasht (temporary and migrant) raiyats. The former had firmer security of tenure while the latter enjoyed more favourable rates of rent, at least in the early phase of absolute deficit labour. The balance of advantage or disadvantage of khudkasht and paikasht status varied in different historical conjunctures.

A motley collection of rural overlords in late-eighteenth-century Bengal conveniently and misleadingly went under the single name of zamindar. To compound the confusion, these varied elements in the Bengal countryside bore no resemblance to the village zamindars but rather were more akin to the talukdars of northern India. The Bengal zamindars embraced at least four separately identifiable categories: (1) the old territorial heads of principalities, such as the rajas of Tippera and Cooch Behar; (2) the great landholding families who paid a fixed land tax and behaved like feudatory chiefs, such as the rajas of Burdwan, Dinajpur, Rajshahi, Jessore and Nadia; (3) the numerous families who had held offices for collecting land-revenue over a number of generations; and (4) revenue-farmers since the grant of Diwani to the Company in 1765.[9] In a bad 'case of mistaken identity'[10] Cornwallis, by a grand proclamation on 22 March 1793 followed up by a barrage of 'regulations', conferred the prized private property right in land to this diverse group of rural overlords unified only in nomencla-

[8] Report of the Amini Commission, 25 March 1778, Home Miscellaneous Series, Vol. 206 (IOR).
[9] W. W. Hunter, *Bengal Manuscript Records*, (London, 1894), pp. 31–4.
[10] Ray, *Change in Bengal Agrarian Society*, p. 73.

ture. Divorced by and large from possessory dominion, these land-lords had received in effect a property right in revenue collection or in the rental of the land rather than in land itself.

The gift of private property was naturally not for keeping. It was a saleable right to be auctioned off if the revenue did not come in by sunset on the appointed day. The revenue demand was pitched high. Before the recipients could savour the mixed treats of property ownership, the inexorable operation of the 'sunset law' rapidly altered the composition of the ranks of the 'propertied' and the 'propertyless'. What happened during the first few years of operation of the Per-manent Settlement was not a great revolution in the sphere of land control but 'a great circulation of titles'.[11] Most of the ten great landholding feudatory families were badly mauled during these years. Contrary to conventional wisdom, the biggest buyers of the revenue rights in land were not the new monied men from Calcutta. The chief beneficiaries at the auction sales were other zamindars, followed by their employees or amlas, and government officials. Calcutta baniyas or merchants finished only third in the race to buy into landed rights.[12]

The great survivor of the era of demolition of giant-scale zamindaris, the Burdwan raj, pioneered the strategy which gave shape and form to the revenue-collecting structure. Faced with the palpable lack of a mechanism to collect rent punctually and effectively, this zamindari granted leases to be held in perpetuity at fixed rents to middlemen known as patnidars, subcontracting as it were a permanent settlement of its own. The patni system was given formal legal sanction by a regulation of 1819 after which it became quite widespread in west Bengal. Patni (literally constituency or settlement) rights were often held over a whole village or even a cluster of villages, with occasional subletting of the rent-collecting function to lower grades of darpatni-dars and sepatnidars. In east Bengal, it was more common to have a plurality of revenue-collecting landlords known as zamindars and talukdars within villages. Tenureholders occupying the space in the rent-collecting hierarchy between the revenue-payer and the raiyat were also known by the generic term talukdars. A great mythology has been created in the literature about the extraordinary degree of subinfeudation of tenures. In reality, it was unusual in much of east

[11] *Ibid.*, p. 252.
[12] Sirajul Islam, *The Permanent Settlement in Bengal: a Study of its Operation 1790–1819* (Dhaka, 1979).

Bengal to have more than two or three layers of rentier rights. Many small talukdars collected rent directly from raiyats. In the southern parts of the littoral districts like Bakarganj, however, subinfeudation was found to be an effective way of spreading reclamation costs in the difficult environment of deltaic forested tracts. Here the haoladars and their subordinates presented a picture of complex and elaborate tenure-trees.

The actual landholding structures within villages were quite distinct from the revenue-extracting structures that had been imposed above them. Research in the 1970s which pointed out this crucial distinction also suggested that the landholding structure was dominated by a class of substantial jotedars or village landlords whom both the framers and the critics of the zamindari settlement had largely ignored.[13] The dominance of the lords of the land was somewhat overdrawn, based on a bold generalization from Buchanan-Hamilton's portrayals of the jotedars of Rangpur and Dinajpur.[14] It is now clear that in the early nineteenth century 'if at the top a new commercial landlord class did not entirely take over the landed estates of an ancient aristocracy, neither did a new peasant landlord class at the bottom appropriate on a massive scale the agricultural lands of a self-sufficient peasantry'.[15]

There continues to be some debate about the extent of differentiation at the landholding level. It is not a question that can be easily or decisively resolved. Bengal, being a permanently settled area, did not have cadastral surveys at regular thirty-year intervals from the early nineteenth century as became the norm in some other parts of India. Fragmentary evidence would suggest that the working peasantry was nowhere an undifferentiated mass, but the scale of inequalities varied from the very slight to yawning disparities, particularly in the frontier regions. Paikasht raiyats could be rich peasants leading a train of dependants, or poor peasants who trekked around with their ploughs in search of favourable terms of cultivation. The latest research on the late eighteenth century suggests that the 'jotedar' thesis about the peasantry polarized between a rich peasant class and untouchable landless groups presents 'a false image of rural stratification' even for

[13] Rajat and Ratna Ray, 'Zamindars and Jotedars: a Study of Rural Politics in Bengal' in *Modern Asian Studies*, 9, 1 (1975), 81–102.
[14] Francis Buchanan-Hamilton, *A Geographical, Statistical and Historical Description (1808) of the District, a Zilah of Dinajpur in the Province, or Soubah of Bengal* (Calcutta, 1883), and *Account of Ronggopur*, Vol. XI, Eur. Mss. D75 (IOR).
[15] Ray, *Change in Bengal Agrarian Society*, p. 271.

that early period. It would be more accurate to speak of two broad strata in the peasantry – 'poor' and 'middling' – since the main distinction was between 'the owners of adequate and inadequate land', a distinction 'often rendered tenuous by the smallness of peasant holdings in *general*'. The 'gap between the relatively rich and the comparatively poor was very small' and 'rich' peasants capable of maintaining a cycle of extended reproduction were 'largely absent'. An over-emphasis on the role of a few substantial jotedars in the 1970s literature also led to an underestimation of zamindari power. The revenue-collecting and landholding structures were distinct and discrete, but not wholly divergent. It is of the utmost importance to investigate the degree to which landlords could also turn themselves into lords of the land through the extension of khamar. Certainly at the turn of the nineteenth century the 'jotedar' was less powerful than both the zamindar and the grain-dealing bepari. The extent of jotedari control over land was defined and circumscribed by the zamindar, while the increasingly commercialized grain market of Bengal required a degree of mercantile specialization by beparis with capital which rendered 'jotedari participation in the trade in agricultural produce' 'minimal'.[16]

Detailed case studies of districts and selected zamindaris between the mid-eighteenth and the mid-nineteenth centuries have shown that, once the property right was lodged with men who did not generally have the bulk of land under their possessory control, there were at least 'four possible lines of development'.[17] First, some zamindars could, by virtue of long residence, 'convert legal title into physical occupation of agricultural lands'. This was amply demonstrated by the Surul zamindars of Birbhum. Many patnidars in west Bengal were not simply rent-collectors but played a supervisory role in cultivation on the substantial fraction of the land they kept as khamar. Second, powerful big zamindars could by bureaucratic survey and management 'equalize assessment rates' and bring about a levelling of the raiyati category. Third, and 'the commonest line of development',[18] new zamindars could 'succeed in raising assessment rates' on inferior raiyats 'by

[16] Rajat Datta, 'Agricultural Production, Social Participation and Domination in Late Eighteenth-Century Bengal: Towards an Alternative Explanation' in *Journal of Peasant Studies*, 17, 1 (October 1989), 68–113; quotations from pp. 78–9, 82, 93. See also Aditee Nag Chowdhury-Zilly, *The Vagrant Peasant: Agrarian Distress and Desertion in Bengal 1770 to 1830* (Wiesbaden, 1984), ch. 3.
[17] Ray, *Change in Bengal Agrarian Society*, p. 274.      [18] *Ibid.*, p. 279.

understanding with village landholders' who enjoyed better rates. It is open to question whether, outside the north Bengal bastion of large jotedars, the zamindars' deals were being struck with land-controlling rich peasants or with village leaders, often known as mathbars, who should more appropriately be seen as constituting a seigneurial sergeant class, ready and able to manipulate the rent-collecting mechanism in a period of enhancements during the nineteenth century. Fourth, absenteeism, internecine conflict and subdivisions could so weaken the zamindars that 'village landlords of peasant stock' would succeed in increasing their margins by 'fomenting combinations of ryots'. If the assumption about the widespread existence of 'village landlords of peasant stock' is relaxed, as the evidence would seem to warrant, the lines of contradiction in this instance can be seen to be drawn between rentiers and a not too disparate peasantry sharing a commonality of interests.

Even 'capitalist' indigo planters had to reckon with the balance between raiyati and khamar in gaining access to land and labour in rural Bengal. There were powerful reasons why capitalist development in the indigo phase of commodity production should have preferred the raiyati variety of production process over khamar or nij. The statistics leave little room for doubting the clear preponderance of the former (see Table 5). Over 80% of the 75,000 bighas of indigo cultivation under the jurisdiction of the largest indigo concern, the Bengal Indigo Company, was of the raiyati kind in the late 1850s. The key to the planters' general preference for the raiyati variety of production process was that it rested on unpaid or grossly underpaid peasant family labour. Evidence given by several planters revealed the cold logic of capitalist development in early nineteenth-century Bengal. Raiyati cultivation, one planter said, cost the raiyats 'nothing [sic] but their time and labour'. Another stated in matter-of-fact fashion that the raiyat 'does everything himself: he weeds, ploughs and his children assist him'.[19] Colonial capital preferred a course in which the cost of labour was, quite simply, 'nothing'.

The social organization of production in the indigo sector was not determined, however, in any mechanistic way by the 'needs' of capital, but was forged at the points of resolution of conflicts between the preferences of colonial capital concerning the spheres and degrees of its

[19] Answer Nos. 743 and 346, Evidence, *Report of the Indigo Commission* (Calcutta, 1860).

Table 5. *The balance between raiyati and nij in the indigo sector*

| Region | Indigo concern | Raiyati | Nij |
|---|---|---|---|
| | | (bighas or %) | (bighas or %) |
| | Bengal Indigo | 61,000 | 14,000 |
| Nadia | Khalbolia | 14,000 | 5,000 |
| Nadia | Kallipole | 6,300 | 200 |
| Nadia | Bansberia | 14,000 | 4,200 |
| Nadia | Shikarpore | 20,000 | 6,900 |
| Nadia | Loknathpore | 8,000 | 2,000 |
| Nadia | Nischindipore | 26,000 | 4,000 |
| Nadia | Katchikatta | 16,375 | 2,825 |
| Pabna | Hizlabut | 7,700 | 4,300 |
| Pabna | Coomedpore | 6,800 | 1,200 |
| Jessore | Sinduri | 35,486 | 4,762 |
| Jessore | Nusibshahi | 15,500 | 4,500 |
| Jessore | Hazarapur | 75% | 25% |
| Jessore | Sericole | 8,000 | 3,000 |
| Rajshahi | Rajapore | 50% | 50% |
| | Salgurmurdia | 10,655 | 2,573 |
| Birbhum | Dambazar | 32,000 (approx.) | 0 |
| Bankura | Bancoora | 35,000 (approx.) | 1,000 |
| Faridpur | Cossimpore | 100% | 0% |

*Source:* Evidence of R. L. Larmour, General Mofussil Manager, Bengal Indigo Company, Answer No. 1,939 and Appendix, Part 1, No. 1, in *Report of the Indigo Commission* (Calcutta, 1860).
(N.B. The following concerns had switched completely to nij: Serajabad of Dhaka, Subancolly of Mymensingh, Serajgunge of Pabna and Ramnagar of Murshidabad. In a handful of others nij had an edge over raiyati. See Chowdhury, *Growth of Commercial Agriculture*, p. 126.)

involvement and the struggle of labour in defence of its material needs and cultural values. The peasantry's tenacious grip on the raiyati right to land was maintained only by paying a very heavy price in the rental and credit markets and in the form of exploitation of family labour. It was resistance by labour that impelled the partial entry of indigo planters into the khamar sector. Since the market in raiyati rights was not well developed and presented numerous barriers to entry, both economic and political, planters' nij cultivation was obtained mainly by buying into tenurial rights between the zamindar and raiyat. This process was initially facilitated by the desire of some landlords to enlist

75

European planters' support in the face of a drive launched by the colonial government in the 1830s to 'resume' underassessed lands.[20] The planter–landlord concordat was shortlived. By the early 1840s the planters, in an attempt to strengthen the security of their tenures, gave qualified support to similar demands of resident raiyats. During the crisis in the indigo economy in the late 1850s they again changed tactics and made a desperate effort to increase khamar at the expense of raiyati cultivation and to enhance rent. The political balance of forces in the Bengal countryside contributed to the failure of this strategy. Indigo cultivation in the late nineteenth century on zerat (the equivalent of nij) rather than assamewar (or raiyati) lands was almost exclusively a Bihar phenomenon.

The different configuration of agrarian social classes in the indigo-growing parts of Bengal and Bihar stemmed from important differences in the relationship between land and capital. The immense power of Bihar landlords flowed from their control over land and varied, if crude, instruments of extra-economic coercion. They still had use for indigo planters in the late nineteenth century as a source of capital in its monetary form. Many landlords of west Bengal playing the dual role of rentier and creditor had, by contrast, already engaged in a process of competition and conflict with the planters in the domain of rural capital. The widespread resort to moneylending by west Bengal landlords should probably be dated to the failure of the Union Bank in 1847 and the consequent inability of the planters to meet the credit needs of the smallholding peasantry. The dramatic increase in rice prices from 1854 opened the opportunity to mix loaning in cash with extensive grain-dealing and grain-lending. Evidence given before the Indigo Commission in 1860 makes clear the deep involvement of zamindars and patnidars of various grades in mahajani.[21] Joykrishna Mukherjee of Uttarpara, who paid Rs 90,000 to the government annually in land revenue, earned 12% to 24% in interest on Rs 100,000 he had 'floating' as rural credit. Srihari Rai of Chandipur, who held zamindari rights over seven villages, was also a mahajan charging interest at 24% on cash loans, 37.5% on mixed cash and grain loans and as much as 50% on grain advances. Small patnidars, like the Basu family of Swarapur in Dinabandhu Mitra's play Nil Darpan, were at

---

[20] Chittabrata Palit, Tensions in Bengal Rural Society (Calcutta, 1975), pp. 109–11.
[21] Report of the Indigo Commission cited by Ranajit Guha, 'Neel Darpan: the Image of a Peasant Revolt in a Liberal Mirror', Journal of Peasant Studies, 2, 1 (1974), pp. 36–7.

the same time petty usurers. Planters' dadni (advances) came to a complete end with the demise of the indigo system in 1860 and was fully taken over by the lagni karbar (moneylending activities) of zamindars and patnidars.

During the early nineteenth century the rentiers of east Bengal were not yet important as creditors. Information from the early nineteenth century is thin, but early twentieth-century settlement reports on east Bengal districts state that 'the tide of agrarian indebtedness commenced to flow' in these parts only from about the late 1880s. It had apparently 'jumped from an insignificant sum' during the thirty years from 1885 to 1915.[22] Settlement and cultivation by smallholding peasant families appear not to have been heavily dependent on externally supplied capital, except in the Sunderban tracts where reclamation costs were high. The clearance of jungle in littoral districts like Bakarganj was financed by Dhaka men 'whose capital was ordinarily small', which led to subinfeudation of reclamation and cultivation rights.[23] Generally, east Bengal zamindars and talukdars merely exercised the rent charge over a mass of atomistic peasant families in possessory control over their smallholdings.

The spread of cultivation in east Bengal in the early nineteenth century represented a recovery of resources by a peasantry fanning out from old and established centres of settlement in districts like Dhaka, Faridpur, Tippera and Mymensingh. It was a labour-intensive process which did not require large initial outlays of capital. The jungly wastes of north Bengal posed quite a different order of challenge to reclaimers. In Rangpur and Dinajpur, men armed with large-scale capital set tribal and semi-tribal labour on the arduous and painfully slow process of transforming a forested wilderness into open plains fit for agriculture. Absentee zamindars, mostly recent buyers of revenue rights over 'lots', had little control over local affairs where the bigger jotedars' power was supreme. The size of their holdings ran from 50 to 6,000 acres. Buchanan-Hamilton found in early nineteenth-century Dinajpur that the top 6% of the cultivating population dominated as much as 36.5% of the land leased by raiyats from zamindars; 52.1% of the agricultural work-force consisted of sharecroppers and labourers without even the semblance of raiyati rights to the lands they ploughed at the direction

[22] F. D. Ascoli, *Dacca Settlement Report (1910–17)*, p. 48; F. A. Sachse, *Mymensingh Settlement Report (1908–19)*, p. 27.
[23] J. C. Jack, *Bakarganj District Gazetteer* (1918), p. 87.

of the jotedars. The same observer noted in Rangpur how the successful combination of grain-lending and grain-dealing with landholding resulted in huge losses to the poor and corresponding gains for the rich at each turn of the agricultural cycle.[24]

Tribal labour was in a less disadvantageous position prior to 1860 in the border regions of west Bengal districts such as Midnapur and Bankura, where the communitarian forms of their social organization had remained substantially intact. Contracts for settlement and cultivation, in reality little more than vague and flexible arrangements, were made between zamindars and tribal communities as a whole, who were represented for negotiating and rent-remitting purposes by their leaders, known as mandals. In the initial labour-scarce phase, mandals were able to extract easy terms for their communities from zamindars and the mandali right was recognized to be permanent, heritable and transferable by custom. The zamindars scrupulously maintained a policy of non-intervention in the relations between mandals and their followers. The closing of the labour–land ratio by 1830 altered the state of affairs as landlords sought to impose more rigid rental contracts based on accurate measurements of landholdings. During settlement proceedings in Midnapur in 1839, colonial officials sided with the zamindars in ruling that mandals were only entitled to the rights of sthani or khudkasht raiyats without any munafa or profit from the rent-collecting function.[25] Despite this adverse decision, intra-tribal relations under the mandali system were able to withstand external pressures until the 1860s.

At the midpoint of the nineteenth century the twin processes of the balance between raiyati and khamar and the interplay of khudkasht (settled) and paikasht (migrant) cultivation had fashioned four basic types of agrarian social structure, three of which displayed some enduring qualities. First, peasant smallholders were in effective occupancy of their work-units, particularly in east Bengal, where rentiers did not exercise possessory dominion over the soil. Second, peasant smallholding was engaged in a continuous tug-of-war with landlords' demesne which was quite substantial, especially in the heart of west Bengal. Successful rentiers over raiyati territory and lords of their extensive khamar, these zamindars and patnidars became deeply involved in credit and in the market in grain as indigo cultivation went

[24] See Ray and Ray, 'Zamindars and Jotedars'.
[25] Chowdhury-Zilly, *The Vagrant Peasant*, p. 139.

into a steep decline. Third, rich farmers had risen to the pinnacles of power in reclamation zones, mainly in north Bengal, where zamindars were weak. Combining control over land and capital, these jotedars commanded the labour of rightless sharecroppers. Fourth, tribal society on the fringes of west Bengal showed some resilience by insulating its internal organization from the broader currents of change. Their mandals negotiated the terms of village settlement on behalf of the whole community.

Colonial law and agrarian society, which had been set on divergent paths at the time of the Permanent Settlement with zamindars in 1793, made a few less than successful attempts at resolving their incompatibility in the ensuing half-century. The obsession with a steady source of revenue ensured that most of the interventions reinforced zamindari power in the early nineteenth century. The economic setbacks and political turmoil of the 1850s finally compelled the government to attempt a redefinition of agrarian law in the raiyats' favour. The shifting demographic balance had made a favourable rent rate dependent on security of tenure from about 1830. The landlords' denial of the clamour for khudkasht status raised by former migrants had spawned increasing tension in agrarian relations, which even the intense dissatisfaction with the indigo system could not wholly sidetrack. The Rent Act of 1859 recorded the transition from an era of migrancy to predominantly settled agriculture by introducing the legal character of the 'occupancy tenant'. Raiyats were now subdivided into three major categories: (1) permanent raiyats paying fixed rents, (2) occupancy raiyats protected against arbitrary eviction and rent increase and (3) non-occupancy raiyats paying the competitive rent. With a rough and ready legal scaffolding now in place, the claim to 'occupancy' status could be asserted with fresh zeal.

## SOCIAL RELATIONS OF PROPERTY AND PRODUCTION, c. 1860–1950

The era spanning the mid-nineteenth to the mid-twentieth century has formed the battleground for political and academic debates about capitalist development and under-development as well as 'peasantization' and 'depeasantization' in the Indian countryside under colonial rule. It was in this period that the 'contrast' between change, denoted by rapid commercialization, and continuity, represented by an apparent stability of agrarian social structures, emerged in stark form. Apologists of empire saw signs of development in the winds of change affecting trade and transport. Nationalist critics noticed little prosperity and deepening poverty, manifested in a spate of famines in different parts of the country in the late nineteenth century. They indicted the colonial government's land revenue policy and identified India's export surplus, far from having any developmental impact, as being the principal mechanism of the drain of the colony's wealth to the metropolis. The debate generated sufficient heat to smoulder until very recently. Romesh C. Dutt, the most eloquent proponent of the nationalists' economic critique of colonialism, was still picked as the main scholarly adversary in a 1980s study of famines in nineteenth-century western India.[26]

The terms of the old debate were quite inadequate for the purpose of exploring the dialectic between capitalist 'development' and the labour process involved in primary production. New breakthroughs have come recently in theoretical works that have treated poverty and famines as matters of relative deprivation rather than absolute dearth and interpretative studies that have emphasized the relational rather than parametric features of regional agrarian developments.[27] The theme of agrarian labour relations, having long suffered scholarly confinement within the shackles of the colonial land revenue administration, is now beginning to be placed in the broader and more relevant context of the colonial political economy and capitalist world markets. The role of credit in linking the domains of land and capital is being recognized, making it possible to explore why capitalist development came to rest in the colonial era on particular forms of labour relations in agrarian regions.

The era of rapid expansion of commodity production for capitalist markets that began in the 1860s saw the redefinition of agrarian property rights as defined by colonial law. Revenue-collecting landlords had to pay for their palpable lack of capitalist enterprise precisely at the moment when the attractions of such an initiative might have been greatest. In the expectation that peasant proprietors would better power the motors of agrarian development, the colonial government

[26] Michelle McAlpin, *Subject to Famine* (Princeton, 1983).
[27] See Amartya Sen, *Poverty and Famines: an Essay in Entitlement and Deprivation* (Oxford, 1981); C. J. Baker, *An Indian Rural Economy: the Tamilnad Countryside 1880–1955* (Delhi, 1984); Sugata Bose, *Agrarian Bengal: Economy, Social Structure and Politics* (Cambridge, 1986).

introduced tenancy legislation in regions of zamindari settlement, such as Bengal, which virtually gave occupancy tenants the position of owner-cultivators subject to the payment of controlled rent. Where the depredations of moneylending non-agriculturists appeared to have been greater, as in the Punjab, than evictions and rackrenting by landlords, colonial law now sought to restrict land alienation from agriculturists to non-agriculturists. The aim in either case was to provide cushioning for a protected and largely self-cultivating tenantry or proprietary peasantry which would meet capitalism's demands of commodity production, while holding down the share of labour in the total social product by utilizing unpaid or underpaid family labour. This reordering of property relations was not a case of an omnipotent colonial capitalism having it all its own way. It was dictated to a significant extent by the feasible range of responses to resistance by peasant labour anxious to maintain entitlement to subsistence. A cardinal feature of this resistance was the security of direct access to a piece of land on acceptable rental terms. Effective occupancy of a smallholding did not imply in the post-1860 period direct entitlement to foodgrains, but the foundation for production-based and trade-based entitlements combining in varying measures cultivation of food-crops and cash-crops. The cash-cropping alternative offered the prospect of not only higher gross income but, more importantly, credit for small peasant families at the most vulnerable moment in the agricultural cycle. A blend of defiance and compromise, peasant resistance succeeded in maintaining a hold on the chief means of production – land – in an age of advancing capitalism, at the cost of collusion in the intensification of intra-family exploitation.

Although the colonial government had reserved the right ever since 1793 to intervene in zamindar–raiyat relations to protect the latter, it had actually avoided doing so until the Rent Act of 1859. The Bengal Tenancy Act of 1885, the product of a Rent Law Commission set up in 1880, went a few steps further in investing the raiyati layer of right to the land with substance and security. It created an important category of 'settled raiyats with occupancy status' who could not be evicted if they had lived and worked in the same village for at least 12 years and whose rent could be increased by only 12.5% once in 15 years. While the landlords had made learned and weighty depositions before the Commission, the raiyats had made their point loudly and clearly in a wave of rent strikes in east Bengal districts. Had they successfully wrested recognition of the relationship to their holdings as a form or fraction of the property right in land? The raiyati right was acknowledged in 1885 to be heritable and made a protected interest to remain unaffected by changes to superior tenurial rights, but the law-makers baulked on the point of transferability. Landlords' pressure groups had made much of the inviolability of the right to choose one's own tenants and raised the bogey of displacement of cultivators by wily 'non-agriculturist' moneylenders. The Bengal Tenancy Act consequently fudged, directing the courts to recognize the transfer of raiyati holdings only where it was sanctioned by custom.

Yet 1885 marked a decisive turning point in a slow but sure movement towards the strengthening of the property component in the raiyati right and its withering in the zamindari right to land. A 1928 amendment to the Bengal Tenancy Act legalized free transferability of raiyati rights, although provisions for the landlords' right of preemption and a 20% fee modified the degree of 'freedom'. Another amendment in 1938 abolished the landlords' fee and gave the preemptive right to co-sharer tenants. A Land Revenue Commission appointed by the provincial government recommended in 1940 the abolition of zamindari and all intermediary rentier interests after payment of compensation to the owners of these landed rights. The recommendation was eventually implemented after independence and partition in East and West Bengal in 1951 and 1953, respectively. Raiyats could then boast the full rights of property ownership.

From the Rent Act of 1859 to the Estates Acquisition Act of 1953, the correspondence between the legal expressions of property relations and the relations of production in agriculture remained approximate at its very best. Tenancy legislation needed some sort of grid and this was provided by the raiyati category. As the Howrah settlement officer proudly declared, the raiyat was 'the pivot of all tenancy legislation. There may be many tenure-holders and there may be many under-raiyats but there can be only one grade of raiyats'.[28] The law, however, had granted protection and privilege to legal personalities who were not in all cases working peasants. There was nothing to deter better-off raiyats subletting to inferior grades of actual cultivators, and nothing to prevent non-cultivating moneylenders and landlords buying into increasingly valuable raiyati rights. Despite all its imperfections and inaccuracies, the Bengal Tenancy Act made possible for the first time a

[28] *Howrah Settlement Report*, p. 50.

detailed investigation of production relations in agriculture by calling for settlement of rent and revenue based on cadastral surveys of each of Bengal's districts. There are limitations in the mass of settlement data churned out between the 1890s and the 1940s. Sharecroppers and labourers who could not aspire to legal rights are only partly visible. The equation of peasant families with male heads of household renders half of the peasant population – women – almost invisible. There is sufficient additional documentary as well as circumstantial evidence, however, to enable historians of this period to penetrate the facade of legal property and explore the relations of material production and social reproduction in the Bengal countryside.

The settlement data not unexpectedly reveal an almost infinite variety of local relationships. A summing up of the details indicates that in early twentieth-century Bengal 'two out of every three tillers of the land cultivated their own ryoti land, subject of course to the power and influence of the zamindars'.[29] Neither the microscopic view nor the aggregated picture makes possible an investigation of continuity and change in agrarian social structure. Few clear reference points are available within these descriptive approaches to examine the processes of 'peasantization' and 'depeasantization' which appear in the literature to be simply separated by the watershed date of 1885. An overall characterization of the relations of production in agrarian Bengal and India can only be attempted through an analytic rather than a descriptive method. The first task in this analytical exercise is to construct a broad typology of agrarian social structure showing some enduring qualities and defined by some basic distinctions in the relationship of the working producers to the owners of the conditions of production, particularly land and capital. The peasant smallholding system, the peasant smallholding–demesne labour complex and the rich farmer–sharecropper system continued from the pre-1860 period to be the three major types of social organization of production. However, the tribal communitarian form disintegrated in the late nineteenth century and became indistinguishable from a rather extreme variant of the smallholding–demesne complex in which the demesne lords dominated. The mandali right slipped from the hands of tribal leaders into those of dikkus or foreigners, moneylending Bengalis from the east and Utkal Brahmins from the southwest. Between the suppression of a

[29] Rajat Kanta Ray, 'The Retreat of the Jotedars?' in *India Economic and Social History Review*, 25, 2 (1988), 246.

major tribal rebellion in the mid 1860s and the imposition of restrictions on the alienation of land from tribals to non-tribals in 1909, the tribal communities lost the superior rights to the better lands in the western fringes of Bengal.[30] The same period saw the rise of a new organizational form in the north Bengal districts of Darjeeling and Jalpaiguri, where tribal migrants from Bihar were pressed into the labour lines of tea plantations. Each of the types of agrarian social structure predominated in certain regions, but the typology presented is structural rather than regional in character. It does not split up Bengal into exclusive regions; quite the contrary, it opens the way for comparisons with analogous structural types elsewhere in India and in the agrarian world generally.

### The peasant smallholding system

During the 1910s the settlement officer of Dhaka district had no question in his mind that 'the settled *raiyat* paying his rent in cash' formed 'the backbone of the agricultural population'.[31] Indeed, most east Bengal districts, where peasant smallholding was the predominant form of the social organization of production, were conspicuous by the absence of a malik class of rentiers-cum-landholders who were so dominant in the agrarian power structure of the upper Gangetic plain. Rent-collecting landlords drawn from the higher Hindu castes and ashraf Muslims thinly overlaid a mass of mostly ajlaf Muslim and Namasudra peasants holding firm rights to occupy and cultivate their smallholdings. Landlords' personal demesnes or khas khamar were of very marginal importance. Survey and settlement in Dhaka, Faridpur and Tippera during the second decade of the twentieth century showed that some 85–7% of the land in each of these districts was occupied by raiyats, an overwhelming majority of whom were working peasants.[32] Faridpur, according to J. C. Jack in 1916, was 'no country of capitalist farmers with bloated farms and an army of parasitic and penurious labourers'; the cultivators, it was claimed, were 'a homogeneous class'.[33]

It would have been more accurate to say that east Bengal peasant families, who had been steadily settling the extensive margins of

[30] McAlpin's Report 1909 quoted in *Bengal Board of Economic Enquiry Bulletin District Bankura* (Calcutta, 1935), pp. 3–4.
[31] Ascoli, *Dacca SR*, p. 71.
[32] *Ibid.*, p. 70; J. C. Jack, *Faridpur Settlement Report (1904–14)*, p. 29.
[33] J. C. Jack, *Economic Life of a Bengal District* (Oxford, 1916), pp. 81–2.

4. Bengal districts in the early twentieth century

cultivation during the nineteenth century, had secured solid rights to their jotes or holdings which were marked by a very limited range of differentiation. The exhaustion of the extensive margins and the utilization of intensive margins under demographic pressure between 1890 and 1920 had seen the emergence of a land-poor peasantry dependent on sharecropping and wage labour. Yet, around 1920, the bargadar in Mymensingh was 'usually a settled ryot of the village, renting his homestead and one or two plots of arable land from the same landlord on a cash rent'.[34] In Dhaka, too, bargadars did not 'on the whole ... constitute a separate class'. Barga cultivation on a small portion of landlords' khamar as an adjunct to predominantly peasant smallholding cultivation was still the norm; a new type of share-cropping on raiyati lands recently bought up by moneylending land-lords was very much the exception.[35] The 'landless labourer' was reported by Jack to be 'unknown in Faridpur and very rare anywhere in Eastern Bengal'.[36] Jack's own evidence and all other contempor-aneous data suggest that dependence on wage labour in early twentieth-century east Bengal was not as rare as landlessness. Indeed, the relatively high rural wage rates in east Bengal reported by the Dufferin enquiry of the 1880s are only explicable in terms of 'the better bargaining position of landholding labourers'.[37] Despite the strong general trend towards 'peasantization' and village-based settled agri-culture during the middle and later nineteenth century, it was still not unusual in the early decades of the twentieth century to engage in short-distance migration from poorer to better-off districts to harvest jute and paddy where the timing of crop cycles permitted.

The sharecropping and labouring strata were not structurally dis-tinct from peasant smallholding resting on recognized raiyati rights. Most workers on the soil were contained within the spectrum stretch-ing from the virtually landowning tenant-cultivator with a small surplus to the dwarfholder who made up his deficit through share-cropping or wage labour. Yet the fact that peasant production was mostly carried out by settled and occupancy raiyats did not mean they constituted an 'independent' peasantry. This was because, although these peasants enjoyed favourable rental relations, they were bound in

[34] Sachse, *Mymensingh SR*, p. 45.      [35] Ascoli, *Dacca SR*, pp. 75–7 and App. XI.
[36] Jack, *Economic Life*, p. 84.
[37] GOB, *Report on the Conditions of the Lower Classes of Population in Bengal* (Dufferin Report, Calcutta, 1888) cited by Willem van Schendel and Aminul Haque Faraizi, *Rural Labourers of Bengal, 1880 to 1980* (Rotterdam, 1984), p. 16.

sets of inequitable credit and market relations. Between the 1880s and 1930 indebtedness within the peasant smallholding system widened and deepened in the context of increased market penetration of east Bengal agriculture and the enlarged credit needs of the peasantry. By 1930 less than a fifth of families of cultivators with secure rights to their holdings still managed to remain free from a permanent cycle of debt.[38] Peasant smallholders were mostly indebted to one of two categories of moneylenders – trader-mahajans interested in the product, often jute, at a low price, and talukdar-mahajans earning usurious interest in an era of falling rental incomes. The two groups of creditors were effective collaborators and not competitors in a scenario where a mahajan had 'as many demands on hand as his capital will sustain'.[39] The indebted peasant was constrained to undertake both the expensive servicing of his debt and the disposal of his crop at harvest time. An important mechanism for appropriating the peasants' surplus, credit simultaneously played a crucial role in the social reproduction of the peasant smallholding structure. It ensured the subsistence of peasant families during the lean phase in each production cycle and regularly replenished the capital fund needed to sustain production. Contrary to some district officers' complaints, a negligible fraction of debts incurred were squandered on litigation or 'thriftless' extravagance. The primary reason for incurring debts in the sowing season was 'the necessity for food and seeds'; borrowed money was also generally used for repairs to homesteads, replacement of cattle, labour costs and, occasionally, marriage.[40]

While some moneylenders undoubtedly dispossessed their peasant debtors for default, the overall tendency of the operation of usury and merchant capital in early twentieth-century east Bengal was to preserve rather than dismantle the peasant smallholding system. As a general rule, so long as the peasant debtor paid the interest he was in 'no hurry to pay off the capital' and had 'no fear of being sold up'.[41] Extracting reasonably regular interest payments over an extended period of time was more profitable for moneylenders with an established clientele, and made for a smoother continuance of an unequal symbiosis in social relations than attempting to seize the fragmented holdings of a heavily indebted smallholding peasantry. So developments in the credit market

[38] Bose, *Agrarian Bengal*, pp. 105–6.     [39] Sachse, *Mymensingh SR*, p. 27.
[40] GOB, *Report of the Bengal Provincial Banking Enquiry Committee*, vol. I, p. 70.
[41] Sachse, *Mymensingh SR*, p. 27.

had only a very limited knock-on effect on the land market. The vicissitudes of the jute economy, where booms were less spectacular and busts more frequent than in the cotton and wheat belts, also ensured that the product market did not create conditions for a systematic and sustained process of differentiation within the peasantry prior to 1930.

The withdrawal of traders and talukdars from the rural credit scene at the onset of the great depression opened the possibility for a qualitative transformation of the relations of production in east Bengal agriculture. However, the fall in land values that accompanied the collapse of prices and credit as well as successful political combinations among peasants meant that the pre-existing landholding structure was not dramatically undermined. Sales of raiyati rights to the land did not increase rapidly during the economic slump between 1930 and 1938. The Bengal Board of Economic Enquiry found in 1935 that 'in 95 per cent of cases the debtors paid nothing and remained in possession of their land without any penalty'.[42] Peasant smallholders did, of course, have to accept a severe penalty in the form of a sharp drop in living standards. While they refused to pay interest, they demanded subsistence loans, a denial of which was the major ingredient in expressions of protest. Only the fact of a generalized liquidity crisis resulting in a decline in food prices helped maintain their entitlements to minimal subsistence.

Even after reducing expenditure to bare essentials, many peasants could not manage without credit. The steady and substantial rise in usufructuary mortgages suggests the entry of slightly better-off peasants into the field of rural credit left vacant by traders and talukdars. These were clearly men who were directly interested in control over agricultural land. In Tippera, for instance, 'the comparatively well-off or "bourgeois" Krishaks' were said to 'hold most of the usufructuary mortgages'; in Mymensingh, usufructuary mortgages were mainly in the hands of 'simple cultivators who had not done any moneylending business before'.[43] When in 1938 the revival of trade and

---

[42] Bengal Board of Economic Enquiry, *Preliminary Report on Rural Indebtedness*, p. 5.

[43] Commissioner Chittagong Division to Chief Secretary, 15 October 1937, Home Political Confidential File 10/73 (Home Dept West Bengal); Collector Mymensingh to Joint Secretary Cooperative Credit and Rural Indebtedness Dept, 27 November 1937, in 'Restriction of Rural Credit – Possible Effect of Debt Conciliation Board', GOB, Revenue Dept, Land Revenue Branch, May 1940 B Progs. 14–57 (Bangladesh Secretariat Report Room).

legislation abolishing the landlords' fee gave a tremendous boost to the velocity of the land market, it was a newly formed peasant elite that gained most from it. It was within this immediate context of concern about massive land alienation that the Land Revenue Commission conducted an enquiry into the transfer of raiyati rights over the past twelve years and the mode of cultivation on transferred holdings.

The results indicate that, in east Bengal districts, 5% of the raiyati area enquired into was transferred. Of the area alienated, 54.1% was cultivated by the purchasers' family, 26.7% by sharecroppers, 16.9% by under-raiyats and only 2.3% by labourers. The area under share-cropping had, therefore, registered a 1% increase, but the number of cultivators mainly dependent on sharecropping was rising at a faster rate. As one expert witness testified to the Commission, 'where there is heavy population and great competition for land, small tenants and agricultural labourers clamour[ed] for and obtain[ed] barga'.[44] The preponderance of smallholding production was underlined in another set of statistics compiled by the Commission: in east Bengal districts as much as 84% of 'agriculturist' families held less than 5 acres, 11% between 5 and 10 acres and only 5% over 10 acres. The process of land consolidation by rich peasants was a weaker and later phenomenon than land subdivision and pauperization among a smallholding peasantry.

The peasant elite which had begun to separate itself out from the bulk of smallholders in the 1930s further strengthened its position during the catastrophic decade of war, famine and partition. As the relative price of jute remained weak and the older categories of mahajans refused to return to the moneylending business, east Bengal peasants suffered heavily in the great famine of 1943 and accounted for a disproportionate share of the massive quantities of total land alien-ated. Most of the 'very severely affected' subdivisions identified by the investigators of the Indian Statistical Institute, where land alienation was greatest, lay in east Bengal. The worst-affected acreage classes were the below-2-acre category for the sales of entire holdings, and the 2–5 acre category for the sales of part-holdings. The chief beneficiaries appear to have been richer peasants, followed by zamindars and grain-dealers.[45] With the wholly landless labourers decimated by

[44] Evidence of Radhakamal Mukherji in *Report of the Land Revenue Commission* (Flood Commission), vol. II, p. 569.
[45] Bose, *Agrarian Bengal*, pp. 162–4.

destitution and death, the devastation wrought by the famine re-emphasized production relations resting on the labour of a pauperized peasantry reliant to a greater degree on sharecropping and part-wage labour. The ownership of the conditions of production, land and capital had undergone a change, but in the immediate aftermath of the famine the principal contradiction appeared from the peasants' perspective to be with those who had denied them subsistence rather than those who had robbed them of their means of production. When after the partition of 1947 a majority of Hindu zamindars, talukdars and traders abandoned the limited amounts of khamar they had possessed to flee across the border, the Muslim peasant elite of the post-1930 generation were able further to entrench themselves in positions of dominance in the agrarian social structure.

## The peasant smallholding–demesne labour complex

The settlement officer of Bankura noted in the early 1920s 'a tendency for much of the land to fall into the hands of the tenure-holders' and the role of the Bauris as a class of 'usually landless men who work[ed] for others'.[46] In this district, 23% of the total area was in the direct possessory control of zamindars and patnidars and 46% under the effective occupancy of raiyats and under-raiyats, while the rest consisted of waste lands over which the landlords wielded the firmer rights of access. Bankura, especially its tribal fringe, may have presented an extreme case, but in much of west and central Bengal rent-collecting landlords, including the large number drawn from the upper Hindu castes, supervised farming on substantial chunks of land which they held as their personal demesnes or khas khamar. Smallholdings of peasants drawn largely from middle agricultural castes like the Mahishyas, Sadgops and Aguris were still preponderant in quantitative terms, but the smallholding sector was structurally dependent on parcels of surplus land and doses of credit from the demesne sector to reproduce itself. A large reserve of low-caste Bagdi and Bauri as well as Santal tribal labour worked the khamar lands. Moreover, the long stretch of rising grain prices from the mid 1850s onwards had contributed to a significant degree of differentiation within the peasantry. The existence of *coqs de village* of peasant origin is revealed not only in official reports but also in the fiction of Tarashankar Bandyopadhyay, which vividly portrays rural society in early twentieth-century Birb-

[46] F. W. Robertson, *Bankura Settlement Report (1917–24)*, p. 67.

hum.[47] The wave of malaria epidemics had also depleted in many instances the working members of small peasant families. The diminution of peasant family labour along with somewhat larger and less fertile average holdings than in east Bengal meant that hired labour formed an important component in the productive enterprise of smallholdings in west Bengal. In Hooghly, for instance, Mahishya peasants were employers of Bagdi, Bauri and tribal sharecroppers and labourers.[48] Only in the Contai and Tamluk subdivisions of Midnapur, which had been since the withdrawal of the salt monopoly in the 1860s a haven free of malaria for Mahishya peasants, were reserves of landless labour non-existent and labour exchange among peasants was common. Overall, extensive landlords' demesnes, surplus lands of rich peasants and labour deficits of smallholders together absorbed the labour of landless bargadars (sharecroppers without occupancy rights), krishans (tied workers paid with a third of the produce), munishes (day labourers) and mahindars (farm servants).

The rentiers within the smallholding–demesne complex were not only substantial landholders but creditors as well. 'As a rule,' in Bankura district in 1924, 'the landlord [wa]s also the moneylender.'[49] The richer peasants were junior partners of the landed gentry in the moneylending and grain-dealing business. Peasant smallholders borrowed money to purchase food and seeds and to pay rent and labour charges. Regular grain advances attached the labour of sharecroppers and wage-workers for the khamar sector. The drain of usury interest to the demesne sector was the price the smallholding sector paid to remain viable in the decades prior to 1930.

The drastic fall in prices and the squeeze on monetary credit during the 1930s slump were a blow to the smaller patnidars and many smallholding raiyats. Unable to pay their rents, many micropropri-etors of Burdwan, Hooghly and Howrah lost their tenures to the Maharaja of Burdwan and other big zamindars and patnidars.[50] Rental arrears as well as the sheer inability to complete the full cycle of peasant production without credit led to a substantial loss of ground for raiyati in the tug-of-war with khamar. Raiyats rapidly lost their occupancy rights as they were resettled as sharecroppers owing a much higher

[47] Tarashankar Bandyopadhyay, *Dhatridebata*; *Ganadebata o Ponchagram*; and *Hansuli Banker Upakatha* (Calcutta, 1971).
[48] M. N. Gupta, *Hooghly Settlement Report (1904–13)*, p. 37.
[49] F. W. Robertson, *Bankura Settlement Report (1917–24)*, p. 17.
[50] Bose, *Agrarian Bengal*, p. 167.

produce rent. The Land Revenue Commission's figures showed that in the twelve years before 1940, 8.5% of the raiyati area surveyed in west and central Bengal districts had been alienated. Of the transferred area, 36.2% was cultivated by the purchasers' family, 31.3% by share-croppers, 25.2% by under-raiyats and 7.4% by labourers. More important, the bonds of dominance and dependence within the pre-existing khamar sector were strengthened as the nexus between grain lending and labour on personal demesnes remained intact. The composition of acreage classes of 'agriculturist' families compiled by the Commission only inadequately captures the extent of social differentiation that characterized the smallholding–demesne complex in the late 1930s. In west and central Bengal, 72% of the families held less than 5 acres, 19% between 5 and 10 acres and 9% over 10 acres.

The declining fortunes of the peasant smallholders in the face of an onslaught by grasping grain-lending landlords and rich peasants during the depression became a full-scale debacle during the war and famine. As erstwhile lenders refused to make advances in an era of skyrocketing prices, 'valuable land [was] sold by the small agriculturist to the larger agriculturists ... for a small quantity of rice or paddy'.[51] Throughout the 1930s and 1940s, while facing a broad provincewide challenge to their role as rentiers, the zamindars and patnidars had increased their direct control over land by expanding khamar and buying up occupancy raiyati rights from smallholders in trouble. The richer peasantry also gained at the expense of their less fortunate compatriots. The hapless condition of dependent cultivators became apparent when sharecroppers in west Bengal were easily cowed by threats of eviction and denials of subsistence loans in 1946 even as the provincial government announced it would consider legislation to improve their lot.[52] Proprietors and tenureholders were merely shorn of their rent-collecting rights by zamindari abolition when it eventually came in 1953. Upper-caste gentry had engrossed land quite as effectively as middle-caste richer peasantry in the preceding decades. Many zamindars and patnidars of old now joined the ranks of big raiyats to continue dominating the relations of production in west Bengal agrarian society.

[51] Commissioner Presidency Division to Secretary Cooperative Credit and Rural Indebtedness Dept, 16 September 1943, GOB CCRI Dept RI Br., B June 1943 Progs. 6–17, Conf. Files 24 of 1943 and 10 of 1944 (West Bengal State Archives).
[52] Subdivisional Officer Sadar Burdwan to Additional Secretary Board of Revenue, 7 March 1947, Rev. Dept LR Br., Progs. B December 1948, Nos. 15–107, File 6M-38/47 (WBSA).

## The rich farmer–sharecropper system

'As elsewhere in North Bengal', the settlement officer of Dinajpur found in the 1930s, the 'jotedar class' was 'socially supreme in the countryside'. These jotedars were not rentiers under the permanent settlement, but rich farmers who after 1885 often held the raiyati right to their very substantial holdings. These might run to several hundred or even thousands of acres of land on which they practised 'large-scale farming', albeit 'not with any large capital sunk in machinery, but through the traditional methods, employing either labourers or adhiars (sharecroppers)'.[53] This type of sharply polarized agrarian structure had originated in the late eighteenth and early nineteenth centuries when large tracts of jungle had been assigned to men of capital to facilitate the difficult task of reclamation. A similar structure evolved in the abadi or reclaimed areas of the Sunderbans in the 24-Parganas during the late nineteenth and early twentieth centuries. The scale of capital involved was larger than in Bakarganj and Khulna and, consequently, no resort was made to the intricate process of subinfeudation. Semi-tribal and tribal labourers were tempted into the arduous clearance projects by the prospect of owning a patch of land of their own. Some were able to cling on to small jotes, but most were reduced to being sharecroppers with no recognized long-term rights to the land they tilled. Production decisions were taken by the jotedars, who claimed half of the crop at the time of harvest as rent. Despite this uniformity in the rental relationship of all adhiars to their jotedars, a relatively favourable land–labour ratio enabled some sharecroppers to amass relatively big operational holdings, which made for varying degrees of dependence among different adhiars. It was next to impossible, however, for adhiars to be able to buy into jotes. By contrast, a comparative glance at Buchanan-Hamilton's surveys of the early nineteenth century and early twentieth-century settlement reports on Dinajpur and Rangpur makes clear the resilience of the bigger jotedars at the apex of the landholding structure.

The larger landholding jotedars, both Muslim and Rajbansi, were deeply involved in the credit and product markets. In the jute-growing parts of Rangpur, trade and moneylending were carried on by Marwaris and east Bengal Sahas in the decades before 1930.[54] The 'village

[53] F. O. Bell, *Dinajpur Settlement Report (1934–40)*, pp. 16–17.
[54] A. C. Hartley, *Rangpur Settlement Report (1931–38)*, pp. 13–14.

"bania", foreign to the cultivator in caste and tradition, and sucking the blood of a depressed peasantry' was not a familiar sight in predominantly paddy-growing Dinajpur.[55] Grain loans at derhi or 50% interest were the most common form of borrowing by sharecroppers. Jotedars also extended cash loans to meet the expenses of cultivation. Repayments were scheduled for the winter harvest but in actual practice could be carried over in the event of a bad year.

By restricting sharecroppers' direct access to the product market, the rich farmers monopolized the profits during the buoyant phase until 1930 but took the brunt of the collapse once the depression struck. As elsewhere, there was a sharp contraction in the circulation of monetary credit which contributed to a precipitous drop in living standards. In instances where adhiars were utterly dependent, grain loans were continued and returns taken in the form of labour service and appropriation of almost the entire grain heap. Where more decentralized sharecropping prevailed and the creditor was not necessarily the jotedar of the adhiar debtor, the flexible system of grain-lending was replaced by a rigid pattern of grain-selling on condition of deferred payment in cash at harvest time.[56]

The role of the jotedars as creditors in the agrarian economy was dented and damaged during the depression, but they were unable to extricate the capital they had locked up in landed rights until the land market revived in 1938. Small jotes were too few and far between in north Bengal for a systematic advance on the smallholding domain to be profitable. According to the Land Revenue Commission's figures, 5.6% of the raiyati area investigated in Dinajpur, Rangpur and Jalpaiguri had been transferred in the twelve years before 1940. Of the transferred area, 27.4% was said to be cultivated by the purchasers' family, 40% by sharecroppers, 29.7% by under-tenants and 4% by labourers. In the abadi south, however, the loss of small peasants' rights and the rise of insecure sharecropping was much more dramatic. Where only twenty years previously some land had been let out in 15-bigha plots under government supervision, large holdings of 500 bighas or more had emerged by 1938 under the control of lotdars and chakdars taking 'advantage of bad years to get lands made khas and . . .

---

[55] Bell, *Dinajpur SR*, p. 25.
[56] F. O. Bell's Tour Diary, Dinajpur, November–December 1939, Bell Papers, Mss Eur D733(2) (IOR).

resettle in bhag'.[57] The period of war and famine saw further expropriation of the occupancy right of small peasants, making the dichotomy between rich farmers and sharecroppers starker than it already had been. But there were big jotedars as well among the sellers of raiyati rights in the post-1938 phase. Their aim was to create a nucleus of capital to invest in the now more profitable urban sectors of the economy. When the war ended, adhiars discovered that at least some jotedars had partially disengaged themselves from their rural commitments. In parts of Bengal where the rich farmer–sharecropper system was the predominant form of the social organization of production, zamindari abolition was practically a non-event.

## The plantation

Tea production in north Bengal from the mid nineteenth century was entirely geared towards a capitalist world market and, on the face of it, spawned 'capitalist' relations of production on mostly British-owned plantations. The ownership of large tea-gardens certainly displayed corporate capitalist forms and the labour force was remunerated in wages. Yet a detailed study of labour on the tea plantations of the Jalpaiguri Duars between 1874 and 1947 has revealed that 'the relation between the planter and the worker was that of master and servant, and not of employer and employee'.[58] An element of extra-economic coercion permeated the relationship. Unlike the interventions by government in the zamindar–raiyat relationship through tenancy legislation, the planter–worker relationship in the tea sector remained unregulated and unconstrained by any kind of reformist legislation during the colonial period.

The earliest British-owned tea-gardens in Darjeeling had utilized immigrant Nepali labour since 1850. The annexation of the Jalpaiguri Duars from Bhutan in 1865 opened the possibility of rapid expansion of tea production. The government obliged by providing cheap tea-grant land to British capitalists, while cheap tribal labour was induced to migrate from the Chhotanagpur area of Bihar, which in the later nineteenth century was in the throes of famine, widespread loss of land rights and abortive rebellion. The first of the British-owned plantations, known as sterling concerns, started production in 1874.

---

[57] Note by Commissioner Presidency Division, GOB Home Poll. Conf. File 333/39 (WBSA).
[58] Sharit Bhowmik, *Class Formation in the Plantation System* (New Delhi, 1981), p. 38.

Bengali entrepreneurs made their debut in 1879 when the Jalpaiguri Tea Company was established. Although the number of tea-gardens and acreage under Indian control increased steadily, they continued to be generally smaller in scale and fewer in number than the British-owned plantations until the 1960s.[59]

The tea plantations developed a strictly hierarchical organizational structure involving four broad categories of employees – management, staff, sub-staff and labour – which were rather more rigidly enforced in the sterling concerns than in the indigenous ones. Family-based, long-term immigrant workers at lowly wages characterized the labour process. Most had been initially cajoled and coerced to move out of their original habitats by local recruiters, usually craftsmen, called arkatis. With agricultural wages in Jalpaiguri ruling twice as high as wages on offer on tea plantations in the 1870s and 1880s, there was little prospect of attracting labour from the immediate vicinity.[60] In the early twentieth century the bulk of the recruiting among tribals was done by sardars, literally leaders, who were themselves tea-garden labourers. Unlike the indentured labourers on the Assam tea plantations further to the east, the recruits to the Duars were technically 'free' labourers since they were not placed under any contracts. Very few among them, however, were able to realize their hopes of one day returning to Bihar to cultivate their own holdings. The labour lines on the plantations were kept strictly insulated from any interaction with the agrarian society that bordered on it. Only upon retirement did coolies settle down in neighbouring bustees or settlements to work as adhiars on jotedars' lands or as temporary hands for the forestry department.

The best analysis of rather fragmentary sources between 1911 and 1946 has suggested that living and working conditions of labour on the Jalpaiguri tea plantations 'remained more or less static'.[61] Labour was generally paid by 'piece work', known as thika. Those engaged in plucking were assigned a certain quantity of leaves as their thika; those involved in pruning and hoeing were made responsible for a specific number of bushes or a particular area. The wage for completing each thika was known as hazri. The hazri of 4 annas per thika for men,

[59] Percival Griffiths, *History of the Indian Tea Industry* (London, 1972); S. Mukherji, 'Emergence of Bengalee Entrepreneurship in Tea Plantations in a Bengal District, 1879–1933' in *Indian Economic and Social History Review*, 13, 4 (October–December 1976), 487–512.
[60] W. W. Hunter, *Statistical Account of Bengal: Jalpaiguri, Cooch Behar and Darjeeling Districts* (Calcutta, 1872), p. 278.
[61] Bhowmik, *Class Formation*, p. 62.

3 annas for women and 6 pies for children remained unchanged between 1920 and 1947.[62] Unwilling to raise the wage rate, the planters allowed partial cost of living adjustments by reducing the thika, which enabled workers to earn more than one hazri a day. The average monthly earnings in 1923 were reckoned to be between Rs 9 and Rs 12 for men, Rs 4 and Rs 9 for women and 'a few rupees' for children; these had increased to rather more precise figures of Rs 14 annas 4, Rs 10 annas 6 and Rs 2 annas 2, respectively, in 1929.[63]

While regular replenishment of the labour force from the tribal catchment areas was the main concern of planters in the pre-independence period, severe retrenchment was resorted to during the 1920–2 slump and the 1930s depression when the price of tea collapsed. As the tea plantations cut back on production, part of the 'surplus' labour was 'released' to the forestry department, while others sought work in the saw mills and sugar factories in Assam. The isolation and lack of organization among tea-garden labourers was such that they could neither fight against redundancy nor clamour for better wages. Often wages were paid through the sardar, who received a commission for each worker under his charge. Capitalistic relations of production in the workplace were significantly tempered by the tribal, communitarian forms of neighbourhoods that lent considerable heterogeneity in real life to the monotonous concept of labour 'lines'. Wages were effectively held down by collusion among tea planters, British as well as Indian, who worked through the India Tea Association (and its local branches) and the Indian Tea Planters Association respectively. The Royal Commission on Labour had stressed in 1931 the crying need for a neutral machinery to fix minimum wages on the tea plantations. Little was found to have changed by the Rege Commission, which made very similar recommendations to ensure fair wages in 1946.[64]

AGRARIAN SOCIETY AND FAMILY LABOUR:
RELATIONS AND PROCESSES UNDER
COLONIALISM

Agrarian historians of India writing in the 1970s and 1980s have tended to discount earlier views of cataclysmic social structural change under

[62] Griffiths, *Indian Tea Industry*, p. 310.
[63] GOI, *Report of the Royal Commission on Labour in India* (Calcutta, 1931), p. 399.
[64] GOI, *Report on and Enquiry into Conditions of Labour in Plantations in India* (D. V. Rege Commission, New Delhi, 1946), p. 76.

the impact of colonial capitalism and emphasized the 'dynamics of continuity'.[65] Even a leading scholar who has observed a 'process of depeasantization' in Bengal and Bihar between 1885 and 1947 believes that it 'did not lead to any basic structural change in the peasant economy'.[66] Descriptive snapshot approaches to levels of differentiation and catalogues of land transfers do not quite enable the issue of change to be meaningfully addressed. But an analysis of the basic, broad types of the relations of production in the Bengal countryside between c. 1860 and c. 1950 does suggest that these showed a remarkable measure of adaptability and resilience. The peasant smallholding system underwent a process of pauperization but was far from being undermined. The smallholding–demesne complex revealed a swing in the balance in favour of the demesne lords but was still recognizable for what it was. The rich farmer–sharecropper system lost a few farmers and gained a few sharecroppers but the dichotomous relationship between them remained as stark as ever. Even the 'capitalist' plantation displayed more continuity than dynamism in retaining well-worn modes of coercion as part of the relations of production.

Yet things did change, not only at the level of the dominant relations of surplus-appropriation, as will be discussed in the next chapter, but at the point of production as well. The processes of pauperization, the changing khamar–raiyati balance and the temporally, spatially and structurally differentiated emergence of a peasant elite constituted important qualitative change at the level of agrarian society during the second century of colonial rule. More subtle, less easily fathomable but highly significant change had occurred within working families. The enhanced labour requirements of rapidly increasing cash-crop production for a capitalist world market were not simply met by macro-processes of demographic and technological change. Capitalist development under colonialism rested heavily on the forcing up of labour intensity within family units actually tilling the land. This had enormous implications as the propeller of a process of change in social relations along lines of gender and generation rather than purely class divisions.

[65] See, for instance, Rajat and Ratna Ray, 'The Dynamics of Continuity in Rural Bengal under the British Imperium' in *Indian Economic and Social History Review*, 10, 2 (1973), 103–28.
[66] Binay Bhusan Chaudhuri, 'The Process of Depeasantization in Bengal and Bihar' in *Indian Historical Review*, 3, 1 (1975), 164–5.

It is well known that many of the specialist tasks involved in the labour-intensive food-cum-cash-crop agriculture of late nineteenth- and early twentieth-century India, such as rice transplanting, jute stripping, cotton picking and tea plucking, were performed by women. Most censuses and surveys, however, show a very low proportion of women in the total agricultural workforce of Bengal. This is because unpaid labour within the peasant family, which formed the bulk of women's contribution to production, was by and large left out of account. Information is fuller on women's participation in certain sectors and stages of production in which remuneration in wages, however meagre, was common. Reasonably accurate measurements of under-reporting in certain kinds of activities such as rice dehusking make it possible to extrapolate the true extent of women's role in providing labour and changes in production relations which that entailed. Any probing of the nature of change in agrarian labour relations between the genders can only be partly evidentiary and partly derived from the logic of rural production patterns under colonial capitalism.

It is striking that in the plantation type of production organization – the tea-gardens of north Bengal – women outnumbered men in the workforce in the early twentieth century. According to the 1921 census figures, there were 56,745 male and 65,938 female workers in the Jalpaiguri Duars.[67] Unlike industrial factories, capitalist plantations in the agrarian sector showed a general preference for family-based rather than individual labour. On tea plantations, in particular, women were more efficient in performing the key task in the production process – the plucking of tea leaves. While it is true that ploughing and harvesting in the more expansive paddy and jute sectors were not generally considered women's work, women were heavily involved in weeding and transplanting during the sowing season and in paddy dehusking and jute stripping after the harvest. Certain activities like husking were 'traditional' occupations, not an innovation of the era of capitalist development. Two processes, which telescoped into each other around 1920, were definitely new in the period from 1860 to 1950: first, the large and increasing component of *unpaid* women's and children's labour in labour-intensive cultivation from the late nineteenth century and, second, a decline in the *paid* component of women's labour as a result of the direct interventions by capitalism in the processing stage of production from the early twentieth century.

[67] GOI, *Census of India 1921*, Vol. V: *Bengal*, Pt 1 *Report* (Calcutta, 1923).

Hand-processing of paddy absorbed a very large proportion of the labour time of rural women of the peasant and labouring classes before the advent of rice mills in the early twentieth century. Working the family dhenki, the wooden instrument used to pound rice out of its husk, required on one estimate at least 300 labour hours per year over and above the time needed for preliminary soaking, boiling and drying.[68] Already in the early nineteenth century paddy dehusking had emerged as a more significant income-earning activity for women than spinning. A budget compiled by Buchanan-Hamilton of a typical adhiar family of Dinajpur in 1808 read as follows:

| | Rs | As | Ps |
|---|---|---|---|
| Profit | | | |
| 15 bighas cultivated with grain produce on average | | | |
| Rs 41–4–0 of which half is his share | 20 | 10 | 0 |
| Out of his 6 leisure months he works for 4 | | | |
| at Rs 1–8–0 a month | 6 | 0 | 0 |
| His wife about the same time as he does | | | |
| only much harder by cleaning rice | 7 | 12 | 0 |
| By spinning 4 as a month | 2 | 8 | 0 |
| | | | |
| | 36 | 14 | 0[69] |

Women employed in dehusking could earn as much as 9 maunds of rice per year, nearly half of the 20 maunds consumed by an average family of five. The rice-equivalent of wages earned by dhenki operators declined steadily in the late nineteenth and early twentieth centuries as the price of common rice increased rapidly.

Paddy dehusking and jute stripping by women became in this period a critical element in the social reproduction of labour relations. The unpaid price of women's labour in the post-harvest stage formed a very important part of unpaid family labour which sustained the economic viability of jute cultivation. Peasants who had small surpluses of paddy to sell had women perform the dehusking operation at home to take advantage of the paddy–rice price differential in the marketplace. The self-sufficiency of many small peasant families rested on expenditure-saving dehusking by women. Land-poor and landless peasant families made up their food deficits with income earned by women in

[68] Mukul Mukherjee, 'Impact of Modernization on Women's Occupations: a Case Study of the Rice-Husking Industry of Bengal' in *Indian Economic and Social History Review*, 20, 1 (1983), 34. The discussion on women's productive role in rice husking is largely based on this excellent article, 27–45.

[69] Cited in *ibid.*, 36.

dehusking paddy for others, an activity that underpinned an agrarian economy that was turned over by credit. As the Dufferin enquiry of the 1880s noted:

A ryot's income is eked out in many ways. His women are always busy husking rice. The mahajan advances paddy to the ryot. The ryot ... carries the husked rice to market and sells it and then repays the mahajan ... When it is remembered what a large amount of paddy comes into the mahajan's hand, nearly equivalent to the rental of the village and that in the well-to-do households the paddy for family consumption is given out to be husked, it will be perceived that an important part in the village economy is played by rice husking.[70]

Until the turn of the century women's income-earning capacity in the husking occupation allowed them a certain autonomy from men in their entitlement to subsistence. During a crop failure in central Bengal in 1896–7 women and children in trouble 'were those of raiyats who had gone in search of work and left their females unprovided for but many of the women [we]re used to maintaining themselves by husking paddy for their richer neighbours'.[71] Since women and girls would 'in no case do earth work', even government relief measures had to get 'husking and jute-twisting from them'.[72]

The census figures of the early twentieth century overlook the category of women engaged only or mainly in domestic husking and seriously underestimate the number engaged in non-domestic husking for wages. The figures reported were 2.1 lakhs in 1901 and 2.7 lakhs in 1911. Careful calculations by one scholar based on rice output and the extent of dhenki use and its yield suggest that the probable numbers were at least ten times higher – 25.2 lakhs in 1901 and 30.4 lakhs in 1911.[73] The rapid switch to mechanized processing in rice mills sharply cut into the employment and income-earning opportunities of rural women. The number of rice mills in Bengal jumped from only 24 in 1911 to 369 in 1946.[74] The takeover by capitalists of the processing stage of rice production resulted in both an aggregate loss of women's employment and income-earning opportunities, and a change in the composition of the workforce engaged in husking. A 1943 survey of rice mills in Birbhum revealed that the workers were mainly men or

[70] Cited in *ibid.*, 30.
[71] Selection of Papers relating to the Famine of 1896–7 in Bengal, Vol. 5, 205, cited in *ibid.*, p. 32.
[72] Selection of Papers relating to the Famine of 1896–7 in Bengal, Vol. 3, cited in *ibid.*, p. 33.
[73] Mukherjee, 'Impact of Modernization on Women's Occupations', p. 35.
[74] *Ibid.*, p. 41.

Santhal women while 'women who formerly earned their living by *dhenki* [we]re socially debarred from seeking employment outside their immediate neighbourhood'.[75]

The large-scale employment of women in paddy dehusking may have been a somewhat special feature of Bengal. All the quantitative data between 1855 and 1920 make clear that unhusked rice or paddy formed a very small proportion of the marketed supply in Bengal while the bulk of grain imports from other parts of India was in the form of paddy, which Bengali women no doubt dehusked.[76] Large-scale use of women's and children's labour in the new intensive commercial agriculture was something which Bengal shared in common with the rest of colonial India. Unfortunately, there is little in the way of hard quantitative information on the involvement of women in jute cultivation. The thorough surveys by the Imperial Council of Agricultural Research in the cotton and sugar-cane tracts during the 1930s revealed very high participation rates of women in the workforce, two-thirds woman-days to man-days in some instances.[77] One analysis of private accounts in a south Indian district uncovered a process of progressive feminization of labour in all agricultural operations other than crop-cutting between 1894 and 1961.[78] It can be surmised that expanded commodity production for the world market between 1860 and 1950 entailed significant shifts in production relations along lines of gender and generation.

The increase in unpaid women's labour over the long-term from 1860 onwards and the curtailment of opportunities for paid labour after 1920 raise interesting questions about implications for intra-family distribution of food in Bengal. An old Bengali adage stated that in a home without a dhenki the daughter-in-law was bereft of all well-being.[79] The loss of women's income-earning opportunities from paddy dehusking around 1920 may have contributed significantly to the gender-bias against women in peasant families' food consumption so glaringly evident today. The state of the evidence makes it difficult to be sure, but complexities informing cultural practices notwithstand-

---

[75] Hashem Amir Ali, *The Rice Industry in Lower Birbhum* (Sri Niketan, 1943), p. 43.

[76] Mukherjee, 'Impact of Modernization on Women's Occupations', pp. 29–30.

[77] Imperial Council of Agricultural Research, *Report on the Cost of Production of Crops in the Principal Sugar-cane and Cotton Growing Tracts, 1938–39.*

[78] M. Atchi Reddy, 'Female Agricultural Labourers of Nellore, 1881–1981' in *Indian Economic and Social History Review*, 20, 1 (1983), 78.

[79] 'Jar ghare nei dhenki mushal, she bou-jhir nei kushal.'

ing, it remains one plausible hypothesis. Women of the agricultural labouring classes, however, suffered economic and sexual exploitation due to their class position and enjoyed relative freedom in their gender roles within their own community.

Whatever the negative effects on distribution at the level of the family and agrarian society, intensive and largely unremunerated family-based cultivation had clear production advantages from the capitalist angle of vision. Capital and capitalists concentrated their control over the product and credit markets and established strategic footholds on the processing stage of production without incurring costs in the labour market. The inverse farm size–productivity ratio which came to light in a series of 1950s surveys had much to do with the kind of agrarian development based on labour intensity within family units that was fostered by colonial capitalism, although it was not immediately recognized as such. The often stark inequities created or exacerbated by changes in production relations along lines of gender and generation have been only recently coming into the spotlight of analysis.[80]

## SOCIAL RELATIONS OF PROPERTY AND PRODUCTION, C. 1950–90

Zamindari property rights, including all intermediary interests between the zamindar and raiyat, were abolished by legal enactments in east and west Bengal in 1951 and 1953, respectively. Erstwhile tenants, therefore, technically became owners of petty property rights in land. In regions where landlords' demesne had been substantial, as in many west Bengal districts, zamindars and patnidars now joined the ranks of the bigger raiyats. The post-colonial state in India was pledged not only to zamindari abolition but also to the dismantling of large-scale property in land. The Land Reforms Act of 1955 imposed a ceiling on land ownership in west Bengal. The ceiling has been progressively lowered and loopholes sought to be plugged through subsequent amendments. Ceiling legislation was successfully evaded by resort to a number of subterfuges until 1967, but since then the strength of a peasant-smallholder-based left movement has resulted in

---

[80] For recent evidence on inequities along gender lines see Amartya Sen, 'Family and Food: Sex Bias in Poverty' in *Resources, Values and Development* (Oxford, 1984), pp. 346–68.

more effective implementation than in most other parts of India. Land ceilings were also imposed through a set of presidential ordinances soon after Bangladesh emerged as a sovereign country in 1971. Ceilings have generally been more liberal and enforcement more lax in Bangladesh than in West Bengal. Tenancies have continued to exist below the raiyati level in both Bengals but did not receive legal sanction as any form or fraction of property except in one instance. A major amendment to the Land Reforms Act in West Bengal in August 1970 made the sharecroppers' right to cultivation heritable. This layer of right to the land, extending over some 5% of the cultivated acreage, has been strengthened further with the issuance of certificates to registered sharecroppers since 1977 so that they can claim their statutory rights. The general tenor of land legislation in post-partition Bengal may be said to have been the defence of petty property.

Despite quite drastic legal redefinitions of the concept of landed property, relations of production in agriculture continued to be resilient to any radical restructuring. Two processes of macro-level change affected the major types of agrarian social structure in the post-1950 era – a sharp rise in the category of landless labour and a significant increase in the capital intensity of agricultural enterprise in pockets of an attempted 'green revolution' through technological innovation. But the primary characteristic of capitalist development resting on peasant family labour appeared to remain a constant through all the alterations in the peasant smallholding system, the smallholding–demesne complex and the dichotomous rich farmer–sharecropper system. Even in the plantation-type structure of north Bengal, the major changes took place in the composition of owners of the tea-gardens. The grosser inequities in the relations of production were simply mitigated by state-sponsored palliative reforms, not undermined in any decisive way.

The types of agrarian social structure that had formed in the late colonial period displayed some broad resilient features as well as elements of qualitative change. Where peasant smallholding had prevailed, a high degree of household mobility within the peasantry and the proliferation of a class of landless labourers did not subvert the conditions of reproduction of the smallholding system as such. One comprehensive study of peasant mobility in east Bengal has characterized the 'overall process' as 'one of downward aggregate shifting of the peasantry as a whole, increasing economic differentiation of peasant households and household mobility mostly within the confines of the peasantry'. As a result, 'an increasingly crushed peasantry' has been 'producing a growing proportion of landless labourers', but 'well-to-do peasants' cannot be described as 'rural capitalists'.[81] This 'net downward trend leading to pauperization' as distinct from proletarianization is also reflected in some of the statistical surveys conducted in the 1960s, 1970s and in the early 1980s.

Since a peasant elite had been emerging in east Bengal from the 1930s and had clearly consolidated their position upon the departure of mostly Hindu zamindars and talukdars after partition, the durability of the peasant smallholding system requires some explanation. One argument emphasizing demographic variables advanced the notion of 'cyclical kulakism' based on an inter-generational circulation of economic as well as social status between families of different acreage classes.[82] Anthropological research demonstrating rather limited opportunities of upward mobility for families of labourers and poor to middle peasants has seriously qualified the validity of this view.[83] Another interpretation stressed 'the barriers to polarization set up by the internal structure of peasant society' which had held back the development of class contradictions at an incipient or 'emergent' stage even as late as the 1970s.[84] Peasant smallholding society undoubtedly presented formidable structural obstacles and dogged political resistance to a capitalist transformation that might threaten the petty property base of small-scale agriculture. But equally, capital, conscious of its own imperatives and the minimum demands of peasant labour, persevered with a strategy of capitalist development resting squarely on peasant family labour which had paid rich dividends under colonialism. It was noted in Noakhali in the 1970s, for instance, that richer peasants leased out their lands in small parcels to several tenants to

---

[81] Willem van Schendel, *Peasant Mobility: the Odds of Life in Rural Bangladesh* (Assen, 1982), pp. 287–8.

[82] Peter Bertocci, 'Elusive Villages: Social Structure and Community Organization in Rural East Pakistan' (unpublished Ph.D. dissertation, Michigan State University, 1970); 'Structural Fragmentation and Peasant Classes in Bangladesh' in *Journal of Social Studies*, 5 (1979), 34–60.

[83] Shapan Adnan and H. Zillur Rahman, 'Peasant Classes and Land Mobility: Structural Reproduction and Change in Bangladesh' in *Bangladesh Historical Studies*, 3 (1978), 161–215; John Wood, 'Class Differentiation and Power in Bondokgrâm: the Minifundist Case' in M. Ameerul Huq (ed.), *Exploitation and the Rural Poor* (Comilla, 1978), pp. 59–158.

[84] Abu Ahmed Abdullah *et al.*, 'Agrarian Structure and the IRDP: Preliminary Considerations' in *Bangladesh Development Studies*, 4, 2 (1976), 217.

'ensure a greater labour input' as each tenant would 'have to devote his surplus family labour to the petty holding he gets'.[85] Even in a Comilla locality, which was the showpiece of state-aided capitalist agricultural development both before and after 1971, 'rich peasants ... were only interested in production increases, not in replacing the existing relations of production with capitalist ones'. Their surpluses were reinvested not in agriculture but in usury, urban employment and trade, and education, as they aspired to join 'the ranks of a shiftless bourgeoisie largely subsisting on foreign aid and concentrated in administrative, poorly-industrialized urban centres'. The prognosis for the future to any acute observer in the 1980s was clear: given the context of peripheral capitalism, there was quite simply 'very little room for breaking the involutionary downward spiral in which agriculture, and with it the entire society, is caught up'.[86]

In the erstwhile peasant smallholding–demesne labour complex which had predominated in west Bengal, a richer peasantry initially had a more substantial presence in the 1950s and 1960s than in east Bengal. The ranks of this class were swelled by zamindars and patnidars of old who lost their rentier rights in 1953 but held on to possessory rights to their khas khamar. The middle-caste rich peasantry, augmented by fractions of the old upper-caste gentry, now formed what came to be popularly called the jotedar class in the west Bengal countryside. Ceiling laws were ineffective in robbing this class of lands already in their possession but acted as a disincentive to further accumulation. A proliferating class of rural proletarians in west Bengal was not simply derived from a process of pauperization of peasant smallholders but had a structurally distinct prior existence. Consequently, forms of labour attachment to the surplus lands of a richer peasantry showed greater variation and more intricate ties of dependency than in east Bengal. At the same time, smallholding cultivation has been bolstered through powerful oppositional political campaigns since the mid-1960s and state initiatives at the provincial level since 1977.

Interestingly, west Bengal districts provided the empirical battleground for a lively debate on the transition to capitalism during the attempted 'green revolution' in the late 1960s and early 1970s. A major

[85] H. Zillur Rahman, *Report from Raipur Thana* (Copenhagen, 1982) cited in Shapan Adnan, 'Peasant Production and Capitalist Development'.
[86] Van Schendel, *Peasant Mobility*, pp. 290–1.

theoretical formulation on the persistence of 'semi-feudal relations' used the krishani form of labour attachment in Birbhum as its empirical reference. Large landowners, it was argued, opted against investing in productivity-raising technological innovations primarily because it would have loosened their 'semi-feudal' relations with indebted krishans who were paid with a one-third share of the crop.[87] The argument about the persistence of 'semi-feudalism' has been questioned from a variety of standpoints,[88] but what is undeniable is the resilience of social relations, at the point of production, and even primary appropriation, to attempts at capital-intensive technological change. Krishani, however, was an atypical and localized form of labour attachment which during the 1970s and 1980s became outmoded even in Birbhum. The dialectic between a surplus (in place of a demesne) sector and a peasant smallholding sector continues to be at the crux of the relations of production in west Bengal agriculture.

Since 1970 various state initiatives including the supply of easy credit have contributed to the stabilization of peasant smallholding. Smallholders are, however, still at a disadvantage in relation to the richer peasants who command a wider portfolio of investments in the agrarian economy and have a clear edge in manipulating developments in the product market. Their surplus lands are cultivated by sharecroppers or various categories of labourers. Although bargadars have been in the political limelight, sharecropping tenancies have been in steady decline in the post-independence period. Sharecropping arrangements in west Bengal showed 'certain extraordinary constancies and certain equally impressive variabilities'.[89] The 50:50 share of the harvest displayed great resilience even though since 1955 sharecroppers were entitled to 60% and since 1970 as much as 75% of the crop. Field research revealed an array of cost-sharing practices for seeds, fertilizers and manure, but significantly 'human labour cost' was 'always the responsibility of the tenant' and with a few exceptions so were the costs of bullocks and ploughs.[90] Far more important in

[87] Amit Bhaduri, 'A Study in Agricultural Backwardness under Semi-Feudalism' in *Economic Journal*, 83 (1973), 120–37.

[88] See Keith Griffin, *The Political Economy of Agrarian Change* (London, 1979); Ashwini Saith, 'Agrarian Structure, Technology and Market Surplus in the Indian Economy', unpublished Ph.D. dissertation (Cambridge, 1978); Shapan Adnan, 'Peasant Production and Capitalist Development'.

[89] Ashok Rudra, 'Share-cropping Arrangements in West Bengal' in *Economic and Political Weekly*, 10, 39, Review of Agriculture (September 1975), A-58.

[90] *Ibid.*, A-60.

sustaining production in the surplus sector has been a class of agricultural labourers, accounting for over a third of the rural population
in the 1980s, without even the limited rights of sharecroppers to the
land they till. Between the 1950s and the 1980s there has been a
perceptible shift in the character of this labour force. The proportion of
mahindars or farm servants has declined, while that of munishes or
day-labourers has risen sharply. Munish-based agricultural production
does not necessarily denote the development of a capitalist labour
market. The credit and labour markets are closely interlinked, and
most munishes are dependent for their survival on subsistence loans
provided by the richer peasants and on food-for-work programmes
sponsored by the state.

The rich farmer–sharecropper system that had prevailed in north
Bengal also witnessed a decline in the number of adhiars and a steep rise
in the number of agricultural labourers, especially during the 1960s.
Census statistics showed a 155% increase in the number of agricultural
labourers in four north Bengal districts between 1961 and 1971, while
the average increase in West Bengal as a whole was about 80%. The
percentage increases in Jalpaiguri and Darjeeling were quite startling –
264% and 249% respectively. A part of this phenomenal increase could
be attributed to changes in census categories. But there had also been a
'genuine' increase in the hired labour force owing to the 'intensification
of agricultural enterprise of two distinct types based on better irrigation' by small, enterprising refugee peasants from east Bengal and
gentlemen-farmers from the mofussil towns. Although the days of the
giant jotedar were over, the dominance of the men who combined
control over some surplus lands with trade and moneylending led
during the 1960s to 'a process of acute impoverishment' and the
emergence of 'a large labouring population which belong[ed] neither
clearly to the traditional form of adhiari nor to that of free hired
labour'.[91] The Naxalite movement, despite its immediate failure, paved
the way for the introduction of measures, including bargadar registration, which curbed the blatant dominance of the jotedars and
brought production relations in the northern and southern fringes
more in line with the rest of west Bengal.

Production relations after 1950 in the tea plantations of north Bengal

[91] N. Bandyopadhyay, 'Causes of Sharp Increase in Agricultural Labourers, 1961–71: a
Case Study of Social Existence Forms of Labour in North Bengal' in *Economic and Political
Weekly*, Review of Agriculture (December 1977), A-124.

represented 'a change from ... the existing master and servant relationship to a relationship of employer and employee' with the latter enjoying 'some legal protection'.[92] From 1952 onwards there was no organized coercive recruitment of workers by the tea-gardens. This had less to do with the changes wrought by independence than with the emergence of a situation of excess labour which placed the workers in a weak bargaining position in extracting the reforms enshrined in the Plantation Labour Act of 1951. The government intervened in 1952 to fix for the first time statutory minimum wages for tea-plantation workers in West Bengal. Between 1952 and the appointment of the Second Minimum Wage Fixation Committee in 1973, the average daily wage increased by a modest 3% per year with men earning Rs 3 and women Rs 2.83 for comparable work. In the late 1960s many British-owned companies sold their gardens to Indian entrepreneurs, while the controlling shares in other sterling concerns passed into Indian hands. The concern of the new owners to maintain the pressure of work on individual labourers in tea production was evident in their insistence on preserving the ratio of 0.9 workers for every acre of cultivation. The workers demanded a ratio of 1.5 during a major strike in 1969, upon which the owners compromised on 1.1. The mid 1970s marked the highpoint of a renegotiation of the terms of employment in the workers' favour. In 1976 the wage differential between men and women was abolished by law, and in 1977 the government-appointed wage committee awarded a handsome wage increase to tea-garden workers so that daily wages in 1978 were double what they had been in 1973.[93] Although political turmoil in the hills in the 1980s makes it difficult to be sure of wage data, it can be fairly said that the promise of vastly improved working and living conditions made in the late 1970s remained largely unfulfilled.

## PROPERTY, PRODUCTION AND POVERTY

Post-colonial reformism softened some of the harsher features of unbridled colonial capitalism but did not wholly undermine the logic underlying the social relations of production in agriculture. Plans for a socialist transformation, in particular, remained long on rhetoric and short on implementation. A labour process primarily utilizing

---

[92] Bhowmik, *Class Formation*, p. 231.     [93] *Ibid.*, pp. 86–95.

the unremunerated work of peasant families, which had been the basis of colonial capitalist development, was seized upon as a potential engine of modernization in the period after independence. Consequently, the most dramatic changes occurred in the legal expressions of property, not at the level of the social organization of production and the poverty of peasants and labourers engaged in primary production.

The historical experience of colonial and early post-colonial Bengal reveals the logical relationship between capitalist development and non-capitalist relations of production. The important strand of continuity in the social organization of production rested on a labour process utilizing the unpaid and underpaid work of family labour. Expanded commodity production for the capitalist world market was achieved efficiently and cheaply without resort to the formal commoditification of labour. The refusal to be reduced to a commodity was itself a success of resistance by peasant labour determined to retain access to a combination of production-based and trade-based entitlement to consumption and subsistence. During the second century of colonial rule, the surplus produced by peasant labour was extracted largely through the economic circuits of debt at the end of the production cycle. But this had to be tempered by the sharing of the responsibility for assuring subsistence and minimal needs of peasant labour through adequate provision of credit by the owners of land and capital at the beginning of the production cycle. It was the lines of credit that tied together the domains of land, labour and capital, and geared agrarian society to undertake production that sustained colonial commerce. Over the long term, agrarian society 'peasantized' during the early nineteenth century may be seen to have fought a drawn-out rearguard action contesting and warding off the tentative forces of 'depeasantization' since the late nineteenth century. The human and social costs of the contradictions between capital and labour in Bengal's agrarian context can be gauged by the direction of change in the different, otherwise resilient types of social structure – the downward spiral of pauperization, the slower but significant shift in favour of demesne lords and a richer peasantry, and the subtle change in gender and generational roles to the disadvantage of women and children. All of these altered entitlement relations, the consequences of which would be dramatically and cruelly evident in the differential impact of famines, especially the catastrophe of 1943, along lines of region, class, gender and generation.[94]

Non-capitalist agrarian production and capitalist economic development were bound in a dialectical relationship. A dissonance between exploitation and operational accountability marked non-capitalist relations of agrarian production.[95] Yet it was the same element of discontinuity that was adopted as the strategy of capitalist development at other levels of the economy. Capital was developed in the sense that it attached the labour capacity of Bengal's working peasantry, robbed it of its creative power and reduced its share in the total social product. The productive role of Bengal's peasantry did not free labour but merely enhanced colonial capital and magnified its dominating power over an increasingly impoverished rural population. The ways in which this power was exercised varied in the different phases of capitalist development shaped by contradictions within capitalism and resistance by labour. An analysis of changes in the predominant modes of exploitation is crucial in any understanding of the complex relationship between peasant labour and colonial capital.

[94] See Sen, *Poverty and Famines*, chs. 6 and 9; Paul Greenough, *Prosperity and Misery in Modern Bengal: the Famine of 1943–44* (New York, 1982), chs. 5 and 6; Bose, *Agrarian Bengal*, pp. 87–97.
[95] Cf. Adnan, 'Peasant Production and Capitalist Development'.

## CHAPTER 4

# APPROPRIATION AND EXPLOITATION

The labour process in agrarian production marked by its predominantly familial character was encumbered by various forms of appropriation imposed upon it. The colonial state, local landlords, metropolitan capitalists, indigenous merchants and moneylenders, and richer peasants were among the many claimants of the surplus produced by the working peasantry. The aim of those who lorded over landed rights and controlled the circuits of capital was to hold down, with the assistance of those who wielded state power, the share of labour in the total social product. Several mechanisms of extracting the surplus were available and generally deployed simultaneously. Yet, while the social organization of production displayed a strong strand of continuity despite important elements of qualitative change, the principal modes of exploitation and relations of appropriation underwent more decisive transitions over the two centuries following the onset of colonial rule.

The extraction of surplus value produced by peasant labour in the forms of rent, interest and profit occurred during the century following the grant of the Diwani to the Company in 1765 within a primary framework of the colonial state's land revenue demand. The Permanent Settlement of the land revenue with the zamindars of Bengal in 1793 was designed to ensure the security and stability of the state's main source of income.[1] As the votaries of free trade got the better of defenders of the Company's monopoly in the 1810s, the need for remittances was added to the major concern about fiscal strength. An assessment of the early experience in Bengal and the new ideological currents of the nineteenth century led colonial administrators to institute varying sorts of land revenue systems in other regions of India. Not only were different strata and segments of the rural populace chosen to be invested with the property right in land revenue collection, but the state desisted from signing away its prerogative to enhance the land revenue demand in the future.

[1] See Ranajit Guha, *A Rule of Property for Bengal* (Paris, 1963); Sirajul Islam, *The Permanent Settlement in Bengal: a Study of its Operation, 1790–1819* (Dhaka, 1979).

A raiyatwari arrangement, ostensibly with the actual cultivators, was introduced in about two thirds of Madras Presidency, while the zamindari system prevailed in the remaining third. Parts of northwestern India were chosen for an experiment with a mahalwari arrangement, with village communities owning joint responsibility for land revenue. The diversity in formal legal structures for land revenue collection did not necessarily reflect very real differences on the ground. The Madras raiyat, for instance, often became in course of time 'in effect a landlord who hired his land out'.[2] The important difference lay in the decision by the colonial state to reserve the right of revenue enhancement, which was usually exercised in the temporarily settled areas during survey and settlement operations carried out at 30-year intervals. In permanently settled Bengal the land revenue demand was initially pitched very high but it could not be increased. Temporarily settled tracts were subject to periodic and often arbitrary enhancements to meet the cash hunger of the colonial state.

The impact of the colonial land revenue demand on the well-being of India's peasantry has been a subject of intense political and scholarly disagreement ever since the later nineteenth century. Nationalist critics of British policy held it to be the single most important factor contributing to poverty and famines. Romesh C. Dutt, in particular, catalogued the rising aggregate collections of land revenue outside Bengal and lamented the disastrous effects of arbitrary enhancements of revenue demand imposed on what he believed to be largely inferior land lately brought under the plough.[3] A recent examination of taluka-level data in Bombay Presidency has suggested that, once rising prices of the second half of the nineteenth century are taken into consideration, 'real' land revenue collections can be seen to have significantly declined.[4] Since the price phenomenon transcended specific regions, wide applicability is claimed for the argument about declining land revenue demand.

There can be little doubt that the state's revenue onslaught, and also the landlords' rent offensive, waned late in the nineteenth century, if

[2] Dharma Kumar, *Land and Caste in South India* (Cambridge, 1965), p. 85; see also Nilmani Mukherjee, *The Ryotwari System in Madras, 1792–1827* (Calcutta, 1962) and Burton Stein, *Thomas Munro: the Origins of the Colonial State and His Vision of Empire* (Delhi, 1990).

[3] Romesh C. Dutt, *The Economic History of India*, Vol. II, *In the Victorian Age* (London, 1904; reprinted Delhi, 1960), pp. 36, 238–9, 252–3.

[4] Michelle Burge McAlpin, *Subject to Famine: Food Crises and Economic Change in Western India, 1860–1920* (Princeton, 1983), pp. 198–202.

these are measured as percentages of the value of the total agricultural product. But from about 1860 onwards the colonial land revenue administration no longer constituted the primary colonial context of surplus-appropriation from Indian agriculture. Although land revenue continued to be a leading item on the list of the state's sources of income well into the twentieth century, the state's measures to gear Indian primary production to wider economic systems including a world market based on capitalism, and especially its financial policies, formed the more important colonial context throughout the second century of British rule.

The simultaneous resort to multiple instruments of appropriation cannot obscure the role of rent, located within the context of the colonial revenue system, as the principal mode of exploitation in Bengal from the late eighteenth to the late nineteenth century. Within a framework of externally financed, expanded commodity production for the world market, the credit mechanism assumed pre-eminence in extracting the surplus between the late nineteenth century and the onset of the great depression in 1930. During the tumultuous decades of the depression and the Second World War, the lease and land markets became the chief channels of expropriation. The post-independence period has seen the rise of new forms of capital markets which have enabled micro-differences in land control to be deployed effectively in the exploitation of landless and land-poor labour.

## THE LANDLORDS' RENT OFFENSIVE AND ITS RETREAT, C. 1799–1885

... the landholders, through their local influence and intrigues, easily succeeded in completely setting aside the rights, even of the Khudkasht cultivators, and increased their rent. (Rammohan Roy, *Exposition of the Practical Operations of the Judicial and Revenue System of India*, Calcutta, 1832.)

Two contradictory tendencies influenced the ability of the landlords to perform their rent-collecting function. The Permanent Settlement of the land revenue with the zamindars of Bengal brought about, as was shown in chapter 3, a dichotomy between large-scale property in revenue collection and small-scale occupancy and production based on peasant holdings. Those who controlled usufruct of the land held a major advantage against those who sought to collect rent but were divorced from possessory dominion over the soil. This was the first tendency which operated against rentiers and towards a potential fall in the rate of rent. The impotence of zamindars squeezed between a grasping state and recalcitrant raiyats was evident during the immediate aftermath of 1793. Defaults by landlords in the payment of revenue led to a massive turnover of property rights. Worst hit in the late eighteenth century was the handful of great territorial zamindar families.[5] Alarmed at the prospect of losing revenues, the Company's state decided from 1799 onwards to bolster the zamindars with coercive powers to extract rent from the tenantry. This was the second tendency which operated against rent-payers and towards intensified 'feudal' exploitation of the peasantry.

The first salvo fired by the state to inaugurate the landlords' rent offensive was Regulation 7 (or Haftam) of 1799. It came to be known as the Law of Distraint because it permitted landlords to distrain crops for arrears of rent and compel the attendance of tenants at their 'courts' or kachharis. The effects were most immediately felt in the old settled districts of west Bengal, especially Burdwan, where in 1811 the peasantry complained 'loudly and grievously of the oppressions of the zamindars and their officers in regard to surplus exactions, abwabs, deductions and distraints'.[6] For all their complaints the peasants were rewarded with Regulation 5 (or Panjam) of 1812. This became known as the Law of Eviction since it stripped away the safeguards for raiyats written into the Permanent Settlement of 1793 and empowered zamindars to make whatever terms with their tenants as they wished, regardless of custom and, if necessary, by evicting old tenants and settling new ones. The legal sanction given by another regulation in 1819 to the creation of patni tenures, resorted to originally by the Burdwan Raj to facilitate the collection of rent, lent further ammunition to rentier landlords.

The coercive powers granted by the Haftam and Panjam Regulations of 1799 and 1812 could not be used indiscriminately in the initial phase,

---

[5] Eleven territorial families had controlled about half of the landed 'property' in Bengal in 1793. The 'rajas' of Rajshahi, Dinajpur, Nadia, Birbhum, Bishnupur, Yusufpur, Muhammadshah and Idrikpur were ruined before the end of the century. The zamindars of Potia in Rajshahi and Jahangirpur in Dinajpur weathered this early storm best; the Burdwan Raj lost nearly a sixth of its territory in this initial phase but recouped its losses in the nineteenth century. See Sirajul Islam, *The Permanent Settlement in Operation*, chs. 4, 5 and 6.

[6] Bengal Revenue Proceedings, 31 December 1811, cited in Aditee Nag Chowdhury-Zilly, *The Vagrant Peasant: Agrarian Distress and Desertion in Bengal, 1770–1830* (Wiesbaden, 1984), p. 143.

except in pockets of high population density. Given the overall context of absolute deficit labour, peasants could still exercise the option of deserting the lands of especially oppressive landlords. During the first two decades of the nineteenth century zamindars, by and large, had to induce peasants to cultivate new lands by offering low rates of rent and remain content with higher absolute incomes accruing from the extensive nature of growth. With the building up of population pressure and the exhaustion of extensive margins in much of west Bengal by the 1820s, the threat of eviction could be deployed to force up rents and other charges.

It was primarily on the basis of reports on conditions in west Bengal districts that J. H. Harrington, a British civilian, drafted a regulation in 1827 providing permanent occupancy rights and fixity of customary rent for khudkasht raiyats.[7] The government, now professing laissez-faire on matters to do with rent, did not enact the draft into law. An enquiry conducted by collector Halhead of Burdwan in 1828 furnished more evidence on rent hikes in west Bengal. In districts like Burdwan and Nadia new cash crops, such as indigo, sugar and cotton, had been introduced and rents had been raised. The jama or rental rate in some parts of Nadia had increased from 1 anna 8 pice to 5 annas 8 pice per bigha (about a third of an acre) within the previous decade and a half. The rates paid by paikasht (non-resident, migratory) raiyats had increased sharply over roughly the same period as extensive cultivation reached its margins. Khudkasht (resident, settled) raiyats, who were in theory and according to their pattas (leases) secure on their holdings so long as they regularly paid rent, were being forcibly displaced by aggressive landlords who made new settlements at higher rents.[8] The plight of khudkasht raiyats was confirmed by the investigations of Rammohan Roy in 1831.[9]

Around 1830 zamindars were in a much more comfortable position in terms of their margin between rent and revenue than they had been in 1799 (see Table 6). According to one very rough comparison, the gross rental increased from Rs 30 million in 1793 to Rs 130 million in 1876, including Bihar districts where increases were much sharper than

[7] J. H. Harrington, *Minute and Draft of Regulation of the Rights of Ryots in Bengal* (Calcutta, 1827).
[8] Report by Halhead, collector of Burdwan. Board of Revenue Proceedings, Range 50, vol. 54, Report No. 46, 7–25 March 1828 (IOR).
[9] Rammohan Roy, *Exposition*, pp. 57–9 and *passim* (Calcutta, 1832).

## Table 6. *The zamindars' cut, 1830*

| District | Revenue Demand | Rent Collected | Balance |
| --- | --- | --- | --- |
| Birbhum | 14,508 | 23,871 | 9,363 |
| Burdwan | 27,360 | 34,652 | 7,292 |
| Dhaka | 2,248 | 3,225 | 977 |
| Dinajpur | 66,562 | 110,041 | 43,479 |
| Jessore | 110,224 | 225,037 | 114,813 |
| Midnapur | 5,045 | 12,906 | 7,861 |
| Murshidabad | 101,882 | 189,631 | 87,749 |
| Mymensingh | 115,941 | 316,732 | 200,791 |
| Nadia | 23,823 | 43,204 | 19,381 |
| 24-Parganas | 6,625 | 8,601 | 1,976 |
| Rajshahi | 40,474 | 84,263 | 43,789 |
| Rangpur | 25,656 | 57,587 | 31,931 |
| Tippera | 20,464 | 31,128 | 10,664 |

*Source:* Reply by Holt MacKenzie, Question No. 2929, *Parliamentary Papers*, XI (1831–2).

*Note:* The figures (in sicca rupees) refer to figures of revenue demand and rent collected in estates under the administration of the Court of Wards in 1830. It is probable that the government did a better job in collecting rents for their formal 'wards' than even the more aggressive zamindars.

in Bengal proper.[10] Another report indicated that the gross rental tripled or quadrupled between 1793 and 1880 in Bihar, while the ratios of increase in some Bengal districts were 1.5 in Burdwan, 1.7 in Midnapur, 1.8 in Nadia and 1.2 in Dinajpur.[11] Much of the expansion in gross rental was derived from extensive agricultural growth, but a part came from the imposition of higher rental rates in west Bengal districts. The year 1830 represented the moment when paikasht rent, so long generally lower, now began outstripping the rates paid by khudkasht raiyats in west Bengal. The same did not happen in east Bengal until very late in the nineteenth century as long as extensive

[10] The 1793 figure is based on the belief that the rental constituted 90% of the revenue demand. The 1876 figure is based on data collected in connection with the implementation of the Bengal Road Cess Act of 1871. On the doubtful assumptions made in estimating these figures see B. B. Chaudhuri, 'Agrarian Relations in Eastern India' in Dharma Kumar (ed.), *The Cambridge Economic History of India*, Vol. II (Cambridge, 1983), pp. 135–6.

[11] *Report of the Government of Bengal on the Proposed Amendment of the Law of the Landlord and Tenant in that Province* (Calcutta, 1881), p. ii.

agricultural growth continued.[12] West Bengal landlords doggedly opposed the acceptance of khudkasht status of raiyats from the 1820s onwards and sought to protect their prerogative of eviction and choice of tenants.

The rent offensive gathered further momentum between 1830 and 1860, driven mainly by extra-economic coercion. One study of these decades has described the results of the zamindars' lathi raj: 'Khud Kasht ryots became rarer day by day. The pargana rate of rent was pushed up by false evidence of dependent ryots. Abwabs were freely collected. The power of distraint was thoroughly abused'.[13] Landlords were not the only stick-wielders in the Bengal countryside in this period. The indigo planters were second to none when it came to coercion. Indigo having become an unremunerative crop from the 1820s, the planters sought special legal dispensations from the state to enforce contracts on hapless peasants. Regulation 6 of 1823 gave the planters a 'lien or interest' in the indigo plants tended by peasants who had accepted advances. Regulation 5 of 1830 prescribed imprisonment for peasants who were unable or unwilling to adhere to indigo contracts. This measure was considered so outrageous that it was repealed after five years and dusted off the shelves again for a six-month period at the height of the anti-indigo agitation in 1860.

More important, the Bentinck administration's efforts to remove the restriction on the holding of land by Europeans bore fruit in the Charter Act of 1833. Planters now began to buy into landed rights, most commonly as intermediary tenure-holders between zamindar and raiyat, and take advantage of the institutions and instruments of intimidation embedded in the zamindari system. 'We require zemindary power,' declared the general manager of the Bengal Indigo Company, 'to conduct our business in the mofussil.'[14] They proved especially eager to use the power to summon peasants to their kachhari, not to extract rent as the zamindars would, but simply to deploy the threat of rent enhancement to force them to grow indigo. They were even prepared to take losses on rent so long as they made unconscionable profits on indigo. It was only after the prospects of indigo were

[12] Sirajul Islam, *Rent and Raiyat: Society and Economy of Eastern Bengal, 1859–1928* (Dhaka, 1989), p. 25.

[13] Chittabrata Palit, *Tensions in Bengal Rural Society: Landlords, Planters and Colonial Rule, 1830–1860* (Calcutta, 1975), p. 94.

[14] Reply by Mr Larmour, general manager, Bengal Indigo Company, No. 2225, *Report of the Indigo Commission.*

doomed in 1860 that some of them made a late and, as it turned out, largely futile attempt to enhance rents and survive in the post-indigo era as landlords.

Already in the late 1850s key officials in the colonial administration had begun a process or rethinking the issues of revenue and rent. A bill was written in 1857 which was eventually passed as Act X of 1859, commonly known as the Rent Act. Assenting to the bill, Viceroy Canning described it as

a real and earnest endeavour to improve the position of the ryots of Bengal, and to open to them a prospect of freedom and independence which they have not hitherto enjoyed by clearly defining their rights and by placing restrictions on the power of the zemindars such as ought long since to have been provided.[15]

A few hard calculations were behind this apparent change of heart. It had been increasingly recognized that the development of India as a market for British manufactured goods would rest on a broadly based expansion of purchasing power of the predominantly rural populace. The emergence of rural India as a major exporter of agricultural raw materials was also not possible without a lightening of the revenue and rent burden.

The Rent Act of 1859 granted the right of occupancy to raiyats in continued possession of their holdings for twelve years, and called for fair and equitable rents. Zamindars could claim enhancements if (1) the area under cultivation increased, (2) the value of the produce rose and (3) higher rates than the one applied to a particular holding prevailed in the locality. The law put limits on the landlords' power of distraint granted in 1799.[16] In short, tenancy legislation was seeking to bring about relative stability among the cultivating classes and to restrict grounds for rent enhancement to economic ones. An initial judicial test of the new law in 1862 appeared to permit dramatic rent increases on the basis of increased value of the produce. But another High Court decision in 1864 in the Thakurani Dasi versus Bisheshur Prasad case laid down a principle of proportion by which rent increases could not exceed the ratio of increase in produce value. The stage was now set for a new phase of struggle over occupancy status and rent in a period of accelerated commercialization and rising agricultural prices.

[15] Resolution of the Governor-General in Council, 29 April 1859, cited in Sirajul Islam, *Rent and Rauyat*, p. 7.
[16] For further details see Sunjeeb Chunder Chatterjee, *Bengal Ryots: Their Rights and Liabilities* (Calcutta, 1864, reprinted 1977).

Once the emphasis shifted from extra-economic forces to economic reasons for rent enhancement, the property–production contradiction came into its own in influencing the ability of landlords to increase the rental demand and collect rent. Where landlords had already accumulated substantial khamar or personal demesne, as in much of west Bengal, they were better able to maintain high rental rates and extract surplus. Zamindars and patnidars of west Bengal not only controlled demesnes, but they had since the late 1840s entered the credit market in the rice sector in a very big way. Most importantly, they were also the principal grain-dealers and well positioned to take the lion's share of profits from a buoyant product market.

Where raiyati decisively predominated over khamar, as in much of east Bengal, landlords were seriously handicapped in raising rental rates. Zamindars and talukdars of east Bengal had not, by and large, diversified their portfolios to include investments in the credit and product markets. They consequently found themselves at a serious disadvantage in attempting to take a share of the fruits of rapid commercialization, including higher incomes from jute, and in the unenviable position of paying higher prices for their articles of consumption. Occupancy of the work-units of production greatly helped the peasantry in thwarting the efforts made by landlords distanced from possessory dominion either to enhance rents on raiyati land or systematically and significantly to increase the proportion of khamar. One detailed study of east Bengal districts in this period has revealed that the 'average rate [of rent] showed a remarkable inelasticity at least since the mid nineteenth century, which gave rise to the tendential fall in the pitch of rent, i.e., the proportion of the rental to the value of the gross agricultural produce'. The pitch of rent is estimated to have been about 15% of the value of gross produce around 1870 and to have declined to between 5% and 10% by the turn of the century.[17] Romesh C. Dutt, who was sent to east Bengal as a young officer to organize relief after the severe cyclone of 1876, discovered that the 'peasantry in those parts paid light rents', had sufficient savings and did not need large-scale relief operations. 'But,' he noted, 'rents in Western Bengal are higher, in proportion to the produce, than in Eastern Bengal.'[18] This differential continued to hold into the twentieth century, even

[17] Nariaki Nakazato, 'Agrarian Structure in the Dhaka Division of Eastern Bengal, 1870–1905' (unpublished Ph.D. thesis, Calcutta University, 1985), pp. 424, 397–9.

[18] Romesh C. Dutt, *The Economic History of India*, Vol. II, *In the Victorian Age*, pp. iv–v.

after the pressure of population became much heavier and the scramble for smallholdings much more intense in the eastern districts of Bengal.

The battle over the issue of occupancy rights and rent was fought and lost, despite victories in minor skirmishes, by the landlords of east Bengal in the 1870s and early 1880s. The peasant proprietor and the occupancy tenant were now the favourites of the colonial state as potential leaders of the crusade for 'improving' agriculture and sustaining India's export surplus. The Bengal Tenancy Act of 1885 sought to give the peasantry of Bengal security of tenure and moderation of rent. A raiyat who had been in continuous possession of any land in a village either himself or through inheritance for twelve years would from now on be recorded as a settled raiyat of the village with occupancy rights to the holdings he possessed or acquired in the future. Rent could only be enhanced once in fifteen years and by not more than 12.5% of the existing rent.[19] The law of 1885 had given formal recognition to the collapse of the landlords' rent offensive.

For much of the late eighteenth and the nineteenth centuries rent had been the principal mode of surplus-appropriation in Bengal. But it was not the only channel of the drain on the resources of the working peasantry. The indigo planters' profits in the first half of the nineteenth century were only indirectly linked to the rental structure after 1833. The zamindars and patnidars of west and central Bengal combined their rentier role from the late 1840s with control over demesnes, credit and the grain market. Occasionally, the oppressive measures were directly applied by colluding richer peasants. From the late 1850s the landlords also made a selective foray into the land market and dispossessed the tribal peoples in the western fringe of Bengal. In the northern districts, such as Dinajpur and Rangpur, the zamindars were generally far removed from actual control over the land and were often absentees. Here the big jotedars, commanding land, labour and credit, collected half the produce as rent from bargadars and often managed to get themselves recognized as raiyats under the categories created by late nineteenth-century tenancy legislation.[20] But overall rent within the zamindari structure of revenue collection remained during the first

---

[19] For further details and a discussion of the background to the Bengal Tenancy Act of 1885 see Asok Sen, 'Agrarian Structure and Tenancy Laws in Bengal, 1850–1900' in Asok Sen, Partha Chatterjee and Saugata Mukherji, *Perspectives in Social Sciences 2: Three Studies on the Agrarian Structure in Bengal, 1850–1947* (Delhi, 1982).

[20] See Shinkichi Taniguchi, 'The Structure of Agrarian Society in Northern Bengal' (unpublished Ph.D. thesis, Calcutta University, 1977).

three quarters of the nineteenth century the main mechanism of exploitation of peasant labour.

The available historical sources enable us to locate rent as the principal mode of appropriation and track movements of gross rental and, more important, variations in the rate of rent and the proportion of rental demand and collection to the value of agricultural produce in different phases. But these still do not allow any precise measure, far less quantification, of the rate of exploitation of labour. Even when rent was the chief mechanism of appropriation, the rate of rent did not provide a proper measure of exploitation since it did not capture the rate of surplus-value being expropriated. The tendential fall in the rate of rent in certain phases did not necessarily denote a lessening of the degree of exploitation. Qualitative evidence on the enormous and multiple pressures being exerted on the productive capacity of peasant labour by the colonial state, rentier landlords and profit-seeking planters would suggest a high ratio of surplus labour to labour necessary for subsistence in any apportionment of labour time and the paltriness of labour's share of value. Yet, the identification of rent as the leading mode of appropriation, as well as the mapping of its broad direction and trends, are in themselves of great significance because of their bearing on any understanding of the opportunities for and effectiveness of resistance to exploitation in nineteenth-century rural Bengal.

## THE TIDE OF INDEBTEDNESS, c. 1885–1930s

'Jedin theke mahajaner shange janajani
Shedin thekei Kalu Sheikher bejay tanatani'
Ever since he made the mahajan's acquaintance
Kalu Sheikh has been in straitened circumstance. (Maulavi Sheikh
Idris Ahmed, *Krishaker Marmabani*, Manaksha, Malda, 1921)

Debt was more insidious than rent as a surplus-extracting mechanism because it was not only a mode of exploitation. Credit, as chapter 3 has shown, played a vital role in material production and in the social reproduction of peasant labour. The creditor, unlike the rentier, had the unique characteristic of giving and taking, nurturing and impoverishing at the same time. The rise of rural credit to the position of the principal relation of surplus-appropriation undoubtedly occurred in the context of rapidly expanding commodity production in rural India for the world market. But debt followed in the wake of increased need for credit, not enhanced creditworthiness consequent on prosperity – a subtle but important distinction often missed by even the more perceptive observers of the rural landscape.[21] 'There is a kind of poverty', the Bengal Provincial Banking Enquiry Committee reported, discounting a prevailing prosperity thesis, 'which, while not amounting to insolvency, makes for precarious and uncertain living, and it is this which is the real cause of indebtedness among agriculturists in Bengal.'[22]

The precise operation of credit as the principal mode of exploitation and the size of its appropriations varied according to the nature of the agrarian social structure. Within the peasant smallholding system predominating in jute-growing east Bengal the credit and product markets were closely interlinked. Credit in the peasant smallholding–demesne labour complex typical of west Bengal substantiated the dependence of labour on the demesnes and facilitated continued rent extraction from smallholders. The rich farmer–sharecropper system pervasive in north Bengal was marked by debt interest as an important component of the jotedars' product share.

It is important to distinguish, certainly with regard to peasant smallholders of east Bengal, the dadni and lagni forms of credit representing merchant and usury capital in the countryside. Both took shape from the later nineteenth century within the framework of a widening market and rising prices for the peasants' product. Merchant capital, which originated in the arenas of high finance in the metropolis, was exchanged and forwarded by the purchasing firms through a network of commission agents to the primary producers. The peasant usually received his dadan or advance from a small trader-moneylender directly dependent on the flow of funds from above. The primary interest of the entire hierarchy of lenders, whether the borrower was contracted to sell to a particular lender or not, was to secure the crop at a low village-level price. In addition to trader-mahajans, some rentier landlords, who had proven too weak to enhance rents or expand demesnes in the face of falling rental rates, found a niche for themselves in the jute-growing areas as usurers in the new principal mode of

[21] For example, Malcolm Lyall Darling, *The Punjab Peasant in Prosperity and Debt* (London, 1925, 1947, reprinted Delhi, 1978). For a critical comment see Neeladri Bhattacharya, 'Lenders and Debtors: Punjab Countryside, 1880–1940', in *Studies in History*, 1, 2 (1985), 339.
[22] *Report of the Bengal Provincial Banking Enquiry Committee 1929–30*, Vol. I, p. 65.

surplus-appropriation. Merchant and usury capital were distinct but they effectively complemented each other in exploiting the working peasantry. Talukdar-mahajans were able to switch from rental to usurious income because of the expansion of the product market. Trader-mahajans were helped, in instances where the peasant was not tied by dadan, in procuring the produce cheaply by the demand for interest on lagni at harvest time. The heavy demand for unsecured loans negated any potential for playing off one fraction of the creditor group against another.

The raiyati–khamar complex in west Bengal displayed a more explicit linkage between control of credit and the rental structure. By and large, the landlords constituted the chief group of creditors supplemented as junior partners by some richer peasants. Lending within the demesne sector was mainly in grain. Peasant smallholding could not reproduce itself in the late nineteenth and early twentieth centuries without money borrowed from the demesne lords, but paid a heavy price in interest payments and was caught in a cycle of impoverishment in the process. The involvement of moneylending landlords in the rice market blurred the distinction between trading and usury capital. Recognizing that credit, not rent, was now the more acceptable and important mechanism of surplus-appropriation, land-lords included rental arrears in the accounts of debt. In the jute-growing parts of the rich farmer–sharecropper system prevalent in north Bengal, some trader-mahajans engaged in the dadan business. But grain loans constituted the bulk of credit, which at this stage underpinned, and was interlaced closely with effective control over land and the product market.

Evidence from the early twentieth century strongly suggests that appropriation through debt interest was larger than rent and that the differential widened during the fifty-year span from 1880 to 1930. There was general agreement with the Dhaka settlement officers' opinion that in east Bengal 'the tide of indebtedness commenced to flow' in the 1880s. By the 1910s the cultivator's 'payments to his landlord in rent, premiums and *abwabs* form[ed] but a small percent-age of his gross earnings; the only danger, and that a vital one [was]... his burden of debt and the consequent domination of the moneylen-der'. The total annual interest charge in the district was estimated to be over Rs 21 million, which was about a fifth of the value of the total product and five and a half times the rental demand. The average rental

demand for each person supported by agriculture worked out at
Rs 2.50 and the average interest demand at Rs 12, nearly a quarter of a
person's average share of the product.[23] If figures from Wards' and
Attached Estates are taken as an indication, the proportion of rent
collected to total rental demand in Dhaka averaged only about 30%
between 1913–14 and 1920–1.[24] In neighbouring Mymensingh, where
rent collection was in a similar dismal state, the settlement officer
found the raiyat's rent to be 'the least important factor in his budget'
but interest 'so high' that 'its payment constitute[d] a severe drain on
the resources of the agricultural population'.[25] Indebtedness in Pabna
in the early 1920s was 'widespread and crushing'.[26] J. C. Jack, who
conducted the most detailed district-level survey of rural indebtedness
in Faridpur early in the twentieth century, did not attempt an explicit
comparison between rent and debt interest payments. He reported,
however, that rent including abwabs as a proportion of the value of the
product declined from 15% in 1860, to 12% in 1880, to 9% in 1900 and
finally to 6% in 1914.[27] Indebtedness, on the other hand, was on the
rise. In 1916 the average indebtedness per cultivator's family was Rs 55,
but since 55% of the families were still free from debt the average per
indebted family was Rs 121. The interest rate was 'never less than 36
per cent, often 48 per cent and more'.[28] By the early 1930s a mere 17%
of cultivators in Faridpur with secure rights in land were reported free
from debt, the family average of total principal debt was up to Rs 217
and the average per indebted family a hefty Rs 262.[29]

The peasants in west Bengal districts such as Burdwan, Bankura,
Birbhum, Howrah and Hooghly were steeped in debt, of which a
substantial part came to consist of rental arrears.[30] Sharecroppers and

[23] F. D. Ascoli, *Dacca Settlement Report (1910–1917)*, pp. 47–50.
[24] *Report on the Wards and Attached Estates* cited in Binay Bhushan Chaudhuri,
'Movement of Rent in Eastern India, 1793–1930' in *Indian Historical Review*, 3, 2 (January
1977), 353.
[25] F. A. Sachse, *Mymensingh Settlement Report (1908–1919)*, p. 27.
[26] D. Macpherson, *Pabna and Bogra Settlement Report (1920–1929)*, cited in Bengal
Board of Economic Enquiry, *Bulletin District Pabna* (Alipur, 1935), p. 6.
[27] J. C. Jack, *Faridpur Settlement Report (1904–1914)*, pp. 30–1.
[28] J. C. Jack, *The Economic Life of a Bengal District*, pp. 77–8, 100–1.
[29] Bengal Board of Economic Enquiry, *Bulletin District Faridpur* (Alipur, 1934), p. 4.
[30] See F. W. Robertson, *Bankura Settlement Report (1917–1924)*, p. 17; Santipriya Bose,
'A Survey of Rural Indebtedness in South-west Birbhum, Bengal in 1933–34', in *Sankhya*, 3,
2 (1937), 151–9; settlement officer, Burdwan–Howrah–Hooghly settlement to director, Land
Records, 9 August 1930, and note by director, Debt Conciliation (West) in 'Settlement of
Debts in Burdwan, Hooghly and Howrah Districts where Rate of Rent is Very High and
Rent Arrears form the Major Portion of the Debt', May 1938, cited in Sugata Bose, *Agrarian
Bengal: Economy, Social Structure and Politics, 1919–1947* (Cambridge, 1986), pp. 166, 130.

labourers on the demesne sector paid for credit with their labour and a good part of the product of their labour. Sharecroppers in north Bengal typically accepted grain loans in the sowing season and were expected to pay back derhi or one and a half times the amount borrowed at harvest time.[31] Credit played a central role in the ability of dominant social groups to appropriate surplus in a variety of ways.

The Bengal Provincial Banking Enquiry Committee calculated in 1929–30 that the total agricultural debt in Bengal amounted to Rs 1000 million – Rs 930 million in money and Rs 70 million in kind. The gross rental demand, by comparison, amounted to just above Rs 150 million, representing six and a quarter per cent of the gross value of the agricultural product.[32] There are serious problems with these aggregated statistical estimates and, consequently, too much store should not be set by them. No attempts were made to compare annual rent and interest payments. Interest rates were reported to vary widely between 12% and 300%, with jute-growing east Bengal districts tending to have higher rates.[33] An average rate of about 15% would produce an interest payment equal to the rental demand, which was roughly double the rent actually collected in any year in the twentieth century.

What the banking enquiry reports of other provinces suggest clearly is that the debt phenomenon as the major surplus-appropriating mechanism of the late nineteenth and early twentieth centuries was all-India in scope. Most of these reports calculated debt as a multiple of land revenue, which was relevant in the predominantly temporarily settled raiyatwari provinces. The multiples were 25.5 in the Punjab, 21 in Assam, 19 in Madras, 15 in Bombay and 12.5 in the Central Provinces. Only the Central Provinces report stated explicitly that interest charges were two and a half times the land revenue demand.[34] Darling calculated for the Punjab, where the land revenue demand in 1929 was Rs 53 million, that the total interest charge amounted to over Rs 150 million, of which Rs 120 million were owed by proprietors and the remainder by tenants and farm-hands. The proprietors' interest burden was, therefore, more than twice their land revenue demand.[35]

---

[31] See F. O. Bell, *Dinajpur Settlement Report (1934–1940)*, p. 25; A. C. Hartley, *Rangpur Settlement Report (1931–1938)*, pp. 13–14.

[32] *Report of the Bengal Provincial Banking Enquiry Committee (1929–30)*, pp. 69–70, 28.

[33] *Ibid.*, p. 198.

[34] All these figures are conveniently compiled and presented in tabular form in Darling, *Punjab Peasant in Prosperity and Debt*, p. 18.

[35] *Ibid.*, pp. 182–4.

The growing convergence in the destinies of diverse agrarian regions in India since the middle of the nineteenth century made certain that they suffered a broadly similar fate in the great depression of the 1930s. Certainly, credit as a mode of surplus-appropriation collapsed, or at least was severely damaged, as a result of this most serious economic crisis of capitalism and the politics of resistance to which it gave rise. In 1930 the worldwide economic cataclysm announced itself in India in the form of a dramatic downslide in the demand and the prices for the country's raw material exports and a sudden stoppage of the flow of foreign funds into the circuits of agrarian credit.

No part of agrarian economy and society in Bengal remained immune from the credit squeeze, but the nature of the impact varied according to the type of agrarian social structure.[36] East Bengal, with its highly monetized economy, was most directly and sharply affected by the liquidity crisis. Most trader-moneylenders were stranded without cash as finance capital stopped pouring in. A great majority of talukdar-moneylenders recovered little, if anything, in interest from peasant debtors badly hit by the price fall and, consequently, had little to lend. A few creditors who commanded more substantial resources simply pulled back from involvement in the unprofitable business of rural moneylending. As an enquiry in Mymensingh revealed, mahajans were 'less willing and also less able to lend money to agriculturists since the commencement of the depression of 1930–31'.[37] Those who held stocks of grain were reluctant to lend, preferring to sell on rigid conditions of partially deferred payment at harvest time. The ties of credit which had underpinned an unequal symbiosis in social relations in east Bengal between trader-mahajans and landlord-mahajans on the one hand and peasant-debtors on the other snapped during the depression. While bringing severe economic hardship to peasant labour, the depression also destroyed the only effective means of dominance available to appropriators divorced from control over land and largely bereft of extra-economic powers of coercion.

The relations of landlord creditors controlling substantial khas khamar in west Bengal with their debtors were not ruptured in quite the same way. Lending in money contracted sharply under the impact

[36] For a detailed analysis of the impact of the depression on rural credit relations see Bose, *Agrarian Bengal*, ch. 4.
[37] Collector, Mymensingh to Joint Secy, Cooperative Credit and Rural Indebtedness Dept, 27 November 1937, in 'Restriction of Rural Credit', GB Revenue Dept Land Revenue Br, May 1940, B Progs, 14–57 (BSRR).

of the generalized liquidity crisis. The centrality of the credit relationship in surplus-appropriation is underlined by the fact that west Bengal landlords who had managed to maintain high rental incomes until 1930 suddenly lost their ability to do so.[38] But a narrow focus on rent has led some historians to draw the mistaken conclusion that west Bengal landlords, like their east Bengal counterparts, finally lost their position of dominance in the 1930s.[39] Demesne lords continued paddy loans to dependent sharecroppers and labourers and took their returns in labour service. The smaller patnidars and peasant smallholders were worst affected by the shrinkage in lending and borrowing in money. Those smallholders who could not reproduce themselves without credit were absorbed as sharecroppers within a grasping demesne sector dominated by the larger zamindars and patnidars.[40] Despite the serious dislocation in the monetary form of credit, the ties of dominance and dependence deepened and widened in the peasant smallholding–demesne labour complex during the depression.

Money credit was reduced to a trickle in the frontier regions as elsewhere. The jotedar creditors of north Bengal continued grain advances to the most hopelessly dependent adhiars from whom they could extract labour and the bulk of the crop. Where more decentralized sharecropping prevailed and control of land and credit were not necessarily concentrated in the same person, grain redistribution moved out of the orbit of credit and into the more rigid domain of the product market. Finding their role as creditors sharply attenuated, many jotedars waited for an opportunity to shift their rural investments into the more promising parts of the urban sector.

At the same time as appropriation through debt interest diminished drastically in the early 1930s, the quest for liquidity and credit brought about a dramatic dishoarding of accumulated treasure in the Bengal countryside. Corroborating evidence from Tamil Nadu and the Punjab suggests that this was a development which transcended specific

[38] One recent work has argued on the basis of selected case studies that some large estates under the Court of Wards, notably the Burdwan Raj, had been able to collect rent efficiently until the economic crisis of the depression. See Akinobu Kawai, *Landlords' and Imperial Rule: Change in Bengal Agrarian Society, c. 1885–1940* (Tokyo, 1986).
[39] See, for instance, Rajat Kanta Ray, 'The Retreat of the Jotedars?' in *Indian Economic and Social History Review*, 25, 2 (1988), 239, interpreting evidence on rent collection adduced by Kawai, *'Landlords' and Imperial Rule*.
[40] Bose, *Agrarian Bengal*, pp. 130–4.

regions.[41] The outflow was triggered in September 1931 by the move of the pound sterling away from the gold standard and the linking of the rupee with the devalued sterling at a fixed exchange rate. By the late 1930s there were no ornaments left to pledge in the rural areas.[42] Short-term profit taking on gold masked the huge disinvestment by agrarian economy and society which the drain of treasure truly represented.

A series of delayed debt legislation in the 1930s marked the formal recognition of the end of the creditors' heyday as appropriators of the agrarian surplus. The key legislative measure in Bengal was the Bengal Agricultural Debtors' Act of 1936, which, like similar laws in other provinces, provided for debt conciliation boards to scale down debts according to the debtors' ability to pay. In addition to giving relief to debtors, it was also designed to benefit moneylenders who 'as a whole had failed to collect any interest, much less any part of the capital of their outstanding loans' since the onset of the slump.[43] The debt boards did a vigorous job of slashing debt obligations, especially in east Bengal. Another measure, the Bengal Moneylenders' Act of 1940, placed low ceilings on interest rates and total amounts recoverable on loans and also sought to register moneylenders. The effect of the 1936 law was to aggravate further the process of drying up of credit. The 1940 law served as a disincentive to moneylenders prepared to consider re-entering the rural moneylending business and was used as a pretext by west Bengal landlord-creditors not to lend grain at illegal interest rates but to sell for large profits in a wartime product market.

The Land Revenue Commission concluded in 1940: 'it would not be too much to say that at present rural credit is virtually non-existent'.[44] Although trade and prices had already taken an upward turn, the agrarian credit market continued to languish during the 1940s. Legislative intervention in the debt problem had something to do with this, but the more important reason was the fundamental relative weakness

[41] Cf. Bose, *Agrarian Bengal*, pp. 119–25, 130–4, 136–40; C. J. Baker, *An Indian Rural Economy: the Tamilnad Countryside 1880–1955* (Delhi, 1984), pp. 302–3; Bhattacharya, 'Lenders and Debtors', pp. 340–1.

[42] Collector, Tippera to Joint Secretary, Cooperative Credit and Rural Indebtedness Dept, 29 October 1937 and collector, Burdwan to commissioner, Burdwan Division, 1 October 1937 in 'Restriction of Rural Credit', GB Revenue Dept Land Revenue Br, May 1940, B Progs. 14–57 (BSRR); F. O. Bell's Tour Diary, Dinajpur, November–December 1939, Bell Papers, Mss. Eur D 733 (2) (IOR), pp. 79–80.

[43] Bengal Board of Economic Enquiry, *Preliminary Report of Rural Indebtedness*, p. 5.

[44] *Report of the Land Revenue Commission Bengal*, Vol. I, p. 76.

of the jute economy of Bengal. Various statistical surveys up to 1946 confirm the long-term shrinkage of rural debt.[45] This seems to be generally true for agrarian regions reliant on non-food cash crops, as evidence from south India indicates; the wheat-based cash economy of the Punjab, by contrast, seems to have witnessed a resurgence of credit in the immediate post-war era, if not already in the later years of World War II.[46] The observant author of the first census report in post-independence Bengal had no hesitation in asserting that '[b]etween 1935 and 1947 both the extent and the volume of debts were definitely smaller than between 1929 and 1935'.[47]

Credit had been the principal mode of appropriation in agrarian Bengal between about 1885 and 1930, but certainly not the exclusive one. Rent, although it was less important, continued to be extracted and in west Bengal was often incorporated into debt. Besides, there was a tendency for some peasants to lose their raiyati rights either to moneylending landlords who extended khamar or to other raiyats. Some raiyats became rentiers, subletting their lands to under-raiyats called korfas, who generally paid double the raiyati rate of rent. A combination of demographic and market pressures also swelled the ranks of the landless dependent on agricultural wage-labour. So in the early twentieth century exploitation of raiyats newly turned into rightless sharecroppers, under-raiyats lacking security or protection against rack-renting and labourers in poor bargaining positions for obtaining remunerative wages extended to perhaps 15% of the cultivated land and nearly 30% of the rural workforce by about 1930. Yet as long as mercantile and usury capital in the countryside effectively reproduced and exploited peasant labour, these other forms were merely adjuncts of the credit relationship as surplus-appropriating mechanisms. Any rupture in the unequal symbiosis between creditor and debtor would have large implications for the conditions of possibility and lines of resistance in agrarian society.

## THE DISPOSSESSION OF LAND, THE 1930S TO THE 1950S

It is not often that agriculturists have to sell off small parcels of their land in order to raise money for the cultivation of the rest of their holdings. The most common

[45] See Bose, *Agrarian Bengal*, pp. 140–3.
[46] Baker, *Indian Rural Economy*, pp. 307–9; Bhattacharya, 'Lenders and Debtors', p. 341.
[47] *Census of India*, vol. VI, Bengal 1A, p. 105.

practice now is to borrow on the usufructuary mortgage of lands. (Additional collector, Dhaka, to commissioner, Dhaka division, 7 October 1937, cited in Bose, *Agrarian Bengal*, pp. 122–3.)

... the busiest place on Contai [was] the Land Registrar's office where land transactions were being conducted till late at night. The seller was in such dire need of cash that he very often paid *baksheesh* to get his transactions settled quickly. (T. G. Narayan, *Famine over Bengal*, Calcutta, 1944, cited in Paul Greenough, *Prosperity and Misery in Modern Bengal: the Famine of 1943–44* (New York, 1982), p. 201.)

The depression damaged credit, the most sophisticated instrument of appropriation available to dominant social and economic groups. The option of seizing land, the principal means of production, had now to be considered in attempting to maintain social and economic control. But land values collapsed during the slump, which made its purchase an unattractive economic proposition. A 1928 amendment of the Bengal Tenancy Act provided for a 20% fee to the superior landlord while legalizing the transfer of raiyati holdings, which further dampened the land market during a sharp economic downturn. The distress of the depression was consequently not reflected in any dramatic increase in land alienation. On the other hand, some groups were interested in the usufruct of the land and smallholders' desperate need of credit provided just the opportunity for attaining that aim. Better-off peasants in east Bengal began to step into the vacuum left by trader-moneylenders and tulukdar-moneylenders. Their preferred method of operation was to use the lease market in land, which explains the rising trend in the numbers and value of the complete usufructuary mortgage at a time when the total number of mortgages being registered went into steep decline (see Table 7). A report from Mymensingh, for instance, stated in 1937 that borrowing 'on the basis of usufructuary mortgage' was 'going on between simple cultivators who had not done any money-lending business before and aboriginals' while there was little credit available 'from genuine mahajans'.[48] In Tippera 'the comparatively well-off or "bourgeois" Krishaks' were 'said to hold most of the usufructuary mortgages'.[49] Peasant creditors positioned

[48] Collector, Mymensingh to Joint Secretary, Cooperative Credit and Rural Indebtedness Dept, 27 November 1937, in 'Restriction of Rural Credit', GB Revenue Dept, Land Revenue Br., May 1940, B Progs., 14–57 (BSRR).
[49] Commissioner, Chittagong division to chief secretary, GB, 15 October 1937, Home Political Confidential File 10/37 (Home Dept, Govt of West Bengal).

Table 7. *Land sales and mortgages in Bengal, 1929–1943*

| Year | Number of sales | Aggregate value of sales Rs. | Number of complete usufructuary mortgages | Value of complete usufructuary mortgages Rs. | Total number of mortgages |
|---|---|---|---|---|---|
| 1929 | 79,929 | 13,016,351 | | | 588,550 |
| 1930 | 129,184 | 20,092,584 | | | 510,974 |
| 1931 | 105,701 | 13,133,716 | 41,353 | 3,013,472 | 376,422 |
| 1932 | 114,619 | 12,445,879 | 41,752 | 2,920,060 | 338,945 |
| 1933 | 120,492 | 11,749,507 | 38,294 | 2,516,784 | 313,431 |
| 1934 | 147,619 | 13,988,950 | 51,066 | 3,230,561 | 349,400 |
| 1935 | 160,341 | 13,986,133 | 60,715 | 3,873,536 | 357,297 |
| 1936 | 172,956 | 15,136,829 | 79,729 | 4,931,051 | 352,469 |
| 1937 | 164,819 | 14,597,687 | 77,232 | 4,941,457 | 302,529 |
| 1938 | 242,583 | 26,731,027 | 53,374 | 3,254,495 | 164,895 |
| 1939 | 500,224 | 63,215,376 | 62,491 | 3,681,815 | 154,780 |
| 1940 | 502,357 | 71,042,013 | 74,200 | 4,837,479 | 160,152 |
| 1941 | 634,113 | | | | 151,553 |
| 1942 | 749,495 | | | | 106,088 |
| 1943 | 1,532,241 | | | | 183,371 |

*Source:* Annual Registration Department Reports. Some of the above figures on the number of sales and mortgages have been cited by K. M. Mukerji, *The Problems of Land Transfer*, pp. 38, 43 and B. B. Chaudhuri, 'The Process of Depeasantization', p. 138.

themselves well to take advantage of the dramatic upswing in the land market which became a notable feature of an inflationary war economy.

Where khamar or demesne was already substantial, as in west Bengal, a further expansion of khamar at the expense of raiyati lands occurred during the 1930s. In a context of widespread defaults on rent and interest payments, the continuance of grain loans in return for labour services on expanded khamar was one way of maintaining agrarian relations of dominance and dependence. But an increase in the number of sales of smaller patni tenures suggests that only the bigger zamindars and patnidars, notably the Maharaja of Burdwan, were able to resort to a strategy of dispossessing both the micro-proprietors deprived of rent and peasants deprived of resources, especially credit, to continue smallholding cultivation.[50] North Bengal jotedars were hit hard by the collapse of the product market and did not have a significant smallholding sector to poach upon in this period. The more resourceful among them seemed keen to find an opportunity of moving their investments out of land into the more buoyant urban sectors. Chakdars and lotdars in the southern fringe of the Sunderbans – where the reclamation process had started much later than in north Bengal – took advantage of the bad years 'to get land made khas and to resettle in bhag'.[51]

The recovery of trade and agricultural prices towards the end of the decade stirred the market in peasant holdings out of its slumber in most parts of India. In Bengal a 1938 amendment to the Bengal Tenancy Act, which abolished the landlords' fee, turned over the preemptive right to purchase raiyati holdings from the landlord to co-sharer tenants and limited the period of usufructuary mortgages to a maximum of 15 years, gave an additional boost to the rising velocity of the land market. But it was the acuteness of the subsistence crisis culminating in the great Bengal famine which caused distress and consequent dispossession of land on a staggering scale. There was a total of 16.4 million occupancy holdings in Bengal in 1940. Between 1940 and 1945, a total of 4.37 million outright sales of whole or part-occupancy holdings was recorded (see Table 8). The Land Alienation Act of 1944, designed to empower small peasants to repurchase holdings, proved totally ineffectual in achieving its purpose.

East Bengal was worst hit by the wave of distress sales of peasant smallholdings. Eleven out of the fourteen subdivisions 'very severely affected' by the famine were in the four east Bengal districts of Dhaka, Faridpur, Noakhali and Tippera. According to an Indian Statistical Institute survey, 12.5% of all families in subdivisions within this category sold land between August 1943 and April 1944, and 3.9% had to sell off all their paddy lands.[52] The strata of peasantry which had started lending on usufructuary mortgage in the 1930s were the principal beneficiaries of the land sales of the 1940s, but some talukdars made gains too. An enquiry in a Faridpur village revealed that 40.5% of the alienated area was purchased by 'cultivators', 17.9% by 'zamindars',

---

[50] See Bose, *Agrarian Bengal*, pp. 166–8.
[51] Note by commissioner, Presidency division, GB Home Political Confidential File 333/39 (WBSA).
[52] P. C. Mahalanobis, R. Mukherjee and A. Ghosh, 'A Sample Survey of the After-Effects of the Bengal Famine' in *Sankhya*, 7, 4 (1946), 337–400.

Table 8. *Land alienation in Bengal, 1940–1 to 1944–5*

Number of sales of occupancy holdings

| 1940–1 | 1941–2 | 1942–3 | 1943–4 | 1944–5 |
|--------|--------|--------|--------|--------|
| 141,000 | 711,000 | 938,000 | 1,491,000 | 1,230,000 |

*Source:* GB Land and Land Revenue Dept, Land Revenue Br., B April/48 Progs. 39–42, File 6M–21/46 (WBSA).

15% by 'office employees', 10.1% by 'traders', 7% by 'jotedars', 5.4% by 'moneylenders' and 4.1% by 'priests and petty employees'.[53] Yet, land alienation in east Bengal in the 1940s did not swell the ranks of landless agricultural wage-labourers who were 'either reverting to sharecropping – sharecroppers with no land, no cattle, or migrating to the cities, or simply dying out'.[54]

Small peasants in other types of agrarian structure were also evicted from the lands they had possessed. As a report on west Bengal districts explained:

The smaller agriculturist, who was forced by poverty to sell his produce before prices rose to their present heights, is now being forced by the same poverty to buy food from the more well-to-do at an exorbitant rate and, in so doing, is forced to give up, by outright sale, his only source of livelihood.[55]

Both landlords and richer peasants were the land engrossers in west Bengal, while rich farmers were the main dispossessors in southern frontier regions. Jotedars of north Bengal were among both buyers and sellers of land in that region.

Between independence and partition in 1947 and the abolition of zamindari in east and west Bengal in 1951 and 1953 respectively, the land market continued to be very active. Partition and zamindari abolition further strengthened the east Bengal peasant elite's control over critical portions of surplus lands. In west Bengal, holders of substantial khamar and richer peasants became the big raiyats of the post-1953 era. During a brief but tumultuous period when the zamin-

[53] K. M. Mukerji, *The Problems of Land Transfer* (Santiniketan, 1957), pp. 62–3.
[54] A. Ghosh and K. Dutt, *Development of Capitalist Relations in Agriculture* (Delhi, 1977), p. 129.
[55] Commissioner, Presidency division to secretary, Cooperative Credit and Rural Indebtedness Dept, 16 September 1943, GB, Cooperative Credit and Rural Indebtedness Dept, Rural Indebtedness Br., B June 1943 Progs. 6–17, Confidential Files 24 of 1943 and 10 of 1944 (WBSA).

dari rubric of rent extraction was finally torn apart and credit relations remained in disrepair, land itself was wrested on a large scale from smallholding peasants who had been the mainstay of agrarian production in colonial Bengal.

## CAPITAL AND LAND AGAINST LABOUR, THE 1950S TO 1990

We will not quote the numerous heart-rending reports on rural poverty in Bengal which have appeared in recent years. Suffice it to say that rural labourers in Bengal expect to starve for part of each year *even* if they are lucky enough to be employed most of the time. Seasonally, their staple food, rice, becomes a luxury food and they have come to view the possession of more than one piece of clothing as a blessing. Poorly fed, clad, housed and cared for, yet forced to work themselves to the bone, their lives tend to be short and, while they last, bitter. (Willem van Schendel and Aminul Haque Faraizi, *Rural Labourers in Bengal, 1880–1980* (Rotterdam, 1984), pp, 69–70)

In the early 1950s the zamindari framework of revenue and rent extraction was dismantled in both parts of partitioned Bengal. Indeed, intermediary rentier interests were abolished in all states of India where the zamindari system had prevailed. Tenancy from now on would refer to the limited amount of subletting for rent that continued below the level of the property-owning raiyat. Moneylending revived in Bengal and elsewhere but the social base of moneylending shifted significantly in some regions. In east Bengal, the dislocations accompanying partition typically resulted in the replacement of Hindu talukdars and traders by the better-off among Muslim peasants as controllers of surplus land and credit. Lending against usufructuary mortgage of land, a popular device in the 1930s, generally represented a large component of credit. Sharecropping tenancies underwent a slow but steady decline, while the use of wage labour registered a sharp increase and the social conditions of existence of labourers became more grim.

In east Bengal, where 18% of rural families had reported wage labour to be their primary source of income in 1939, the proportion rose to 21% in the early 1960s and to anywhere between 25% and 38% according to various studies by the late 1970s. Wage labour may have been a subsidiary source of income for another 11% to 24% of rural families. Around 1980 nearly 50% of rural families, or some 40 million people, were wholly or partly dependent on wage labour. Prior to

1947, not only had west Bengal possessed a more numerous class engaged in wage labour, but this class was also structurally distinct, unlike the land-poor and landless in east Bengal, from the peasant smallholders. West Bengal shared with the east the trend of rising proportions of wage labour since partition. By the late 1970s about one third of rural families were wholly reliant on wage labour, while nearly another 30% were partly dependent on it. A total of some 20 million people in west Bengal had, therefore, become wholly or partly dependent on wages.[56]

During the late colonial era agricultural wage rates had shown fluctuations but no clear downward trend. Since partition the trend appears to be one of 'decisive decline', especially in east Bengal. Between 1974 and 1982 the food-grain equivalent of the average daily wage rate in east Bengal was just under 2 kilograms of rice, a dramatic decline compared to estimates of just below 6 kilos to nearly 9 kilos in the late nineteenth and early twentieth centuries.[57] In west Bengal, the average male daily wage rate (the female rate was 10% to 20% lower) in the late 1970s was 3.2 kilograms of rice, a slight improvement on the 2 to 2.5 kilograms estimated for the late nineteenth and early twentieth centuries. But real wages underwent a steady decline from a base of 100 in 1947 to 72 in 1965, reached their nadir between 1966 and 1968, and thereafter experienced a modest recovery.[58]

The problem of wages was accompanied by the vicissitudes of employment in a situation of absolute surplus labour. A lowly paid rural workforce faced increasing difficulties in finding adequate work opportunities. So it is not surprising that massive increases in agrarian appropriation through holding down the wages of labour occurred at the same time as there was a slackening of labour attachment by various forms of extra-economic compulsion. Although labour had never been 'bonded' in modern Bengal in quite the same way as in neighbouring Bihar, 'tied' labour was used until the mid twentieth century on khamar and jote holdings in parts of west and north Bengal. But during the 1960s and 1970s the krishani form of labour attachment in

[56] Willem van Schendel and Aminul Haque Faraizi, *Rural Labourers in Bengal, 1880–1980* (Rotterdam, 1984), pp. 43–5; see also F. Tomasson Jannuzi and James T. Peach, *The Agrarian Structure of Bangladesh: an Impediment to Development* (Boulder, 1980), pp. 20–1.

[57] Van Schendel and Faraizi, *Rural Labourers*, pp. 67–8.

[58] N. Krishnaji, 'Wages of Agricultural Labour' in *Economic and Political Weekly*, Review of Agriculture (September 1971), A149–A151; A. V. Jose, 'Agricultural Wages in India' in *Economic and Political Weekly* (25 June 1988), A55.

Birbhum, for instance, all but disappeared.[59] More importantly, the proportion of mahindars or farm servants dwindled all over west Bengal while that of munishes or day labourers soared. According to one estimate, day labourers represented 83.6% of the total number of agricultural labourers by 1979; only 10.9% were attached and 5.5% were semi-attached.[60] It is technically 'free' labour that has been so freely exploited in recent decades in both east and west Bengal. Freedom from the older forms of attachment has not loosened the stern discipline imposed by economic forces. Hopelessly poor day labourers are generally recipients of khoraki or subsistence loans from their employers. Since the 1970s 'credit relations' have been 'a pivotal element in the structuring of contractual labour relations'.[61]

While landlessness explains to a large extent the predicament of the exploited, landedness alone does not explain the dominance of the exploiters. For one thing, post-independence agrarian reforms, despite all their loopholes, have irrevocably undermined the possibility of appropriation based primarily on large landholdings. In order to translate relatively small advantages in landholding into effective social dominance, involvement in new forms of capital and commodity markets has been indispensable. An insightful local study in west Bengal found the 'rich peasant landowners' portfolio of investments' to 'include, prominently, local retail businesses', and 'a kind of speculation on the price of paddy' was identified as 'the motor' of the agrarian economy.[62] In east Bengal moneylending and petty trade not only substantiated the dominance of richer peasants but also afforded limited opportunities of upward mobility to the more skilful and entrepreneurial among the rural poor.[63]

Although Bengal did not experience a 'green revolution' in the later

[59] The krishani system, under which tied indebted labourers were paid with one-third of the crop, was the empirical reference for Amit Bhaduri's celebrated article 'A Study in Agricultural Backwardness under Semi-Feudalism' in *Economic Journal*, 83, 120–37. On the erosion of krishani see Khoda Newaj and Ashok Rudra, 'Agrarian Transformation in a District of West Bengal' in *Economic and Political Weekly*, Review of Agriculture, 10, 13 (29 March 1975), A22–A23.

[60] Pranab Bardhan and Ashok Rudra, 'Types of Labour Attachment in Agriculture: Results of a Survey in West Bengal, 1979' in *Economic and Political Weekly* (20 August 1980), 1483.

[61] Van Schendel and Faraizi, *Rural Labourers*, p. 97.

[62] John Harriss, 'Making out on Limited Resources: or, what happened to semi-feudalism in a Bengal district' (University of East Anglia mimeograph, 1979).

[63] For a useful summary of findings of various village studies on this question see Shapan Adnan, *Annotation of Village Studies in Bangladesh and West Bengal: A Review of Socio-economic Trends over 1942–88* (Dhaka, 1990).

1960s and 1970s on the scale of northwestern India and parts of Pakistan, certain pockets witnessed technological innovation in the form of new fertilizers and higher-yielding seeds. Richer peasants generally consolidated their edge in landholding by their ability to have better access to this capital-intensive agricultural technology. The same groups have tended to be better able to siphon off flows of aid in rural Bangladesh. Control of new capital-intensive inputs, institutional credit and foreign aid has provided important leverage in the relations of appropriation. Even a socialistic initiative – the nationalization of banks in India in 1969 – has not had the intended effect of releasing the rural poor from their relations of dependence. State-supported credit has benefited the middling to richer peasantry rather than the land-poor and landless labourers.

Land and capital have always been inextricably intertwined in the agrarian history of Bengal. Yet in the context of narrowing differences in patterns of landholding, manipulation of a range of new sorts of capital investments in the agrarian economy has been critical in ensuring that the odds of life in rural Bengal remain tilted against labour.

## TRANSITIONS IN THE RELATIONS OF APPROPRIATION

The shifts in the predominant modes of appropriation in rural Bengal over the two centuries since 1770 are quite as important as the processes of continuity and change in production relations in providing a nuanced understanding of the social and political history of peasants and rural labourers. The key transitions had a close bearing upon and were influenced by labour resistance. If the predominating relation of exploitation moulded to an extent the character of protest, the conditions of possibility of subverting it were opened up by contradictions in the broader land and capitalist economic systems in which it was embedded. The great anti-rentier and anti-creditor movements of the 1880s and 1930s, for instance, constituted revealing flashpoints illuminating the crucial axes of the relationship of peasant labour with the controllers of land and capital.

Straddling the domain of the economic and the political, shifting relations of appropriation both sought to define and were acted upon by the mental world of the exploited. A mode of exploitation, even during an extended and apparently unchallenged period of its domination, did not preside over a pulverized consciousness. Tacit acceptance of the social rules set by dominant groups was hardly ever untainted by an undercurrent of rejection. Having refined the fine art of the possible, the consciousness of the subordinated classes lent articulation to successful movements of resistance whenever chinks in the chief mechanism of appropriation came under sufficient strain and widened to reveal a potentially fatal crack.

# CHAPTER 5

# RESISTANCE AND CONSCIOUSNESS

Modern Bengal's agrarian history was forged at the points of contest and compromise between the colonial state and the dominant land-holding and capital-controlling classes on the one hand and the subordinate sectors of smallholding and labouring society on the other. A combination of material need and culturally informed value of the smallholding and landless labouring majority generated imperatives which challenged those deriving from the colonial, land-holding and capital-controlling establishment. The demands of smallholders and labourers for subsistence, security and social conditions reflective of their notion of human dignity sought to resist and restructure relations governing access to land, work, consumption and production imposed upon them. The course of agrarian history was influenced by an undercurrent of everyday resistance to inequities and periodic surges of effective resistance which dismantled the established structures of domination.

The older historiography of agrarian India generally privileged the landed and the powerful. Recent trends in scholarship have aimed at restoring to the subordinate social groups their 'subjecthood' in the making of history.[1] Reacting against the concentration on insurgency or the dramatic instances of revolt in the literature on resistance, some writers have begun to stress the importance of the less ubiquitous but more frequent acts of defiance.[2] Yet, paradoxically, an over-emphasis on the everyday processes of contest and compromise might obfuscate the reality of social dominance and leave a less than accurate impression of the 'active' agency of labour resistance contributing to a form of social equilibrium. Moreover, everyday resistance along class lines to ensure subsistence from the peasant smallholding often entailed impli-

---

[1] Evident in the work of individual scholars in the 1970s and 1980s, these tendencies found their most organized expression in the work of the subaltern school. See Ranajit Guha (ed.), *Subaltern Studies*, Vols. I–VI (Delhi, 1982–90); also, Ranajit Guha, *Elementary Aspects of Peasant Insurgency in Colonial India* (Delhi, 1983).

[2] This group of historians has drawn inspiration from James C. Scott, *Weapons of the Weak* (New Haven, 1985). See Douglas Haynes and Gyan Prakash (eds.), *Contesting Power: Resistance and Everyday Social Relations in South Asia* (Delhi, 1991).

cit complicity in domination along lines of gender and generation. The 'weapons of the weak' were rarely able to defend more than minimally defined norms and needs within a context of an unequal symbiosis in social relations. The timing and character of the more formidable movements of resistance, which attacked the predominant relations of exploitation, remain significant themes for historical interpretation.

Beyond acknowledging the creativity and initiative of peasants and labourers as historical actors, there is little agreement among various historians of subordinate social groups' resistance and consciousness on the questions of organization and spontaneity, individual and collective rights, identification along lines of community, class and nation and, above all, the status of the economic, political and cultural in explanatory schemes. In order to be able to analyse and interpret the changing forms of agrarian resistance over the two centuries since 1770, it is important to recognize that many of these apparently dichotomous categories in fact overlapped to a significant degree, that their meaning and content altered over time according to the historical context and that motive and opportunity together moulded the consciousness of peasant labour and created the moment of effective resistance.

Among the multiple lines of debate in the historiography of consciousness and resistance, the issue of organization and spontaneity is easiest to deal with. The rudimentary or localized nature of organization in the early phases of resistance did not imply that protest was spontaneous in the sense of being unpremeditated or pre-political. The risks were too high for participants to be able to afford not to calculate them in the light of alternative strategies.

The matter of individual versus collective rights is by contrast far more complex. Since the colonial state imposed a 'modern' form of government but withheld rights of citizenship from its subjects, the scope for articulating and asserting political demands as individuals was severely limited. But pre-colonial notions of individual material rights including rights to land co-existed with and were more pervasive in many regions than communitarian rights.[3] The colonial rule of

---

[3] Irfan Habib stated categorically on peasant rights to land in the Mughal empire, 'No evidence exists for communal ownership of land or even a periodic distribution and redistribution of land among peasants. The peasant's right to the land ... was always his individual right' (Irfan Habib, *The Agrarian System of Mughal India* (Oxford, 1963), p. 123). This may well be an overstatement of the case for the existence of the individual right to land since the effective exercise of this right was mediated by clan membership across large parts of

property laid down in the late eighteenth century and tenancy legislation initiated in the late nineteenth century strengthened the conception of individual rights to land and other resources. Colonialism had managed to confer and confirm individual rights of property while depriving and denying individual rights as citizens.

This contradiction in the colonial legal framework ensured that claims to justice based on material needs and indigenous as well as borrowed cultural norms had to seek social bases of solidarity and communitarian forms of expression. Class identity resting on a shared perception or experience of poverty was certainly one basis of 'community'. Religion, language, tribe, caste and place of origin were some of the other social identities available as organizing principles around which to structure communitarian demands. Since the later nineteenth century the language of colonialism has tended to reserve the term 'community' to refer to social affiliations determined by birth, among which religion and caste occupied a privileged place. The dominant discourse of Indian nationalism, accepting the methodology while rejecting the substance of colonial knowledge, increasingly sought to privilege the all-encompassing nation over particularist ties. The peculiarly Indian connotation of the word 'communalism' emerged out of this in part contradictory and in part mutually reinforcing interaction between colonialism and nationalism. It referred primarily if not exclusively to the religious bond and acquired a pejorative undertone. It is necessary, therefore, to distinguish the communitarian struggles of subordinate social groups, including peasants and labourers, in which religion was a component of organization and ideology, from communal conflicts which used the colonial constructions of political categories along lines of religion. What influenced the choice of certain social identities over others in forging the 'community' of resistance and when and why 'communitarianism' flowed into the 'communal' mould are crucial issues for historical analysis.

The 'class' versus 'community' twist to debates about the com-

north India. The concept of individual shares in the community's resources was even more widely prevalent in south India. In a view diametrically opposed to that of Habib, Partha Chatterjee has claimed that all rights, including the right to land, derived from being members of the community. See Partha Chatterjee, 'Agrarian Relations and Communalism in Bengal' in Ranajit Guha (ed.), *Subaltern Studies* I (Delhi, 1982) and 'More on Modes of Power and the Peasantry' in Ranajit Guha (ed.), *Subaltern Studies* II, especially pp. 316–23. Such a claim can only rest on a narrow definition of individualism as an exclusive characteristic of 'bourgeois' culture. Fresh theoretical insights and empirical research are needed to clarify the concept of the role of the individual in pre-capitalist economies and pre-bourgeois cultures.

position and ideology of resistance stems from divergent views on the 'primacy' of the 'economic' and 'political' in agrarian history. Some 'materialist' interpretations may have gone too far in regarding communitarian articulations of protest as mere facades for essentially economically determined class struggles, but nor can politics and culture be seen in isolation from economic structures and processes. The previous chapters have shown how structures and processes of demography, commercialization, production and appropriation represented a combination of economic, political and cultural phenomena and were shaped by the tussle between domination and resistance. Economic and political processes not only operated within a cultural context and were moulded by it, but were also important constitutive elements of culture and consciousness.

As agrarian society became increasingly tied to wider economic systems based on capitalism, the conditions of possibility for effective resistance would often be opened up by the contradictions of capitalism in the upper echelons of its structure which undermined predominant modes of exploitation at the regional level. This is not to claim any neat equation between 'economic' crisis and political unrest, not to mention the motivating ideology of resistance. The 'meaning' of an economic crisis varied according to the type of agrarian social structure that it affected and was mediated by normative social values that it violated. The dialectic between property and production within each type of social structure had a bearing on power relations in the countryside and, consequently, set some initial handicaps which influenced the outcome of resistance. Beyond these structural possibilities and constraints lay a significant area of political indeterminacy. This chapter attempts to interpret the changing forms of agrarian resistance from the fakirs and farazis of the early colonial period to the naxalites of the post-colonial era with reference to both structures and mentalities.

## COMMUNITARIAN RESISTANCE UNDER EARLY COLONIALISM, C. 1770–1850S

Rural society in early colonial Bengal was subjected to four sorts of pressures: first, the colonial imperative of settling and 'peasantizing' a highly unsettled and mobile society; second, the extraction of a high colonial land revenue demand initially through revenue-farmers and from 1793 through 'property-owning' zamindars; third, the forced cultivation of indigo between the 1820s and 1860; and fourth, the intrusion of the colonial state and settled agrarian society into tribal economy and society on the Bengal–Bihar border during roughly the same period. In addition, the decisive undermining of the artisanal economy around 1820 threw many weavers into the ranks of agricultural labour and forged a potential link between weaver and peasant discontents.

Between 1763 and 1800 the chief contributors to political turmoil in rural Bengal were organized armed bands of 'holy' men, sannyasis and fakirs, who conducted a series of incursions and looting raids into Bengal. These groups, which generally congregated at the pilgrimage centres and fairs of northern India, were greatly augmented in the later eighteenth century by demobilized soldiers of the various Mughal successor states and little kingdoms. The colonial state held these wandering peoples in deep suspicion and felt threatened by them at a time when its revenue-collecting machine was seeking to establish a Pax Britannica over a sedentarized agrarian society. It is difficult to determine the nature and extent of local peasant involvement in the armed actions of sannyasi- and fakir-led militias from the denunciatory colonial records of the period or the romanticized view of sannyasi rebels in the late-nineteenth-century fiction of Bankim Chandra Chattopadhyay. There seems to be some evidence that poverty-stricken Bengali peasants swelled the ranks of the fakir raiders led by Shah Majnu in the aftermath of the great famine of 1770, especially during the winter months of 1772–3. The sannyasis and fakirs were certainly discriminating in choosing the mofussil factories and revenue offices of the Company, the kachharis of rich landlords and the granaries of merchants as the main targets of their attack.[4]

The fakirs were imbued with a notion of the legitimacy of the eighteenth-century state system which was in the process of being subverted by the Company's state and its agents. Fakir leaders typically took the title 'shah'; sannyasi chiefs also aspired to kingly authority within their spheres of control. The superimposition of late-nineteenth-century revivalism, including the 'bande mataram' hymn to the mother country, has blurred the religious ideology of

[4] See Jamini Mohan Ghose, *Sanyasi and Fakir Raiders of Bengal* (Calcutta, 1901); Nikhil Sur, *Chhiattarer Manwantar o Sannyasi–Fakir Bidroha* (The 1770 Famine and the Sannyasi–Fakir Rebellion) (Calcutta, 1982), pp. 45–67.

sannyasi rebels, which appears to have been less rigidly distinctive or hierarchical in the late eighteenth century. The fakirs were believers in syncretist forms of Sufism and visited a network of dargahs of pirs in the districts of Malda, Rangpur, Dinajpur, Mymensingh and Faridpur during their periodic incursions. While some clashes occurred between sannyasi and fakir groups and factions within them, the two most important leaders, Shah Majnu and Bhabani Pathak, were on friendly terms and co-ordinated the activities of their respective followers. The sannyasi- and fakir-led movements belong in their social composition and ideology to an era prior to the colonial consolidation of settled and hierarchically defined rural society based on a rekindling of the 'high' traditions rather than the popular syncretism of both Hinduism and Islam.

The best-known instance of anti-revenue uprisings before the Permanent Settlement – the 1783 dhing in Rangpur – witnessed a partial link between the fakir movement of Shah Majnu and Shah Musa and peasant resistance against the oppression of Deby Sinha, a revenue-farmer for the East India Company. An up-country merchant, Deby Sinha had plundered the revenues of Purnea on the Bengal–Bihar border and served Warren Hastings' Board of Revenue before being appointed dewan to the young Raja of Dinajpur and ijaradar or revenue-farmer of the parganas of Rangpur, Edrakpur and Dinajpur in north Bengal. His heavy-handed coercion of the peasants ignited a major anti-revenue revolt which raged across several parganas during January and February of 1783. As the call to rebellion was broadcast by the beat of drums, large crowds of raiyats gathered and collectively attacked landlords' kachharis and the East India Company's granaries. A number of landlords were killed and their money and papers stolen before the kachhari buildings were razed. The rebels decamped with Deby Sinha's revenue records when they attacked his kachhari. The high point of the dhing was celebrated in a popular ballad: 'Thousands of peasants marched together. They took with them their staves, picks, sickles and choppers ... They hurled a lot of stones and brickbats which came down thudding on all sides. Some people had their bones broken by the missiles. And Deby Sinha's mansion was reduced to a heap of bricks.'[5]

At the first signs of unrest Deby Sinha had sought the assistance of

[5] Cited in Ranajit Guha, *Elementary Aspects of Peasant Insurgency in Colonial India* (Delhi, 1983), p. 137.

Goodlad, the collector of Rangpur, and of the Company's government in Calcutta. So what began as an agrarian jacquerie was quickly transformed into a battle against the Company's troops. More important, the insurgents sought legitimacy by invoking the symbols of the pre-colonial state system. Their leader, Dirjenarain, was given the title of 'nawab', the honour of being carried in a regal palanquin and the authority both to impose a tax known as dhing kharcha to finance the uprising and to sanction or validate acts of looting and violence. The dhing was put down by the superior military force of the Company, but Deby Sinha was removed from his post and some of the worst excesses of the revenue-farming system were redressed.[6] Another example of an anti-colonial peasant revolt centring around the revenue question comes from Birbhum in 1786. The revenue enhancements proposed by collector Keating were fiercely resisted by peasants who had been leading an agricultural recovery in the aftermath of the devastating famine of 1770. The protesters of 1786 were beaten back but 'ryots in thousands' had better success in a 'no-rent campaign leading to forcible land seizures' once they were joined by disbanded ghatwals, soldiers of the Birbhum raj, in 1789.[7]

Revolts by zamindars figure very prominently in a broad typology of forms of dissidence in the range of revolts all over India between 1800 and 1860. In addition, there were conflicts between landlords and tenants, tension between settled peasants and wandering tribes and protests by dispossessed artisans in urban centres.[8] Zamindari and zamindar-led broad-based agrarian revolts were directed against not only the higher land revenue demand of the colonial state but also the erosion of kingly authority of rural magnates in many parts of northern and southern India. Bengal provides something of an exception to this general phenomenon. The wave of dispossession of zamindari rights in the wake of the 1793 Permanent Settlement and the stripping away of the landlords' judicial and police functions provoked little political turmoil in rural Bengal. Not only were there more individual gainers than losers in the scramble for zamindari rights, but the lack of

[6] See Narahari Kaviraj, *A Peasant Uprising in Bengal, 1783* (New Delhi, 1972); Suprakash Ray, *Bharater Krishak-Bidroha o Ganatantrik Sangram* (India's Peasant Revolts and Democratic Struggles) (Calcutta, 1966), pp. 87–93.

[7] Ranjan Kumar Gupta, 'Agricultural Developments in a Bengal District: Birbhum, 1793–1852' in *Indian Historical Review*, 4, 1 (July 1977), p. 67.

[8] C. A. Bayly, *The New Cambridge History of India: Indian Society and the Making of the British Empire* (Cambridge, 1988), pp. 170–1.

zamindari possessory dominion over land and the absence of kin-based vertical ties in rural society made it difficult for Bengal zamindars under pressure to mobilize the countryside.

Some zamindari participation in movements against the colonial land revenue establishment occurred in certain exceptional circumstances, such as the early phase of the periodic Chuar rebellions in western Bengal between 1799 and 1832. The Chuars, literally outlandish fellows, were paiks or soldiers of the local rajas of Midnapur. In the late 1790s the colonial state began to resume rent-free service tenures held by these groups. The Chuars, who rose in rebellion to defend their old rights to land, were joined by poor peasants in their attacks on rent-collectors, but also received the initial backing of dispossessed zamindars, including the Rani of Midnapur and the Raja of Cossijurah, who seized this opportunity to attempt to reclaim some of their lost privileges and have the revenue assessments of their estates reduced.[9] By the second decade of the nineteenth century, however, the sarkar–zamindar alliance on the revenue and rent question had been solidified by a series of colonial regulations which bolstered the power of the landlords.

Between the 1810s and the 1850s peasant grievances concerning rent and indigo came to the fore in movements of agrarian resistance. So long as the demographic situation remained relatively favourable, desertion and migration were the most common strategies resorted to by peasants anxious to avoid paying enhanced rents. Refusal to fulfil indigo contracts after taking advances – what planters and pro-planter magistrates referred to as 'deliberate fraud' – was the usual early form of resistance against an unremunerative forced cultivation. This sort of everyday resistance clearly had serious limitations in terms of effectiveness in changing relations of exploitation. Evidence from the 1820s suggests that the landlords were being increasingly successful in enhancing rents and that the balance of power was clearly tilted against the peasantry. In many parts of west and central Bengal, peasants accepted advances from indigo planters to meet their rent obligations and subsistence needs but resorted to all manner of subterfuge, including taking advances from rival planters, to avoid fulfilling their contracts. Under these circumstances, the planters raised a clamour for tough laws giving them the same powers of distraint enjoyed by

[9] See Aditee Nag Chowdhury-Zilli, *The Vagrant Peasant: Agrarian Distress and Desertion in Bengal, 1770–1830* (Wiesbaden, 1984), pp. 130–6.

landlords in order to be able to enforce contracts. Between 1823 and 1835 the colonial state, by and large, obliged the planters with a series of legal measures with the help of which they cowed the disaffected peasants.

Rural society was astir throughout the first half of the nineteenth century, but the early 1830s – a period of severe worldwide economic depression – and the late 1840s – an era of another international crisis emanating from London – saw more than usual unrest. The external shock of 1830, which resulted in the crash of the managing agency houses, drastically lowered prices and reduced the flows of credit. It not only deepened poverty in absolute terms but unsettled pre-existing social relations. Many peasants found themselves tied to contracts to grow an unremunerative cash crop in return for paltry advances from indigo factories at a time when rental demands continued to be stringent. A perceptive magistrate of Dhaka pointed out in 1830 that the spurt in the incidence of fraud about which the planters brought complaints 'frequently originate[d] with the planters themselves'. 'No man is more alive to his own interests,' he elaborated,

than a Bengali ryot, and if he can gain 4 annas more by cultivating indigo than by cultivating any other crop, he is not likely to forego the advantage. If, on the other hand, which is too frequently the case, an advance has been forced upon a needy ryot, either by the overbearing power of the planters or by the more weighty pressure of his own wants and necessities, and the amount received does not afford him a sufficient remuneration for his labour, there is no wonder that he should be found wanting in the fulfilment of the planters' expectation.[10]

Apart from very widespread reliance on strategies of avoidance, the 1830s and 1840s witnessed one striking bidroha or revolt led by Titu Mir centring on Barasat in 1831, and a more sustained campaign of resistance by the farazis of east Bengal. Titu Mir's bidroha was initially directed against rent-collecting landlords, quickly broadened out to include indigo planters among its targets and ended up as an armed confrontation with the coercive wings of the colonial state. While small peasants formed the bulk of the rebels, they were joined by a significant number of dispossessed jolas or weavers. The farazi movement also counted zamindars, planters and the sarkar as its enemies.

[10] Cited in Benoy Chowdhury, *The Growth of Commercial Agriculture in Bengal* (Calcutta, 1967), p. 158.

Farazi rebels attacked zamindars' kachharis and indigo factories; their principal leader, Dudu Mian, was repeatedly arrested by the government. Both the Barasat revolt and the farazi movement were communitarian struggles permeated by a religious ideology, in particular the spirit of puritanical religious reform aimed at curbing the syncretist indulgences of the Islam practised in rural Bengal.

Titu Mir well knew what zamindari coercion to extract rent was all about, having spent his early adult life as a mercenary in the service of landlords. During his pilgrimage to Mecca he was influenced by the wahabis, and made the acquaintance of Sayyid Ahmed of Rai Bareilly, whom he met again in Calcutta in 1821. During the 1820s Titu Mir and his followers preached in the areas surrounding Barasat against the pir-based mediational forms of Islam, a variety of syncretist customs and rituals practised by the local Muslims, and against the evils of usury. In 1830 the campaign of religious reform began to take on a perceptibly anti-landlord stance. The local landlord, Krishnadeb Ray, mistaking bullying tactics to be the best means of asserting authority, announced a beard tax of two and a half rupees on all followers of the 'wahabi' faith. Faced with sullen non-cooperation on the part of the peasants, he attacked Sharparajpur, Titu Mir's home village, and razed its mosque. On 6 November 1830 Titu Mir's followers returned the compliment by attacking Punrah, Krishnadeb Ray's residential village, where they killed a cow in the public marketplace, splattered its blood over the walls of a temple and also looted some shops.

At Punrah, Titu Mir proclaimed the illegitimacy of the Company's government. In a bold act of inversion he declared himself the representative of Muslim sovereignty in India and demanded revenue from the zamindars. Later he also took the title of 'badshah' and formally appointed the leader of the weaving community his 'vazir' and a nephew as commander of his forces. Between November 1830 and November 1831 Titu Mir's bidroha spread across the districts of Nadia and the 24-Parganas as well as parts of Faridpur. Peasants stopped paying rent to the landlords and abandoned cultivating indigo for the planters. Wealthy Muslim landlords and other Muslim dissenters were not spared by the rebels. Titu Mir and his band of followers successfully repulsed a number of armed offensives by zamindars, planters and government troops until on 14 November

1831 their famous bamboo stockade in the village of Narkelberia near Barasat wilted before the vastly superior firepower of the Company's forces.[11]

Emphasizing the acts of desecration by the antagonists in the Barasat bidroha, a leading historian of subaltern resistance and consciousness has commented that '[i]t was this fight for prestige which was at the very heart of insurgency'.[12] The quest for dignity certainly figured prominently in the revolt but it was also about more mundane matters. The *Calcutta Gazette* described how during a raid on an indigo factory by Titu Mir's men there was no 'wanton destruction' but 'papers were destroyed most probably by the villagers for the purpose of destroying the records of their own debts'.[13] A similar combination of motives inspired the farazi movement based in the district of Faridpur between 1837 and 1848. It began in 1820 when Haji Shariatullah returned from Mecca to launch a campaign of religious reform. Although opposed to the practice of religious mediation, the Haji could do no more than modify the pir–murid (spiritual leader and follower) relationship, which smacked of servility, with the ustad–shakred (teacher–student) model. It was under the leadership of his son, Dudu Mian, that the movement acquired a radical anti-landlord and anti-planter character. Acknowledging only Allah's sovereignty over land, Dudu Mian called upon his followers in the 1830s not to pay rent and to disobey the dictates of the planters to sow indigo. The community of reformist religion provided an important basis of rebel solidarity. The farazis exhibited a special antipathy to taxes imposed by landlords to defray the expense of Hindu religious ceremonies. In 1837 they were reported to have desecrated temples of Hindu landlords by killing cows, entering places of worship wearing clothes stitched with cowhide and, in one case, destroying a number of Siva lingas.[14]

The more powerful farazi campaigns against zamindars and planters brought them into conflict with the sarkar as well. The government responded to the widespread destruction of property in Faridpur in 1838 by sending troops from Dhaka and placing Dudu Mian under

[11] See Biharilal Sarkar, *Titu Mir*, ed. Swapon Basu (Calcutta, 1981); Ray, *Bharater Krishak-Bidroha*, pp. 216–33. Sarkar's biographical tract was first published in 1898 in the literary magazine *Bangabasi*.

[12] Guha, *Elementary Aspects of Peasant Insurgency*, p. 75.

[13] Cited in *ibid.*, p. 51.

[14] Muinuddin Ahmad Khan, *History of the Fara'idi Movement in Bengal, 1818–1906* (Karachi, 1965), pp. 17–19.

arrest. The demolition of a major indigo factory owned by Dunlop at Panch Char and the abduction of his chief assistant in December 1846 elicited a strong military response and resulted in another spell in prison for Dudu Mian. The Farazis made some tentative attempts at claiming independent statehood. Farazi elders generally presided over courts and paid scant respect to colonial legal institutions in areas where they were influential. As the movement spread from its principal base in Faridpur district to parts of Khulna, the 24-Parganas, Pabna and the Bikrampur area of Dhaka, Dudu Mian appointed regional representatives whom he called 'khalifas'. In a considerable area of east Bengal the Farazis had successfully subverted the legitimacy if not the reality of the power of the sarkar, zamindar and planter.

The Barasat revolt and the farazi movement are simply two of the more prominent examples of communitarian resistance in this period inspired by a religious ideology. The Pagalpanthi movements in Mymensingh in 1825–7 and 1832–3 share many similar features. Elsewhere in India, the Mapilla rebellions of the Muslims of Malabar in 1802, the 1830s and 1847–52, also combined religious reform of their society and political protest against predominantly Hindu landlords and British revenue officials. Since the more pervasive syncretist beliefs straddling lines of both community and class did not enable predominantly Muslim peasantries to contest the symbols of authority underpinning agrarian power structures, material grievances may well have given a fillip to campaigns of religious reform. These in turn more effectively supplied the processes of negation and inversion in peasant resistance with a legitimizing ideology and a social basis of solidarity.

The communitarian resistance of the Santals drew on the solidarity of tribal social structures and a strong sense of territoriality in the face of the economic incursions of outsiders. Santal resistance on the Bengal–Bihar border in the first half of the nineteenth century culminating in the great hool of 1855–6 had much in common with the revolt of the Bhils in western India in the 1820s and the uprising of the Kols in Bihar between 1829 and 1833. During the hool the Santals, led by Sido and Kanhu, violently resisted the inroads made by dikus or foreigners among whom they included both the British, who were engaged in an onslaught on their forests, and the Indian moneylenders who were grabbing their best lands.

The insurrection of 1855–6 was preceded by a phase of dacoities in which Bengali moneylenders were the chief targets. The hool itself lasted from June 1855 to February 1856 and spread rapidly in the Bihar districts of Bhagalpur, Singhbhum, Monghyr and Hazaribagh, and the Bengal districts of Birbhum, Bankura and parts of Murshidabad. It began with a gathering of some 10,000 Santals on 30 June 1855 at Bhaganidhi, where it was decided to send letters of complaint against the depredations of moneylenders to key officials of the colonial government. The rebellion dramatically announced itself a few days later with the assassination by Sido of Mahesh daroga, an officer who had consistently favoured the moneylenders in their disputes with Santal peasants. Although primarily directed against moneylenders who were encroaching on their lands and imposing high rents on the basis of acreage rather than the number of ploughs, the hool quickly developed into a fully fledged armed confrontation between the rebel fauj or army and the state's military forces. The insurrection reached its peak in September, when the Magistrate of Birbhum reported gloomily that the western half of the district was in rebel hands. The Santals fought bravely against a much better-equipped army, but by February 1856 the hool was effectively repressed.[15]

This celebrated instance of tribal revolt at the mid-point of colonial rule witnessed a complex convergence or mingling of tribalism, religious communitarianism and class consciousness. In its emphasis on tribal rituals such as serpent worship at the onset of the rebellion, the hool displayed its chiliastic character. The collective nature of the uprising by Santal men and women was modelled largely on the cooperative style of their work ethic and organization. At the same time this great tribal revolt against Hindu moneylenders and landlords chose to appropriate rather than desecrate some of the religious practices and cultural mores of the dominant classes. The rebels in Birbhum, for instance, held a Durga puja (worship of the Mother Goddess) with great fanfare before plundering the property of wealthy Hindus. The grain and cattle that were pillaged were generally distributed according to tribal custom, which gave a larger share to the majhis or headmen than to the common Santals. Yet the class consciousness of the rebels becomes evident in the high level of inter-tribal cooperation achieved among various Santal sub-groups and a deliberate decision not to attack the non-tribal poor. British officialdom, already beginning to view Indian society through the

[15] See K. K. Datta, 'The Santal Insurrection of 1855–57' in K. K. Datta, *Anti-British Plots and Movements before 1857* (Meerut, 1970), pp. 43–152.

rigid, distorting prism of 'tribe and caste', wrote about the discriminating choice of enemies by the rebels in terms of 'exempted castes'. But it requires no more than an elementary exercise in deconstruction of the language of colonialism to see that in the Santal hool, even more so than in the Kol insurrection that preceded and the ulgulan (1899) of Birsa Munda which followed it, 'class solidarity triumphed over ethnicity'.[16] This, however, was a consciousness of class which sprang from and was distilled out of the bonds of community. In the altered economic and political context of the latter half of the nineteenth century, peasant resistance in the non-tribal areas would begin to forge class identities that emerged from newly reinforced individual rather than pre-existing communitarian rights.

## COMMUNITY, CLASS AND COLONIAL LAW IN PEASANT RESISTANCE: THE LATER NINETEENTH CENTURY

Changes in the broader economic context and political structure during the 1850s brought some new pressures but also opened unprecedented opportunities for effective peasant resistance. As one perceptive writer has noted, 'The violations of [indigo] contracts *through frauds* were just the expressions of ... antagonism *at a particular level of its development*. The final and most mature form of this expression was the peasant's fight to overthrow the entire system.'[17] The rising costs of indigo production and increased prices of alternative cash crops and rice after the mid 1850s supplied the motive and opportunity for a revolt to destroy the 'entire system'. Both the state and the moneylending landlords of west and central Bengal had an interest in promoting the new agricultural exports and the rice sector respectively. The indigo-growing peasants could take advantage of the planters' erosion of support among government officials and key dominant classes in the rural areas as well as an increasingly assertive urban intelligentsia.

The impact of the Rent Act of 1859, which reflected the altered priorities of the colonial state, was felt in the indigo sector and beyond. It took away the legal sanction behind some forms of extra-economic coercion in extracting the agrarian surplus, and tried to give a stimulus

---

[16] Guha, *Elementary Aspects of Peasant Insurgency*, p. 188.
[17] Chowdhury, *Growth of Commercial Agriculture*, p. 159.

to tenant-led agricultural growth by stressing economic factors on the question of rent determination. It introduced the legal concept of occupancy rights for individual tenants which would form the basis for moderation of rent. The battle lines were drawn between landlords and tenants over the issues of occupancy and rent, especially in those parts of east Bengal where the spoils of the new jute cultivation raised the stakes. The emphasis in colonial tenancy law on individual rights of occupancy appeared to rob peasant resistance in Bengal of the overtly religious communitarian character it had displayed earlier in the nineteenth century and lent a legalistic and class dimension to the anti-rent agrarian movements in east Bengal in the 1870s and 1880s.

Although wider economic changes created the conditions of possibility for the blue mutiny of 1859–60 and the rent strikes of 1873–85, the agrarian class structure and the dialectic between property and production laid down a set of handicaps in these political contests. Indigo was grown both in west and central Bengal and in Bihar. While in Bengal moneylending landlords had emerged since the late 1840s as rivals of the planters in the credit market, the Bihar indigo scene continued to be dominated by a partnership of landlords who supplied coercive power and planters who provided the necessary finance. Bengal had also developed a larger intelligentsia, which enabled indigo peasants to count, at least to begin with, on a broader range of support from other social classes than their counterparts in Bihar. High landlordism between the Rent Act of 1859 and the Bengal Tenancy Act of 1885 was exerted with more vigour in west than in east Bengal. But the stronger possessory dominion at the point of production exercised by the peasantry of east Bengal and the loose and distant property rights wielded by the rentier landlords, who unlike their west Bengal counterparts had not yet entered the product and credit markets in a big way, made certain that the anti-rent challenge was far more overt and effective in the east than in the west.

Rumblings of discontent against unremunerative indigo cultivation had been heard throughout the late 1850s, but signs in the late summer of 1859 that the government was no longer standing solidly behind the planters proved to be the signal for a full-scale 'mutiny'. Already in March 1859 Magistrate Eden of Barasat had upheld the peasants' right to grow whatever crops they preferred. In August 1859 he went a step further, stating that the police had a duty to protect peasants in the possession of their land even if they had broken indigo contracts. 'It is possible,' Eden wrote, 'that the ryots whose promises or contracts are admitted may still have many irresistible pleas to avoid the consequences the planter insists upon.'[18] Once his deputy magistrate Hem Chandra Kar issued a parwana on 20 August 1859 based on Eden's decision, the news was broadcast by beat of drum at all the major mofussil bazaars of west and central Bengal. The peasants were emboldened to assert their freedom from the burden of indigo once and for all.

The blue mutiny spread quickly from Barasat across the districts of Nadia, Jessore, Murshidabad, Faridpur, Malda, Pabna and Rajshahi. Indigo factories were set ablaze, plants were destroyed, planters' employees were assaulted and killed, and dissenters were scrupulously boycotted if not coerced. As the enquiry ordered by the lieutenant governor revealed, 'A regular league was ... formed against indigo cultivation, oaths were subscribed to by both Hindus and Musalmans. Ryots of one village were called upon, by the beat of drum, to assist those of another ... and proceeded in large bodies to any alleged threatened spot.'[19] There was some truth in the planters' charge that the peasants were often encouraged by 'numberless small *talookdars* who ha[d] very strong *mahazuni* interests to promote'.[20] Moneylending landlords did not, of course, oppose the planters 'for quite the same reason as the rest of rural society'.[21] The peasants also received support from urban-based lawyers and writers. Several lawyers from Calcutta defended peasants in court cases. Dinabandhu Mitra's play *Neel Darpan* exposed the horrors of the indigo system, and Harish Chandra Mukherji's newspaper *Hindoo Patriot* carried graphic reports on the course of the rebellion.

By February 1860 the indigo planters of Bengal were reeling under the concerted attacks of the peasants and their allies. In an attempt to save the indigo system from complete decimation, the government revived the infamous Regulation of 1830 to enforce contracts for one indigo season in March 1860. The rebels suffered some setbacks under the operation of this law, but it ceased to be in force in September 1860.

[18] Cited in *ibid.*, p. 202.
[19] Blair B. Kling, *The Blue Mutiny: the Indigo Disturbances in Bengal, 1859–1862* (Philadelphia, 1966), p. 93.
[20] Answer No. 2910 by James Forlong, a planter of Nadia, in *Report of the Indigo Commission* (Calcutta, 1860).
[21] Ranajit Guha, 'Neel Darpan: the Image of a Peasant Revolt in a Liberal Mirror' in *Journal of Peasant Studies*, 2, 1 (October 1974), p. 24.

Having failed to force contracted peasants to grow indigo and seeing no prospect of expropriating raiyati land and expanding nij cultivation, the planters made an attempt to enhance rents in their capacity as landlords under the provisions of the Rent Act of 1859, especially on the grounds that the value of agricultural produce had increased. The peasants responded with a successful no-rent campaign on the planters' estates. This was sufficient to worry zamindar-mahajans, who had initially backed the peasant rebels but now decided 'to decelerate on their collision course'.[22] The damage to the indigo system in Bengal, however, was irretrievable. Although the rebellious peasantry had scored an important victory, one outcome of the blue mutiny was to leave the moneylending and grain-dealing landlords as the dominant class in rural west Bengal. A different configuration of class forces in Bihar, where the landlord–planter concordat against peasant grievances remained solid, ensured that the oppressive indigo system survived there into the twentieth century.

The peasants of west and central Bengal, who had so decisively undermined the indigo system by 1862, remained subject to the high rental demands in the late nineteenth century of landlords who not only controlled substantial demesnes but also engaged in profitable moneylending and grain-dealing. The source of the conflict in east Bengal was the attempt by some rentier landlords to circumvent the pro-tenant provisions of the Rent Act to increase rents in an era of rising prices. In particular, these landlords sought to prevent the accrual of occupancy rights, which would have assured moderation of rent, by shifting their tenants around different holdings in the village and getting them to accept new kabuliyats foregoing their legal right to occupancy. Unable directly to serve notices of rent enhancement, they also tried to consolidate various illegal abwabs with the juridical rent in the new kabuliyats.

The landlords' lack of possessory dominion placed them at a disadvantage in carrying through their programme of subverting the progressive aspects of the Rent Act. The peasants easily saw through the manipulations of the landlords and combined to resist them. In May 1873 an agrarian league was formed in the Yusufshahi pargana of Pabna district to fight back against the impositions of the Banerji, Tagore and Sanyal zamindar families of the area, one of the earliest to have turned to jute cultivation. Although the leading historian of the

[22] *Ibid.*, p. 29.

Pabna disturbances denies the official view that the 'prosperity' of raiyats was a causal factor in the tensions,[23] the battle was at least in part about the share-out of the higher gross income brought in by jute. The league began by filing petitions seeking protection against the illegal acts by zamindars and raising subscriptions to meet litigation expenses. Later there was some rioting and organized passive resistance. The central theme of this protest movement was the refusal to pay rent. Large crowds were called upon by beat of drums or the blowing of buffalo horns to gather together to defy landlords or terrorize dissenters. The militant phase of the Pabna protests lasted from May to December 1873 and had a powerful demonstration effect on the peasantry in other districts of east Bengal. Agrarian leagues on the Pabna model organized rent strikes in the mid 1870s in Bogra, Rajshahi, Dhaka, Mymensingh, Faridpur, Tippera and Bakarganj.

Unlike the early nineteenth-century movements which had questioned the legitimacy of the colonial state, the protesting Pabna peasants declared their wish to be the raiyats of the distant and just Queen of England.[24] They appear to have been encouraged by Lieutenant Governor Campbell's decision in July 1873 to permit peaceful combinations of peasants. The peasants also received sympathy if not support from professional groups divorced from any direct link to landed interests. Romesh C. Dutt restored the perspective in the Calcutta press, which was being flooded with the laments of 'fugitive zamindars crowding in Calcutta or suffering zamindars writing from Pabna' when he wrote in 'An Apology for the Pabna Rioters': 'When the zamindar wants to increase his share of the produce, the ryot will bear no more – the last straw breaks the camel's back.'[25] Once the Rent Law Commission appointed in 1879 commenced deliberations on a new tenancy law, professionals who had formed the Indian Association in 1876 broke with the landlords and organized numerous ryot sabhas in various districts. The Bengal Tenancy Act of 1885, which gave 'settled' raiyats the right of occupancy if they had cultivated any land rather than a particular holding in a village for twelve years, applied to Bengal as a whole. West Bengal-based landlords fought hard

[23] See K. K. Sen Gupta, *Pabna Disturbances and the Politics of Rent, 1873–1885* (Calcutta, 1974); 'Agrarian Disturbances in 19th Century Bengal' in *Indian Economic and Social History Review*, 8 (1972), 192–212.
[24] Sen Gupta, *Pabna Disturbances*, p. 42.
[25] Archydae (pseudonym for Romesh C. Dutt), 'An Apology for the Pabna Rioters' in *Bengal Magazine* (September 1873).

to safeguard their interests and did not forgive the professional allies of
east Bengal peasants during the rent controversies of the 1870s and
1880s. J. M. Tagore, a west Bengal landlord, complained bitterly about
pro-peasant bhadralok to a member of the Viceroy's council:

They are for the most part east Bengal men, joined by some English-returned
natives, who also hail from that part of the country. Many of them have seen
something or read still more of the doings of the Irish agitators ... They go to the
ryots, pretend to be their friends, sow seeds of dissension between them and the
Zamindars, and thus set class against class.[26]

Of the two contradictions along lines of class and religion in anti-rent
agitation in late-nineteenth-century east Bengal, especially Pabna, the
former undoubtedly 'prevailed and dictated its overall character'.[27]
Most landlords in Pabna were Hindus who formed just below 10% of
the district's population. The great majority of the people were
peasants, 70% of them being Muslims. The agrarian league's activities
were unambiguously anti-landlord rather than anti-Hindu in character
and it meted out punishment to waverers and dissenters without regard
to religious affiliation. The most prominent leader of the movement,
Ishan Roy, who was looked upon as 'Bidrohi Raja' or 'rebel king',
happened to be a small Hindu landlord and trader. He was ably
assisted by Shambhu Pal, a disaffected Hindu zamindar's amla, and
Khoodi Molla, a Muslim rich peasant. The social origin of the
leadership, however, cannot be adduced to make a determination of the
character of the movement. The riddle of incongruence in both class
and religious terms between the leaders and the rebellious peasantry
was 'a function of *décalage*', significant only as 'an index of the want of
correspondence between the objective character of the mass action of
the peasantry and the level of their consciousness'.[28]

The emphasis on class identity based on individual rights defined in
colonial law in the late nineteenth century requires some further
explanation and clarification. This after all was also a period of
redefinition of caste and religious identities. A part of this was
stimulated by colonial initiatives to enumerate and rank-order castes
through the decennial censuses, and to invest religious affiliations with
greater supra-local significance than before. Between 1872 and 1911,

[26] Cited in B. B. Chaudhuri, 'Peasant Movements in Bengal, 1850–1900' in *Nineteenth Century Studies* (Calcutta, 1973); see also, B. B. Chaudhuri, 'The Story of a Peasant Revolt in a Bengal District' in *Bengal Past and Present* (July–December 1973), 220–78.
[27] Guha, *Elementary Aspects of Peasant Insurgency*, p. 172.      [28] *Ibid.*

several castes changed their nomenclature and claimed higher ritual status: the Kaibartas of west Bengal became Mahishyas, the Chandals of east Bengal Namasudras, and the Koches of north Bengal Rajbansi Kshatriyas. The colonial invention of the 'Muslim' political category for purposes of differential political patronage was preceded by a relatively autonomous round of debates at mahfils between votaries of reformist and mediational Islam. Between the 1870s and 1910s, many Bengali Muslims in rural areas adopted Arabic names for the first time in place of indigenous Bengali names, and shed some, though not all of their syncretist cultural practices.[29] Yet it is easy to over-emphasize the scale and scope of the Muslim 'redefinition' of identity. The pervasive pir-based mediational and syncretist form of Islam had been for some time facing challenges from reformist sects which had been better able to provide an ideological threat to inequitable power relations in the countryside. This had enhanced the internal fragmentation of Bengali Muslim society, for the repair of which efforts were made through a process of intense dialogue in the late nineteenth century. Bengali Islam made a number of formal concessions to reformist critics. The gulf between reformist and mediational Islam was partially bridged in a particular historical conjuncture, but the contradictions were far from wholly or finally resolved.[30]

A leading agrarian historian of Bengal has noted that peasant movements in this period were 'rarely organized on caste lines' and that 'the new caste solidarity movements only marginally affected the peasant movements, except in some cases, such as the Chandal movement in Faridpur in the 1870s'.[31] The Faridpur example from the 1870s is a significant demonstration that caste solidarity could promote primarily class-based agrarian demands. Although class predominated over religion in the anti-rent movements, there is evidence from Pabna that the 'spirit of combination' was facilitated because 'social alliance was easier among the Muslims'.[32] The rebels were also influenced by

[29] See Rafiuddin Ahmed, *Bengal Muslims: the Redefinition of Identity, 1876–1906* (Delhi, 1982); on the resilience of syncretism, see Asim Roy, *The Islamic Syncretistic Tradition in Bengal* (Princeton, 1983).

[30] On the dialogue and debate between different strands of Islam and their connection to colonial initiatives in Punjab, cf. David Gilmartin, *Empire and Islam* (Berkeley, 1989) and Ayesha Jalal, 'Post-orientalist Blues: Cultural Fusions and Confusions' in *Indian Economic and Social History Review*, 27, 1 (1990), 111–18.

[31] B. B. Chaudhuri, *The Transformation of Rural Protest in Eastern India, 1757–1930* (Presidential Address, Modern Indian History Section, 40th Session, Indian History Congress, Waltair, December 1979), p. 37.

[32] Sen Gupta, *Pabna Disturbances*, p. 39.

the farazi creed which was now in the process of working out an accommodation based on compromises with the main current of Bengali Islam.

The strength of the class structures of domination in west and north Bengal limited the caste movements to seeking improvements of social status rather than challenging the established social order. In east Bengal, caste and religious movements played a role, even if a marginal one compared to the class dimension, in bringing the zamindars' rent offensive to a final grinding halt. But the internal compromises within Bengali Islam and the assertion of its exclusivity came at the very moment of an important transition in the predominant relations of surplus-appropriation in agriculture. Some landlords who had failed to enhance rent or increase khamar at the expense of stoutly defended raiyati rights now joined traders to find a place for themselves in the expanding credit market. The ties of credit underpinned a symbiosis, albeit an unequal one, in the east Bengal countryside until 1930. The demands of the predominantly Muslim peasant associations at the turn of the century stressed issues of social status, such as the courtesy of a seat in the zamindars' kachharis and being addressed with the respectful apni rather than the colloquial tui.[33] Redefined Islam offered an exploited peasantry modes of cultural dissent but not the means to mount an assault on a complex and subtle form of appropriation.

Late-nineteenth-century India witnessed a variety of forms of resistance. Major insurrections may have been less frequent than in the first half of the century, but tribal revolts and the Mapilla rebellions show some degree of the continued importance of older communitarian forms of struggle. Yet a class emphasis drawing on individual rights under colonial law, so clearly evident in the blue mutiny and the rent strikes in Bengal, was also discernible in uprisings in other parts of India, such as the Deccan riots of the mid 1870s. An early indication that the colonial legal framework was an inadequate basis for the articulation of peasant demands came in the no-revenue campaigns in Assam and Maharashtra in the 1890s. In the twentieth century the links and discontinuities between Indian nationalism and agrarian resistance would emerge as a major theme in the history of peasant labour.

---

[33] See Abul Mansur Ahmed, *Amar Dekha Rajnitir Panchas Bachhar* (Fifty Years of Politics as I saw it, Dhaka, 1968), pp. 13–14.

## NATION, COMMUNITY AND CLASS IN PEASANT RESISTANCE UNDER LATE COLONIALISM: THE TWENTIETH CENTURY

The process of colonial extraction from the late nineteenth century until the end of the British raj can only be fully comprehended in the context of the linking of regional agrarian economies to a capitalist world market. With the effective integration of the domains of land and capital, the broad features of the colonial political economy, especially the government's financial policies, had acquired greater potency and relevance than its revenue-extracting mechanism per se. The state continued, of course, to preside over a revenue and rent-collecting structure, but attempted to project an image of arbiter rather than appropriator through ambiguous interventions in landlord–tenant relations. The state's financial difficulties also led to the deeper penetration of its bureaucratic arms into local affairs, which occasionally elicited strong reactions from rural society against outside interference.

Credit, something that peasant labour both needed and resented, formed the nub of surplus-appropriating relationships at the primary level in this period. For moneylending talukdars and traders in east Bengal it was practically the only source of their control over peasant smallholders. The landlords of west Bengal combined their role as creditors and rentiers with substantial landholding in a demesne sector. The rich farmers of north Bengal interlaced the credit relationship with their control over land and the product market to dominate the labour of sharecroppers. The variations in the agrarian social structure opened the prospect of alternative political expressions of resistance. A major economic crisis, such as the great depression of 1930, severely damaged the networks of credit. Its impact was felt across the board, but mediated by varying social relationships it was experienced differently by peasant labour in different structural contexts.[34]

The diverse political articulations of resistance were shaped not simply by structural variations and possibilities but by peasant perceptions and assessments of these. A sensitivity to the question of peasant 'consciousness' is especially important in studying a phase of resistance for which the historiographical emphasis has been on the

[34] For a more elaborate substantiation of this argument see Sugata Bose, *Agrarian Bengal: Economy, Social Structure and Politics, 1919–1947* (Cambridge, 1986), chs. 6, 7 and 8.

theme of 'mobilization'. While illuminating the wider social connections and new organizational forms of struggle, the story of mobilization tends to obfuscate the subjecthood of the peasantry as political actors. Consciousness, on the other hand, can too easily be misconstrued as static collective mentalities from the distant past. Yet consciousness was not solely determined by the pre-existing bonds of community, but was constantly reformulated in response to changing historical contexts, even if mental conceptions of power relations did not exactly match the structural features of domination and resistance.[35] The interaction of social structures and mentalities shaped the composition, intensity, organization and ideology of a variety of major types of agrarian resistance in twentieth-century Bengal.

## The anti-moneylender breakthrough and the class–community dialectic in east Bengal

The tendency towards the assertion of a specifically Muslim self-consciousness among peasants of east Bengal in the late nineteenth and early twentieth centuries did not typically lead to overt political conflict. Indebted peasants were bound in unequal but symbiotic relationships with moneylending landlords and traders. The insensitivity to Muslim concerns and peasant imperatives on the part of the early nationalist mobilizers of the countryside during the Swadeshi movement resulted in a brief spell of rioting against mostly Hindu landlords and moneylenders in the districts of Mymensingh and Tippera in 1906–7.[36] This was the earliest instance of peasant jacquerie with its combination of class and communitarian concerns being at least partially overdetermined by the Muslim communal category

[35] Partha Chatterjee correctly emphasizes the particular importance of peasant consciousness in varying political articulations of protest. In outlining three principal 'modes of power', however, he appears to exaggerate the resilience of the 'communal' mode and the key role of pre-existing communal consciousness in peasant resistance in late colonial Bengal. His 'tentative and hypothetical comments' on modes of power under capitalism acknowledge 'the intrusion of new extractive mechanisms into the agrarian economy, often with the active legal and armed support of a colonial political authority, leading to a systematic commercialization of agriculture and the incorporation in varying degrees of the agrarian economy into a larger capitalist world market ...' The 'analytical problems' of characterizing the relations of production or state formations 'in these situations', according to him, are 'numerous' (Partha Chatterjee, 'More on Modes of Power and the Peasantry' in Ranajit Guha (ed.), *Subaltern Studies*, II (Delhi, 1983), pp. 346–8). The Bengal peasantry found itself involved in precisely one of these situations, which rendered the formation of a collective 'consciousness' far more complex and subject to recent change than the influence of its age-old communal heritage which Chatterjee tends to stress.

[36] Sumit Sarkar, *The Swadeshi Movement in Bengal, 1903–1908* (Calcutta, 1974), pp. 444–64.

newly invented by the British raj and being deployed to split up a broad nationalist front. After a stable period of economic boom between 1907 and 1913, the difficult years of the First World War saw the emergence of predominantly Muslim peasant political associations which made moderate demands for rent and debt remission as well as social respectability. The peasant discontents of the post-war slump of 1920–2 were successfully drawn into the wider non-cooperation movement orchestrated by the Indian National Congress. Peasants enthusiastically responded to the calls by nationalist leaders not to pay local taxes and occasionally went beyond the nationalist programme to resist the impositions of landlords and moneylenders.[37] Although the fate of the Khilafat in Turkey undoubtedly agitated the peasantry, the agitation, predominantly Muslim in composition, focussed more on economic issues than on religious ones. As the economy returned to a more even keel, the symbiosis in social relations ensured a phase of relative political quiescence in the east Bengal countryside.

At the first signs of weakness in the product market in 1926–7, the markets in the mofussil towns became sites of social conflict. This was a time when mass nationalism was in abeyance, and elite groups within both the Hindu and Muslim communities were arrayed against each other in the legislature and in the competition over white-collar jobs along the lines of communal categories defined by the colonial masters. So the Muslim attacks on Hindu religious festivals in east Bengal districts were not simply expressions of communitarian resistance against the cultural symbols of the power of landlords and traders, but were influenced by the communal antagonisms in the colonial arenas of organized politics.

The exploitative social symbiosis in the rural interior was not ruptured until 1930. The most severe crisis to date in the worldwide economic system of capitalism was reflected in the Bengal countryside in the form of a plunge in prices and a sharp contraction in monetary credit. Small trader-moneylenders and talukdar-moneylenders had no liquid cash to lend and the more substantial creditors withdrew from rural moneylending. The role of credit in seeing smallholding peasants through lean months and bad years had lent an element of reciprocity to an exploitative relationship. Now that the erstwhile mahajans rendered themselves redundant to the process of social reproduction,

[37] Rajat Ray, 'Masses in Politics: the Non-Cooperation Movement in Bengal 1920–1922' in *Indian Economic and Social History Review*, 11, 4 (1974), 343–410.

they lost their primary source of power in ordering social relations. With the dropping of the benevolent garb, the old deference on the part of peasants towards mahajans disappeared. Peasant debtors combined to refuse to pay interest, to repudiate their debt bonds but also initially to demand subsistence loans. The depth and length of the economic crisis of the 1930s meant that unlike earlier ruptures the tears in social relations were not repaired. During the 1930s and 1940s landlords who were reduced to their rentier role and traders who remained as grain-dealers rather than lenders were marked out as the targets of peasant resistance.

One of the earliest and more revealing of the anti-moneylender uprisings occurred in the Kishoreganj subdivision of Mymensingh district in July 1930.[38] The usual modality of protest was for large crowds of peasant debtors to surround the house of a moneylender and demand back the documents that recorded their debts. If the moneylender did not oblige, his house was looted and burnt. There was considerable debate among contemporaries whether Kishoreganj had witnessed a 'class battle' or a 'communal outbreak'. The evidence bears out the district magistrate's characterization of the disturbances as 'primarily economic'; moneylenders were clearly selected as the main targets. Most of the moneylenders were Hindus, but Muslim moneylenders had also received threats and the property belonging to the recalcitrant among them had been plundered. The importance of class in defining to a large extent the 'community' of resistance suggests that peasant protest had not yet been fully suborned by the predominantly urban brand of communalism.

This was in spite of the deliberate attempts by the colonial state to prevent Muslim discontents from being channelled into the broad stream of the civil disobedience movement and its willingness to turn a blind eye to Muslim attacks on predominantly Hindu economic and political interests. The Kishoreganj rioters were under the impression that they had been given carte blanche by the government and were somewhat bewildered when troops were sent in to stop disorder from careering out of control. The dying words of a victim of police shooting were: 'ami British governmenter proja, dohai British government' (I am a subject of the British government, have mercy on me).

The government was largely successful in limiting Muslim peasants'

[38] For a detailed analysis see Sugata Bose, 'The Roots of Communal Violence in Rural Bengal: a Study of the Kishoreganj Riots 1930' in *Modern Asian Studies*, 16, 3 (1982), 463–91.

participation in civil disobedience except in some districts, notably Tippera, where the peasant and Congress movements tended to coalesce. But even here peasant resistance acquired a greater degree of militance after Congress had called off the first phase of civil disobedience. One of the more radical peasant demonstations was organized in Comilla on the occasion of a visit by Subhas Bose in May 1931, a couple of months after the Gandhi–Irwin truce. Despite instances of convergence, the autonomy of radical peasant resistance from Congress-led mass nationalist campaigns has become clear from recent research on different regions of India.[39] Among the demands raised by krishak samitis (peasant associations) in Tippera were the limitation of debt interest, the reduction of union board taxes and free legal defence in rent suits. The success of the propaganda against payment of interest and rent to moneylender-landlords was attributed by local observers to the recent breakdown in credit relations. Krishak samiti meetings were often held near mosques on Fridays after Jumma prayers, but an indignant official complained that instead of 'the true spirit of Islam' only 'socialism of a wild nature' was advocated.

The government's repressive measures in 1932 drove both the nationalist and peasant movements underground, but resistance erupted between 1932 and 1935 in the form of 'dacoities', in which erstwhile talukdar- and trader-moneylenders were principal targets. The resumption of open politics following the passage of the Government of India Act of 1935 revealed the growing confidence and strength of the krishak samitis in east Bengal. On the eve of provincial elections in 1937 based on a greatly extended franchise, local krishak samitis began to forge provincewide connections. Specific demands for the scaling down of debts through the recently established debt settlement boards and revisions of the rental and land transfer arrangements in favour of peasants were now encapsulated within the generic call for 'the abolition of the zamindari system'. It was not uncommon to demand the abolition of zamindari and amendments to the Bengal Tenancy Act in the same breath, even though the acceptance of the former would have rendered the latter irrelevant.

When the Krishak Praja Party led by Fazlul Huq formed a coalition government with the Muslim League at the provincial level after the 1937 elections, it was compelled to renege on its election promise to

---

[39] Cf., for instance, Bose, *Agrarian Bengal*, ch. 6 and Gyanendra Pandey, *The Ascendancy of the Congress in Uttar Pradesh, 1926–34* (Delhi, 1978), chs. 3 and 6.

abolish the Permanent Settlement with the zamindars. It did, however, enact an important amendment to the Bengal Tenancy Act into law in 1938. Reversing the anti-tenant position it had taken in the late 1920s, the sizeable Congress opposition led by Sarat Chandra Bose in the Bengal legislature consistently attacked the government for not going far enough in protecting not only the raiyats but also the strata of the poor peasantry that did not enjoy raiyati status. Partly a matter of political strategy, it was also an index of the growing radicalization of a significant section of Bengal's urban-based intelligentsia.[40] Despite the efforts of left-wing Congress and communist workers, the KPP–League ministry managed to take much of the kudos in east Bengal districts for the 1938 amendment of the Tenancy Act, the work of debt settlement boards and the Bengal Moneylenders' Act of 1940.

The late 1930s also saw the linking of provincial Muslim politics with the specifically communal stance of the All-India Muslim League. Alignments along communal categories in the national- and provincial-level electoral arenas increasingly cast their imprimatur on the battle lines in the east Bengal countryside. Although communal riots in 1941 in the urban and rural areas of Dhaka led Fazlul Huq to distance himself from the Muslim League, privileged co-religionists were succeeding in directing Muslim peasant resistance into a communal mould.

Different historians have variously sought to explain the apparent lack of resistance and the 'fatalism' of the Bengali peasantry during the great famine of 1943. According to one view, 'fatalism' represented

the continued acceptance in a crisis of the very values which hitherto had sustained the victims: that submission to authority is the essence of order, and that men and women, adults and children, patrons and clients, rulers and ruled stand in different relations of necessity to the establishment of prosperity.

Seen in the context of a culturally specific construct of prosperity, 'fatalism' is interpreted as an 'active adaptation' in the minds of dying victims to the crisis of famine.[41] However, the long history of resistance by peasant labour up to the early stages of the 1943 famine and the resumption of struggle at the end of the war suggest that the absence of protest during the depths of the crisis is better explained in

[40] Bose, *Agrarian Bengal*, pp. 204–14; Partha Chatterjee, *Bengal 1920–1947: the Land Question* (Calcutta, 1984), pp. 172–82.
[41] Paul Greenough, *Prosperity and Misery in Modern Bengal: the Famine of 1943–44* (New York, 1982), pp. 270–1.

terms of the pulverizing physical and mental devastation brought on by large-scale mass starvation, the knowledge of the repressive capacity of the colonial state and the problems of political organization and leadership.[42]

It is in analysing the processes of abandonment by authoritative male decision-makers during the famine that arguments emphasizing economic, political and cultural factors can be woven together to provide new insights into the dilemmas of resistance. Abandonment occurred at the levels of the state, agrarian society and family. Failure on the part of the state to provide relief clearly stemmed more from economic misjudgement and political expediency than from a culturally determined decision not to play its projected paternalistic role. Rural elites failed to extend life-saving credit not simply as a matter of cultural choice not to fulfil 'traditional obligations' towards dependants deemed inessential to the reconstitution of prosperity, but because of the economic and political forces that had significantly altered social relations during the 1930s.

The point about a cultural ideal of prosperity being turned into an ideology of abandonment in a crisis has force at the level of the family. In innumerable instances male heads of household took the decision to break up the family. While some undoubtedly went in search of relief for their families, the evidence of gender and generational bias against women and children in famine victimization is compelling. Apart from receiving smaller shares of inadequate relief, many women were driven to prostitution and children were sold or left to die.[43] But here too cultural predilections cannot be divorced from economic and political imperatives. The conspicuous success of resistance by peasant labour since the mid nineteenth century, not only in Bengal but across much of India, had been the defence of the peasant smallholding. The struggle to hold on to this key means of entitlement to subsistence had entailed, as chapter 3 has shown, a hefty price and compromise in the form of everyday exploitation of women's and children's labour. The abandonment of women and children to death and destitution has to be seen in the context of the massive and unprecedented land alienation occasioned by the great famine of 1943.

During the period of war and famine, a populist faction of the

[42] Sugata Bose, 'Starvation amidst Plenty: the Making of Famine in Bengal, Honan and Tonkin, 1942–45' in *Modern Asian Studies*, 24, 4 (1990), especially pp. 724–7.
[43] See Greenough, *Prosperity and Misery*, chs. 4 and 5.

Muslim League led by Abul Hashim gained considerable ground among the peasantry of east Bengal and many former KPP workers assembled under the League's banner. The vague and undefined demand for a Pakistan came to encapsulate not only the Muslim demand for dignity and self-determination but also the economic aspirations of the peasant masses. When the final round of peasant resistance in pre-partition east Bengal took place in 1946, a Muslim League ministry was at the helm of the provincial government. Although the League did not directly instigate the riots that broke out in Tippera and Noakhali in October 1946, the disturbances had large implications for communal relations at all levels of politics. Food shortages and soaring prices were more important ingredients in the disaffections of the peasantry in Noakhali and Tippera than specifically Muslim political demands. In one village the governor of Bengal discovered that the shops of traders who 'had made fortunes in the 1943 famine' had been turned into 'a desolate ruin of charred timber and twisted corrugated iron sheets'.[44] But the presence of demobilized soldiers and the growing communalization of politics in the past decade meant that the 1946 riots were different from the uprisings of the early 1930s in at least two important ways. First, the attacks conducted in quasi-military style involved an unprecedented degree of personal violence including rapes of women unheard of before and, second, abductions and conversions to Islam figured prominently in the activities of the rioters. The Noakhali riots coming in the wake of the Great Calcutta Killings of August 1946 sowed deep apprehension among Hindus about their future in a Muslim-majority province claiming separate statehood.

The credit crisis of 1930 had snapped the bonds between a predominantly Hindu rural elite, who retained feeble rentier rights, and the bulk of the mostly Muslim smallholding peasantry. Peasants in a smallholding structure with as yet limited differentiation lived under common yet individually fragmented conditions of social and economic existence. Religious–communitarian identity under these circumstances imparted the social bases of solidarity to articulate class-based political demands. During the final decade of colonial rule the communalism of organized political arenas left deep imprints on peasant resistance and proved to be the lever which enabled upper-class Muslims to appropriate the fruits of agrarian struggles. The Hindu

[44] Cited in Bose, *Agrarian Bengal*, p. 227.

landlords and traders, redundant and on the defensive on the east Bengal rural scene since 1930, made their final exit in the years after the partition along religious lines in August 1947.

## The limits of agrarian nationalism in west Bengal

The generally stronger ties of dominance and dependence in the demesne labour–peasant smallholding complex that predominated in west Bengal were a major factor in the relatively muted nature of resistance by peasants and labourers. The landlords' control over demesne lands, credit and the product market meant that they possessed more diversified and resilient instruments of hegemony than their counterparts in east Bengal. Moreover, the existence of a structurally distinct class of landless labour and their employment on labour-deficient peasant holdings quite as much as on landlords' demesnes engendered significant conflicts of interest which undercut the potential for political alliances between smallholders and the landless against landlords and the rich-peasant class. The depression did not damage relations of dominance within the khamar sector, and it weakened peasant smallholders vis-à-vis demesne landlords. Rural west Bengal did witness some brief bursts of anti-colonial agitation which took the form of broad-based agrarian reaction against government interference in local affairs. But only in some exceptional areas, such as Midnapur, the Arambag subdivision in Hooghly and Burdwan in the late 1930s, did these acquire a high degree of fervour and intensity.

The Contai and Tamluk subdivisions in Midnapur formed a vibrant pocket of demographic and agricultural growth in a region in the grip of malarial decline in the decades leading to 1920. They also did not possess a separate reserve of landless labour although tribal peoples inhabited neighbouring subdivisions. A powerful Mahishya caste movement striving for upward mobility had at least in part lent local society a vertically segmented character. Contai and Tamluk were nearing the margins of extensive growth when the colonial state intervened with the Village Self-Government Act of 1919. It caused deep resentment among the smallholding peasantry since it entailed a 50% increase in the chaukidari tax. The Mahishya richer peasants as well as some of the landlords were faced with an option. They could either collaborate and control the new institutions of local self-government, or lead a mass agitation against their operation. As an historian of peasant resistance in southwest Bengal explains, 'Economic and social leadership had already passed into their hands; now by joining the anti-Union Board movement, they emerged as local political leaders of the new mass mobilisation.'[45] The withdrawal of the offending Act in December 1921 gave peasant nationalism in Midnapur its first confidence-boosting victory.

During three major waves of nationalist mass agitation in 1920–1, 1930–4 and 1942–4, rural Midnapur displayed remarkable multi-class solidarity against outside interference. In the intervening periods internal class conflicts surfaced but did not acquire very threatening proportions. This is a pattern that is also noticeable in some of the other classic examples of Gandhian mass nationalism, such as the recurring agitations by the upwardly mobile Patidar peasantry in Gujarat.[46] In the aftermath of the non-cooperation movement, some poor peasants and sharecroppers demanded better terms and complained that their more fortunate caste fellows were not following the ideals of Mahatma Gandhi. Those who held surplus land were unmoved and their representatives voted against a proposal to strengthen the rights of sharecroppers in 1928.

The issue of the salt tax and the burden of other revenue demands in a context of falling prices once again unified the Midnapur countryside against the bureaucratic arms of the colonial state in 1930. A local official in Tamluk wrote gloomily, 'The ordinary cultivator, even when reasoned with, simply squatted on his haunches and laughing sarcastically said, "We know how powerful the sirkar is ... we find the District Magistrate and the Additional District Magistrate coming round to us, villagers, begging us to pay our taxes."'[47] Seeing the futility of begging and unable to bear the taunts, the District Magistrate ordered the police to fire on crowds of anti-tax demonstrators. The resort to repression only provoked an outbreak of revolutionary terrorism in which three successive British district magistrates of Midnapur were assassinated.

The unity of the rural rebels gave way to internal class conflicts in the

[45] Hitesranjan Sanyal, 'Dakshin-Pashchim Banglay Jatiyatabadi Andolan II' ('Nationalist Movement in South-west Bengal') in *Chaturanga*, 38, 3 (October–December 1976), 198–9. See also Sanyal, 'Congress Movements in the Villages of Eastern Midnapore, 1921–1931' in Marc Gaborieau and Alice Thorner (eds.), *Asie du Sud: Traditions et Changements* (Paris, 1979), pp. 169–78.

[46] See David Hardiman, *Peasant Nationalists of Gujarat Kheda District 1917–1934* (Delhi, 1981); Jan Breman, *Of Peasants, Migrants and Paupers* (Delhi, 1985).

[47] Cited in Bose, *Agrarian Bengal*, p. 238.

interregnum in 1931 between the first and second phases of the civil disobedience movement, and continued to simmer throughout the late 1930s. Congress leaders tried at different times with varying degrees of success to arbitrate compromise solutions. Overall, the poor peasants and sharecroppers were able to win some concessions through a process of collective bargaining. Despite the inter-class tensions, Midnapur rural society reacted to the wartime interventions in the region's economy by the colonial state with another striking display of agrarian solidarity. The implementation of the 'denial policy', especially the removal of stocks of paddy from the coastal areas, was fiercely resisted. The Midnapur peasantry responded to the Congress call to launch the 'Quit India' movement with enthusiasm but worked out the modalities of the struggle through careful deliberation. On 29 September 1942 large crowds of peasants simultaneously attacked six police stations in the Contai and Tamluk subdivisions. A military counter-offensive by five companies of troops and the dislocations caused by a catastrophic cyclone in October 1942 were met with stoical resolve. By the end of the year the local Congress organizations had set up parallel administrations which requisitioned food for relief work, regulated the crop share between landholders and sharecroppers and prevented the export of paddy from the district.[48] The military might of the state and the onset of famine gradually broke the back of this movement of resistance during 1943. In peasant society's defence against the depredations of war and famine women resisted stubbornly and suffered disproportionately. In 1942 many women became targets of physical attack and rape by the army and police for punitive purposes; in 1943 they were victims of cold abandonment to the ravages of hunger.

Apart from Midnapur, agrarian nationalism scored successes in the Arambag subdivision of Hooghly during the non-cooperation and civil disobedience campaigns, and in Burdwan between 1936 and 1939 against an arbitrary and extraordinary increase in a canal tax. The tendency of class struggles within the peasantry to recede during the strong tides of multi-class nationalism has been sought to be explained in terms of the absence of 'an ideological transformation of peasant consciousness'.[49] At the same time structural constraints continued to

[48] For details see Bose, *Agrarian Bengal*, pp. 244–50.
[49] Partha Chatterjee, 'The Colonial State and Peasant Resistance in Bengal, 1920–1947' in *Past and Present*, 110 (February 1986), 169–204.

stifle the prospects of effective resistance in much of west Bengal. The tebhaga movement among sharecroppers for a two-thirds instead of a half share of the crop flared briefly in a small pocket of Tamluk in 1946–7 but soon lost strength. Elsewhere in west Bengal there was no bargadar agitation but, as a report from Burdwan pointed out, 'a movement amongst the landlords, jotdars and big cultivators against the proposed Tebhaga Bill'.[50] The dependent were easily cowed by threats of eviction and suspension of subsistence loans. The demesne lords and rich peasants crossed the threshold of independence with their power over peasant smallholders, sharecroppers and labourers substantially intact.

## Sharecroppers' agitations in the frontier regions

Until as late as 1939 one heard of 'no revolts of adhiars, or adhiar class consciousness' in north Bengal.[51] The impact of the world depression did not immediately rupture social ties as in the peasant smallholding structure of east Bengal, but nor did it clearly strengthen relations of dominance and dependence as in the peasant smallholding–demesne labour complex in west Bengal. Where rich farmers controlled large concentrations of jotes, grain loans were continued to dependent adhiars, but in cases of decentralized sharecropping grain redistribution was taken out of the orbit of credit and subjected to the rigid rules of the product market. In the southern delta, where reclamation was more recent, holders of lots dispossessed small peasants of raiyati rights, but in north Bengal there was no significant smallholding sector to prey upon. The jotedars, who had earlier monopolized the profits from the product market, had borne the major brunt of its collapse. Some of them were anxious to extricate themselves from their agrarian quandary and invest in the more promising sectors of the urban economy. So the slump loosened the stranglehold of the jotedars as creditors in the agrarian economy and set some of them to think about a shift away from the rural sector when the economic situation permitted it.

The first class-based adhiar challenge to jotedar dominance in north Bengal occurred in 1939–40 when land and crop prices were on the road to recovery. Adhiars who held relatively large operational

[50] Cited in Bose, *Agrarian Bengal*, p. 251. The Bargadars Bill was notified in the *Calcutta Gazette* by the provincial government on 22 January 1947 in response to the tebhaga agitation that was raging in north Bengal.
[51] F. O. Bell, *Dinajpur Settlement Report 1934–1940* (Calcutta, 1941), p. 22.

holdings led the movement demanding more direct access to the market and a larger share of the harvest. The agitation centred at first on the issue of tolls collected at hats or village marts by the jotedars. The demand for interest-free seed loans, a ceiling of 25% interest instead of the usual 50% on grain loans for subsistence and the abolition of all extra demands above the customary half share promised a bigger portion of the grain heap and drew the more indigent sharecroppers into the movement. The political leadership was provided by communist members of the krishak sabha, many of them détenus who had been recently released. Rajbansi and Muslim adhiars were arrayed against Rajbansi and Muslim jotedars. Haji Mohammad Danesh, a local lawyer and leader of the movement in Dinajpur, showed considerable skill in not permitting the communal categories of provincial politics to affect the character of this peasant agitation. The district magistrate of Dinajpur acknowledged that there was 'no communal question involved in this movement' and that '*the clash*' was '*really between the Adhiars and Jotedars*'.[52]

Adhiar–jotedar tension continued to simmer between 1941 and 1945, but the pro-communist krishak sabha refrained during the war from intervening in it. A major revolt erupted in the autumn of 1946 and reached its peak during the winter harvest of 1946–7. It was initially led by the bigger adhiars anxious to play the market during the post-war era of high agricultural prices, but the poorer adhiars were soon enthused by the call for tebhaga or a two-thirds share of the crop. The Bengal Provincial Krishak Sabha adopted the sharecroppers' programme once it had been launched, but sought to channel it against the more substantial jotedars. As the adhiars began to carry away the harvest to their own yards and fish collectively in jotedars' ponds, serious armed confrontations took place between the jotedars and the police on the one hand and the adhiars on the other. The poorly equipped adhiars put up a spirited resistance and upon hearing of the publication of a Bargadars Bill on 22 January 1947 disregarded the advice of the Krishak Sabha and broadened their attack to include all jotedars, big and small. This contributed to 'new social tension' and 'new complications'.[53] With a limited class and regional base of support, the adhiar agitation could not contend against the repression let loose by the police. The tebhaga movement, along with the

52 Cited in Bose, *Agrarian Bengal*, p. 259.
53 Sunil Sen, *Agrarian Struggle in Bengal, 1946–47* (Calcutta, 1972), pp. 49–50.

Telengana insurrection which began in 1946, are examples of how in structural situations of clear-cut class dichotomy a perceived weakening of landlord or rich-farmer resolve and uncertainties at the level of the state can provide the impulse for class-based agrarian revolts.[54] The class consciousness achieved in the process of struggle persisted in the post-independence period in these regions. For political radicals, tebhaga and telengana have been the faint glimmers of an Indian peasant revolution that was not to be.

## PEASANTS INTO CITIZENS?

When in 1947 the Krishak Sabha called off the tebhaga movement and agreed to give the new governments in India and Pakistan an opportunity to fulfil the hopes independence had roused, it was giving the 'bourgeois' states the benefit of the doubt that they would be able to assure equal citizenship rights for all their peoples. In formal terms India moved swiftly to establish a democratic political system based on universal adult franchise, while Pakistan (and since 1971 Bangladesh) faltered on its first uncertain steps towards representative government and slipped into lengthy spells of military dictatorship. Yet even the relatively successful democratic experiment in India created disharmonic social systems characterized by a lack of fit between rights enshrined in the constitution and the ability of members of disadvantaged groups to assert them.[55] Affirmative action in the form of reservations of seats in representative institutions for scheduled castes and tribes and agrarian reform designed to benefit the rural poor did not easily melt down the structures of domination. Agrarian resistance therefore made partial use of the 'bourgeois' political framework, but also articulated itself in agitations and revolts relying on the solidarities of class and community.

The departure of Hindu landlords and traders from east Bengal within a few years of the 1947 partition enabled the Muslim peasant elite to consolidate their position in the agrarian power structure by adding portfolios in trade and moneylending to their edge in landholding. But as long as the region was cast in the role of an internal agricultural colony whose earnings from jute exports were siphoned

[54] Cf. D. N. Dhanagare, 'Social Origins of the Peasant Insurrection in Telengana (1946–51)' in *Contributions to Indian Sociology*, 8 (1974).
[55] See André Beteille, *Studies in Agrarian Social Structure* (Delhi, 1974).

off by industry and the centralized state apparatus located in the western wing, the internal class contradictions did not come to the fore in peasant agitations. In the altered context of both the class configuration and the state structure, religion lost its force as a social basis of solidarity and a legitimizing ideology for agrarian resistance. As early as 1954, provincial elections recorded the demise of the Muslim League and the growing strength of the Awami League and the Krishak Sramik Party, which gave a regional and linguistic communitarian expression to disaffections of the urban intelligentsia and the peasantry.[56] It was this broad alliance which gave the agitation for provincial autonomy its potency in the 1960s and laid the foundation for the sweeping victory of the Awami League in East Pakistan in the first nationwide elections based on universal adult franchise in December 1970. The more class-based stance of the National Awami Party proved to have been out of tune with both structural imperatives and the level of peasant consciousness.

The weakness of class-based agitations, not to mention revolts, in post-partition east Bengal, stemmed partly from the disparate and fragmented nature of a predominantly smallholding structure in which religious and linguistic affiliations imparted a sense of community and defined the social bases of solidarity for effective resistance. In addition, the localization of politics under the auspices of a military–bureaucratic state between 1958 and 1971 and again from 1975 to 1991 bolstered the powers of patronage and social control of local peasant elites. Recognizing the crucial role played by the broad masses of the smallholding peasantry in the movement for independence, Sheikh Mujibur Rahman announced a package of populist economic measures and land reforms in 1972 including a presidential ordinance imposing a land ceiling of 33 acres. The half-hearted implementation of reforms, the failure to repair a war-torn economy and, finally, the famine of 1974 eroded support for the Awami League government before the military seized state power in 1975. The policies of two successive military regimes aimed at localizing political activity and privatizing the supply of key agricultural inputs successfully fractured the potential for supra-local class-based resistance.

By contrast with east Bengal and indeed much of the South Asian subcontinent, post-independence west Bengal has witnessed explicitly

---

[56] See A. H. Ahmed Kamal, 'Decline of the Muslim League in East Pakistan, 1947–54' (unpublished Ph.D. dissertation, Australian National University, 1989).

class-based articulation of resistance by peasant labour. An attempt made in 1948-9 to revive the tebhaga movement scored some local successes, especially in the Kakdwip area of the 24-Parganas, before it was firmly repressed. Mixing the hard reality of repression with a semblance of reform, the Congress government in West Bengal state passed the Bargadars Act of 1950, which legislated a statutory 60:40 share of the harvest for bargadars in place of the customary half. This provision was incorporated into the Land Reforms Act of 1955 which also provided for low land ceilings. Yet during the first two decades of independence the big raiyat category, which included landlords who lost their rent-collecting rights in 1953 but retained sizeable portions of their personal demesnes, as well as the richer peasants, retained a significant measure of dominance in the west Bengal countryside and provided the power base of conservative Congress governments. Land ceilings were effectively circumvented through false, benami registration of deeds in the names of family members and dependants. It was only in the late 1960s that communist-led land-grab movements eventually dented the dominance of the big raiyats and an electoral challenge by the leftist parties based on the support of the middling peasantry dislodged the Congress party from power.

Soon after the assumption of office by a United Front government appeared to suggest the weakening of the repressive capacity of the state, a class-based agrarian uprising took place in the northern part of west Bengal which caught the imagination of radicals far beyond the locale in which it occurred. The epicentre of the revolt was Naxalbari in the Siliguri subdivision of Darjeeling district. It began in March 1967 with the forcible dishoarding of jotedars' paddy stocks. By May 1967 the deeds and documents of jotedars were being burnt, their bullocks and implements seized and their land redistributed among the landless poor.[57] On 25 May several peasant rebels were killed in an incident of police firing, and on 10 June the first jotedar was assassinated. The revolt was led by local peasant committees formed by the extreme left wing of the Communist Party of India (Marxist), (C.P.I.(M)), a party whose mainstream was the chief constituent of the United Front government. The Chinese leader Mao Zedong hailed the Naxalbari uprising as 'a peal of spring thunder' of the Indian revolution; but, to mix Mao's favourite metaphors, it turned out to be one which failed to

[57] Kanu Sanyal, 'Report on the Peasant Movement in the Terai Region' in Samar Sen et al. (eds.), *Naxalbari and After*, Vol. II (Calcutta, 1978).

'spread like a prairie fire'. Even at its peak the revolt was confined to the three thanas of Naxalbari, Phansidewa and Khoribari, covering an area of less than 300 square miles and a population of approximately 150,000. It had the active involvement of perhaps 15,000 to 20,000 poor peasants. By the autumn of 1967 the Naxalbari uprising was crushed.

The Naxalite cause was taken up by radical students in urban centres including several belonging to Presidency College in Calcutta, who went out to preach the doctrine of annihilating the jotedar, the class enemy. The author of the annihilation policy was Charu Majumdar, who had served his apprenticeship in agrarian agitation in the north Bengal district of Jalpaiguri during the tebhaga movement of 1946–7 and who became in 1969 the chairman of the new Communist Party of India (Marxist–Leninist). Although the numbers of adhiars had dwindled and the numbers of landless labourers had swelled during the 1960s, north Bengal still possessed a sharply polarized agrarian class structure dominated by jotedars. Elsewhere the oppressive class enemy was not so easily distinguishable. Naxalite students had some success in organizing agrarian resistance in the tribal areas of Debra and Gopiballavpur in Midnapur and parts of Birbhum but, by and large, their message was rejected. Once the anticipated widespread agrarian revolution failed to materialize as the countryside refused to accept the declared policy of annihilating individual class enemies, the Naxalite movement degenerated into an erratic campaign of terrorism in the urban jungle of Calcutta. Elsewhere in India the Naxalites orchestrated a serious revolt in the Srikakulam area of Andhra Pradesh. More importantly, the Naxalbari uprising, limited though it was in its geographical spread, had a disproportionate impact on political psyches in India and helped stir a section of the ruling groups out of a sense of complacency. One sympathetic scholar has likened it to the 'pre-meditated throw of a pebble' designed to bring forth a series of ripples in placid waters.[58]

The Naxalites of Bengal, disowned by the mainstream leftist parties, were repressed by the coercive arms of the state by 1972. The C.P.I.(M), the principal constituent of the United Front, refrained from armed struggle of the Naxalite variety, but organized land-grab agitations during the late 1960s. In 1969 alone the central government noted 346 incidents of forcible occupation of benami land totalling

[58] Sumanta Banerjee, *India's Simmering Revolution: the Naxalite Uprising* (London, 1984), p. 92.

about 300,000 acres, mostly in the districts of 24-Parganas, Burdwan, Midnapur, West Dinajpur and Malda. The main centre of the C.P.I.(M)'s radical agrarian campaign in the late 1960s was the Sonarpur area in the southern part of the 24-Parganas, which exhibited a clear class dichotomy between jotedars and poor peasants.[59] Internecine conflict within the left paved the way for the return of the Congress party to power for five years through the rigged state elections of 1972 and dealt a temporary setback to the cause of peasant resistance.

Since 1977 the state of West Bengal has been governed by the Left Front led by the C.P.I.(M). It has followed a cautious but clearly class-based policy of consolidating its electoral power base in the rural areas among the middling peasantry including sharecroppers. Firmly entrenched in the elected panchayats or local governments from the village level upwards, the C.P.I.(M) has provided one of the most stable and at the same time moderately progressive state governments in independent India. But its repeated electoral successes have been achieved only by nurturing a peasant smallholder base of support and not delivering anything of substance of the poorest of the landless rural poor. In so doing the C.P.I.(M) has merely strengthened the middling peasantry's attachment to petty landed property. Its modest land redistribution programme amounted to little more than the redistribution of poverty. During the late 1970s the Left Front government loudly trumpeted its Operation Barga, a drive to record the names of sharecroppers. An amendment to the Land Reforms Act in 1970 had raised the crop-sharing ratio to 75:25 in favour of the sharecroppers and made their right to cultivation hereditary. Operation Barga, directed by the bureaucracy rather than peasant front organizations, was designed to enable sharecroppers to claim their statutory rights. The undue emphasis on sharecroppers, who constituted well under 10% of the rural workforce, did not threaten the smallholding middling peasantry and initially had a psychological demonstration effect on the landless agricultural labourers, contributing well over a third of the rural workforce, that some palliative reforms might come their way. But the failure of the government to supply inputs and credit through institutional channels perpetuated the dependent status of the landless khetmajurs. During the 1980s the C.P.I.(M) implemented

[59] See Swasti Mitter, *Peasant Movements in West Bengal: Their Impact on Agrarian Class Relations since 1967* (Cambridge, 1977).

food-for-work programmes for these labourers and launched localized and carefully controlled agitations for the implementation of the minimum wage legislation. Being ardent believers in the labour-intensive economic efficiency and political resource base represented by the smallholding middling peasantry, the C.P.I.(M) has not only attempted to keep political resistance by the landless labourers on leash but, applying the authoritarian organizational principle of democratic centralism, has kept its women's-front organizations firmly subord-inated. It has reinforced the patriarchical values of the landed strata and done nothing to alter the exploitative gender division of labour within peasant families. The C.P.I.(M) has 'flourished [electorally] by renouncing radical politics and women's liberation'.[60]

The greatest success of agrarian resistance over the past two centuries – the defence of the peasant smallholding – has until the closing decade of the twentieth century involved a measure of implicit complicity in domination along lines of gender and generation. The colonial era witnessed the effective dismantling of predominant relations of exploitation at particular historical conjunctures by the forces of resistance, for instance appropriation through the mechanisms of rent and debt in the 1880s and 1930s, respectively. The promise of an end to oppression through the institutionalization of equal citizenship rights in the post-colonial state system and political order has been redeemed at best very inadequately and imperfectly. If the trans-formation of peasants into citizens entails instilling 'a national view of things in regional minds' and a 'process by which the language, gestures and perceptions of national politics penetrate[s] the country-side',[61] this has been achieved by India's national project in the realm of rhetoric but not in reality. The building of the nation-state using some of the pillars of the colonial state did not turn subjects into citizens despite the extension of universal adult franchise. The dialectic between domination and resistance continues to be played out in India's differentiated agrarian regions along lines of clan, caste and community. These organizational and ideological affiliations are not of primordial origin but are linked in complex ways to historically changing class-based social relations of production and exploitation.

[60] Amrita Basu, 'Democratic Centralism and Decentered Democracy: Dilemmas of Women's Resistance in Contemporary India', paper presented at a conference on Democracy and Development in South Asia, Tufts University, April 1990.
[61] Eugen Weber, *Peasants into Frenchmen: the Modernization of Rural France* (Stanford, 1976), pp. 485–96.

In the Gramscian narrative of emancipation the 'concept of citizen' was to 'give way to the concept of comrade'.[62] In West Bengal a bold but tragic attempt was made in the late 1960s and the 1970s to reject the frustrating pursuit of the bourgeois version of individual citizenship and achieve the fraternal bonds of cameraderie that unite the disposs- essed. In the sobering aftermath of that struggle Bengal's peasant labourers have both exercised the right to vote and waved their red flags. They may well be a step ahead of their counterparts in most other parts of India but they are still far from enjoying the liberty and fraternity that would be their destiny if peasants did indeed achieve the full-blown rights of either equal citizens or comrades.

[62] Antonio Gramsci, *Selections from Political Writings 1910–1920* (New York, 1977), p. 100.

# CONCLUSION

An integrated analysis of the themes of demography, commercialization and agrarian social structure makes possible an assessment of their role as determinants of the direction and nature of socioeconomic change over the long term in colonial and post-colonial Bengal. Some of the conclusions to emerge have broader theoretical and comparative relevance.

Dramatic changes in the river system of rural Bengal should modify the belief of historians of the *longue durée* that geographical structures represent constants in historical time. While the Bengal delta may well have been prone to extraordinary ecological turbulence, recent research is making clear that colonial India as a whole was subjected to substantial environmental change in the nineteenth century largely as a result of human agency in the form of state interventions. Demographic trends set broad parameters within which rural production occurred, but showed no concordance with output after the mid nineteenth century. Even in the early phase it is important not to elevate correlations to the status of causal relationships. From the 1820s fluctuations in the wider economic systems cast a stronger influence on the regional agrarian economy than movements of population. Changes in prices and the availability of credit flowing from supra-regional economic systems based on capitalism had a significant bearing on even the subsistence concerns of peasant labour. Peasants who had resorted to cash-cropping were especially vulnerable to downturns and periodic crises in the world economy. Population increase generally provided a positive impulse to innovation in agricultural techniques but was blocked or aborted by social and political obstacles embedded in the complex layers of property and possessory rights to the land which underpinned the agrarian power structure.

The landlords who were granted property rights in revenue collection in 1793 were by and large divorced from possessory dominion over land. Some landlords, especially in west Bengal, however, came to control substantial amounts of khas khamar or personal demesne but many more, especially in east Bengal, held minimal khamar land and simply exercised the rent charge over raiyati land occupied and worked by peasant smallholders. Of the five major types of social organization of production identified in this volume – the peasant smallholding system, the demesne labour–smallholding complex, the rich farmer–sharecropper arrangement, the plantation and the tribal communitarian form – the first four displayed a remarkable degree of adaptability and resilience, despite processes of pauperization, the changing khamar–raiyati balance in favour of the former, and the structurally and temporally differentiated emergence of a peasant elite since the onset of the second century of colonial rule. A subtle but significant change also took place at the point of production along lines of gender and generation. The development of colonial capital resting heavily on peasant family labour meant the forcing up of the intensity of unpaid and underpaid women's and children's labour. The 'man with the plough' provides at best an incomplete image of peasant labour in the colonial context.

The colonial state, concerned with the stability of revenue receipts, armed the rentier landlords with considerable legal powers of extra-economic coercion which laid the foundations of a revenue and rent offensive during the first half of the nineteenth century. But the structural contradiction between property rights in revenue collection, and possessory rights as well as production based on peasant small-holdings, resulted in a tendential fall in the rate of rent in the late nineteenth century. The tendency was much more emphatic in the peasant smallholding system predominating in east Bengal, where the amount of landlords' personal demesne was extremely small. In much of west Bengal where the rentiers also held substantial demesne and controlled credit, rental rates continued higher and rental arrears were eventually consolidated under accounts of debt. The issue here is more complex than is captured in debates in European historiography over whether an economically determined fall in the rate of rent or the political balance of class forces has played a more important role in the decline of landlords' feudal power and the rise of agrarian capitalism. The historical experience of colonial Bengal and India as a whole suggests, first, that assumptions about the telos of capitalist transformation of production relations had best be avoided and, second, that differences in the nature and degree of the structural contradiction between large-scale property in revenue and small-scale possessory control and production based on peasant smallholdings imposed different sets of handicaps in the contest between rentier landlords and the working peasantry. In other words, the character of the material relations of production ensured that the outcome of the political struggle was not wholly indeterminate.

The waning of the offensive to extract surplus value through mechanisms of revenue and rent saw the colonial state worried about peace in the countryside and ready to gamble on expectations of 'improving' occupancy tenants rather than 'failed' improving landlords. Even before the passage of the landmark Bengal Tenancy Act of 1885 granting security of tenure and moderation of rent, the peasantry had resorted to expanded commodity production for the world market. Rentier landlords, who had proved too weak to surmount structural obstacles in the way of expanding demesnes when faced with falling rental rates, found a niche for themselves in jute-growing areas as usurers in the now predominant relations of surplus appropriation through the credit mechanism. The colonial rhetoric about the improving initiative of occupancy tenants was little more than an expression of pious hopes. The strengthening of tenant rights facilitated the process of twisting agrarian economy and society to an export orientation. But a formidable combination of problems concerning the public good, and social and political imperatives, meant that neither the colonial state nor the rentiers and creditors, nor even the working peasantry, played an effective role in accelerating the forces of production. Peasant labour clung on to the basic means of production – land – but became increasingly dependent on merchant and usury capital. Their labour capacity was effectively attached to enhance the dominating power of colonial capital. It is not that peasant labour did not resist. But an undercurrent of everyday resistance notwithstanding, the conditions of possibility of effective resistance that could dismantle the prevailing system of production, or at least break down the predominant mode of surplus appropriation, were opened up by contradictions within capitalism, resulting in crises in wider economic systems at the supra-regional level.

Once the initial handicaps imposed by the dialectic between property and production and the conditions of possibility created by contradictions within economic systems have been noted, one enters the explanatory domain where politics is master. This volume has considered at least two remarkable instances of effective resistance, which illustrate better than anything else the salience of alternative configurations of political forces as determinants of agrarian change. The first is the collapse of the system of indigo production in Bengal in 1860 and the second is the end of the creditor's heyday, especially in jute-producing east Bengal, in 1930.

Despite the same context of a general economic crisis which formed the background to the blue mutiny, indigo cultivation was virtually wiped out from Bengal while it further entrenched itself in neighbouring Bihar. The bulk of indigo was grown in Bengal on raiyati or peasant lands. The common opposition of peasants and landlords involved in credit operations in the rice sector ensured that the strenuous efforts by European indigo planters to increase nij or demesne lands at the expense of raiyati ended in decisive failure. In Bihar, by contrast, the alliance between the maliks' or landlords' power and the planters' money forced a massive expansion of indigo cultivation on zerat or demesne rather than assamewar or peasant lands.

The depression of the 1930s, the biggest cataclysm in world capitalism, also had a differential impact on various types of agrarian social formations. The bond-snapping character of the credit crisis was most acute in the highly monetized agrarian society of east Bengal, where zamindars and talukdars held distant and feeble rent-collecting rights over their peasant debtors. Peasant resistance effectively delivered the coup de grace to the principal relations of appropriation through debt. But since food also moved out of the orbit of the credit market into that of the product market, the full extent of small peasant vulnerability became clear later during the 1943 famine. Where a system of peasant smallholding–demesne labour predominated, as in west Bengal, continuance of grain loans in the demesne sector strengthened the ties of dependence while the smallholding sector suffering from low prices and the absence of monetary credit lost much ground to grasping demesne lords. There were further variations in the precise character and timing of the social impact of the worldwide economic crisis on the two other major types of agrarian structure – the plantation and the rich farmer–sharecropper formation.

The regional heritage of agrarian power structure occupies, therefore, a key location in the hierarchy of determinants that have shaped the process of change over the long term in colonial India, although other elements opened up conditions of possibility and established critical sets of handicaps. That legacy was also the rich cultural repository of an array of identities out of which peasant labour selected social bases of solidarity and created shifting communities and ideologies of resistance in their confrontation with the owners of land and colonial capital.

# BIBLIOGRAPHICAL ESSAY

## Introduction

Scholars of colonial India have long been entranced by the intractable problem of 'land tenure', and enamoured of the age-old institution of 'village communities'. While H. S. Maine provided the classical descriptive outline of the optical illusion of India's self-sufficient village communities in his *Village Communities in the East and West*, 3rd edn, London, 1879, B. H. Baden-Powell compiled a more hard-headed, if encyclopaedic, account of *The Land Systems of British India*, Oxford, 1892. A sophisticated early critique of the land systems established by the British was contained in Romesh C. Dutt, *Economic History of India*, Vol. II, *In the Victorian Age*, London, 1904, reprinted Delhi, 1960. The more intense of the late-nineteenth-century debates continued to provide the points of departure for the burgeoning scholarship on South Asian agrarian history in the 1970s and 1980s.

'The return of the peasant to South Asian history' was heralded in the title of Eric Stokes' final essay in an insightful twelve-essay collection *The Peasant and the Raj: Studies in agrarian society and peasant rebellion in colonial India*, Cambridge, 1978. Its publication marked roughly the midpoint of two extraordinarily productive decades in the publication of research monographs and articles on the agrarian and labour history of different regions of colonial India. Notable among the publications which contributed to broader debates about agrarian change under colonialism are Shahid Amin, *Sugarcane and Sugar in Gorakhpur*, Delhi, 1984; C. J. Baker, *An Indian Rural Economy: the Tamilnad Countryside, 1885–1955*, Oxford, 1984; Himadri Banerjee, *Agrarian Society of the Punjab, 1849–1901*, New Delhi, 1982; Crispin N. Bates, 'Regional Dependence and Rural Development in Central India: the Pivotal Role of Migrant Labour' in *Modern Asian Studies*, 19, 3 (1985), 573–92; Neeladri Bhattacharya, 'The Logic of Tenancy Cultivation: Central and South-east Punjab' in *Indian Economic and Social History Review*, 20, 2 (1983), 121–70; Sugata Bose, *Agrarian Bengal: Economy, Social Structure and Politics, 1919–1947*, Cambridge, 1986; Jan Breman, *Of Peasants, Migrants and Paupers: Rural Labour Circulation and Capitalist Production in West India*, Delhi, 1985; Dipesh Chakrabarti, *Rethinking Working-Class History: Bengal, 1890–1940*, Princeton, 1989; Neil Charlesworth, *Peasants and Imperial Rule: Agriculture and Agrarian Society in the Bombay Presidency, 1850–1935*, Cambridge, 1985; Partha Chatterjee, *Bengal: the Land Question, 1920–1947*, Calcutta, 1984; Binay Bhushan Chaudhuri, 'The Process of Depeasantization in Bengal and Bihar, 1885–1947' in *Indian Historical Review*, 2, 1 (1975), 105–65; Sumit Guha, *The Agrarian Economy of Bombay Deccan, 1818–1941*,

Delhi, 1985; Dharma Kumar, *Land and Caste in South India: Agricultural Labour in Madras Presidency in the Nineteenth Century*, Cambridge, 1965; David Ludden, *Peasant History in South India*, Princeton, 1985; Thomas R. Metcalf, *Land, Landlord and the British Raj: North India in the Nineteenth Century*, Berkeley, 1979; Gyan Prakash, *Bonded Histories: genealogies of labour servitude in colonial India*, Cambridge, 1990; Rajat and Ratna Ray, 'The Dynamics of Continuity in Rural Bengal under the British Imperium' in *Indian Economic and Social History Review*, 10, 2 (1973), 103–28; Ratnalekha Ray, *Change in Bengal Agrarian Society, 1750–1850*, Delhi, 1979; Asok Sen, Partha Chatterjee and Saugata Mukherji, *Perspectives in Social Science 2: Three Studies on the Agrarian Structure in Bengal, 1850–1947*, Delhi, 1982; Asiya Siddiqi, *Agrarian Change in a North Indian State: Uttar Pradesh, 1819–1833*, Oxford, 1973; Elizabeth Whitcombe, *Agrarian Conditions in Northern India: the United Provinces under British Rule, 1860–1900*, Berkeley, 1972; and Anand Yang, *The Limited Raj: Agrarian Relations in Colonial India, Saran District, 1793–1920*, Berkeley, 1989. Many of the differences of emphasis in these works on the relative importance of the contexts of revenue or credit relations, the 'primacy' of political or economic factors as determinants of agrarian change and the dialectic between material elements and culture/consciousness are addressed and critically evaluated in the text of this volume.

The research already under way by individual scholars on subordinated social groups including peasants and agricultural labourers was given a further impetus by the collective endeavour of Ranajit Guha (ed.), *Subaltern Studies*, Vols I to VI, Delhi, 1982–1991. Scholarship on peasants under colonial rule was also enriched by stimulating work on intermediate social groups between the state and agrarian society, notably C. A. Bayly, *Rulers, Townsmen and Bazaars: North Indian Society in the Age of British Expansion, 1770–1870* (Cambridge, 1983). There are resonances in modern South Asian history and historiography of several larger debates on the role of demography, commercialization and class structure in agrarian change, such as T. H. Aston and C. H. E. Philpin (eds.), *The Brenner Debate: Agrarian Class Structure and Economic Development in Pre-Industrial Europe*, Cambridge, 1985, especially the contributions of M. M. Postan and John Hatcher, Emmanuel Le Roy Ladurie, Robert Brenner and Guy Bois.

### 1 Ecology and demography

Recent scholarship on the agrarian history of South Asia has not been enriched by a close study of geographic structures. The best definitive works on the rural ecology of the Gangetic plain and the Bengal delta were written in the first half of this century. These include Birendra Nath Ganguli, *Trends of Population and Agriculture in the Ganges Valley*, London, 1938; Radha Kamal Mukerji, *The Changing Face of Bengal: a Study in Riverine Economy*, Calcutta, 1938; and S. C. Majumdar, *The Rivers of the Bengal Delta*, Calcutta, 1942. It is only in the past couple of years that a concern about environmental issues has begun to make its influence felt in the realm of economic history and political economy. The problem of floods in the Bengal delta has been addressed in James K. Boyce, 'The Political Economy of Flood Control in Bangladesh' in Sugata Bose and Ayesha Jalal (eds.), *Democracy and Development in South Asia* (forthcoming) and Shapan Adnan, *Floods, People and the Environment*, Dhaka, 1991.

The relationship between population and production from the mid eighteenth to mid nineteenth century has been the subject of enquiry of both contemporary reports and articles and more recent scholarly publications. Belonging to the former category are G. Campbell (ed.), *Extract from the Records of the India Office relating to Famines in India, 1769, 1788*, Calcutta, 1868; Report of the Amini Commission printed in R. B. Ramsbotham, *Studies in the Land Revenue History of Bengal, 1769–1787*, Calcutta, 1926; W. B. Bayley, 'Statistical View of the Population of Burdwan' in *Asiatick Researches*, 12 (1816); N. Alexander, 'On the Cultivation of Indigo' in *Transactions of the Agricultural and Horticultural Society of India*, 3 (1836); W. W. Hunter, *Annals of Rural Bengal*, reprinted Calcutta, 1975; and W. N. Lees, *The Land and Labour of India*, London, 1867. The more recent articles and monographs include Binay Bhushan Chaudhuri, 'Agricultural Growth in Bengal and Bihar: Growth of Cultivation since the Famine of 1770' in *Bengal Past and Present*, 95 (1976); Nikhil Sur, *Chhiattarer Manwantar o Sannyasi–Fakir Bidroha* [The Famine of 1770 and the Sannyasi–Fakir Rebellion], Calcutta, 1982; Aditi Nag Chowdhury-Zilli, *The Vagrant Peasant: Agrarian Distress and Desertion in Bengal, 1770–1830*, Wiesbaden, 1984; Ratnalekha Ray, *Change in Bengal Agrarian Society c. 1760–1850*, Delhi, 1979; and R. K. Gupta, *The Economic Life of a Bengal District: Birbhum 1770–1856*, Burdwan, 1984. For other regions of India the demographic dimension of agrarian production is treated in detail in Simon Commander, 'The Agrarian Economy of Northern India, 1800–80', unpublished Ph.D. dissertation, Cambridge, 1980; Sumit Guha, *The Agrarian Economy of the Bombay Deccan, 1818–1941*, Delhi, 1985; and Dharma Kumar, *Land and Caste in South India*, Cambridge, 1965.

From the late nineteenth century onwards, quantitative data on trends in demography and agricultural production are more abundant and reliable and can be gleaned from a range of official publications including census reports, district gazetteers and settlement reports. A useful survey of the latter half of the nineteenth century is available in Binay Chaudhuri, 'Agricultural Production in Bengal, 1850–1900: Co-existence of Decline and Growth' in *Bengal Past and Present* (1969). The problem of disease and mortality was investigated by C. A. Bentley in *Report on Malaria in Bengal*, Calcutta, 1916; *Malaria and Agriculture in Bengal*, Calcutta, 1925; and with S. R. Christophers in *The Causes of Blackwater Fever in the Duars*, Simla, 1908. A more recent article on this issue is Ira Klein, 'Malaria and Mortality in Bengal, 1840–1921' in *Indian Economic and Social History Review*, 9, 2 (1972), 132–60. Two important statistical studies of acreage, yield and output are George Blyn, *Agricultural Trends in India, 1890–1947*, Philadelphia, 1966, and M. M. Islam, *Bengal Agriculture 1920–1946: A Quantitative Study*, Cambridge, 1979. An early record of the building up of population pressure on land in the post-1920 period is contained in M. Azizul Hugue, *The Man behind the Plough*, Calcutta, 1939. There are numerous folk poems on the perils of migration, of which one particularly good example is M. Abdul Hamid, *Pater Kabita* [Verses on Jute], Juriya, Assam, 1930. The causes of twentieth-century famines and their demographic consequences are discussed in Amartya Sen, *Poverty and Famines: an Essay in Entitlement and Deprivation*, Oxford, 1981; Paul Greenough, *Prosperity and Misery in Modern Bengal: the Famine of 1943–44* (New York, 1982); M. Alamgir, *Famine in South Asia: Political Economy of Mass Starvation in Bangladesh*, Cambridge, MA, 1980; and Sugata Bose, 'Starvation amidst Plenty: the Making of Famine in Bengal, Honan and Tonkin, 1942–45' in *Modern Asian Studies* (1990). A powerful critique of Malthusian and neo-Malthusian fallacies is offered for the post-independence period in James K. Boyce, *Agrarian Impasse in Bengal: Institutional Constraints to Technological Change*, Oxford, 1987. The class and gender implications of a high-fertility regime in late-twentieth-century Bengal agriculture are analysed in Willem van Schendel and Aminul Haque Faraizi, *Rural Labourers in Bengal, 1880–1980*, Rotterdam, 1984; Mead Cain, 'The Economic Activities of Children in a Village in Bangladesh' in *Population and Development Review*, 3, 3 (1977), 201–27; Mead Cain et al., 'Class, Patriarchy and Women's Work in Bangladesh' in *Population and Development Review*, 5, 3 (1979), 405–38; Naila Kabeer, 'Gender Dimensions of Rural Poverty: analysis from Bangladesh' in *Journal of Peasant Studies*, (1991), 241–62; and Shapan Adnan, 'Conceptualising Fertility Trends in Peripheral Formations' in *Determinants of Fertility Trends: Theories Reexamined*, Liege, Belgium, 1983.

## 2 Commercialization and colonialism

A clear statement of the connection between the colonial revenue demand and the commercialization of Indian agriculture is to be found in Daniel and Alice Thorner, *Land and Labour in India*, Delhi, 1965. The price responsiveness of Indian agriculture has been examined in Dharm Narain, *The Impact of Price Movements on Selected Crops in India*, London, 1965. A recent comprehensive treatment of the theme of commercialization in different agrarian regions of India is available in K. N. Raj et al. (eds.), *Essays on the Commercialization of Indian Agriculture*, Delhi, 1985. Literature on the centrality of the subsistence ethic in peasant economic and political behaviour, especially James C. Scott, *The Moral Economy of the Peasant*, New Haven, 1976, has found resonances in studies of the process of commercialization in Indian agriculture.

The main lines of debate about colonialism and agrarian commerce within the 'mode of production' paradigm are captured in Hamza Alavi, 'India and the Colonial Mode of Production' in *Economic and Political Weekly*, 10 (1975), 1236–62; 'India: Transition from Feudalism to Colonial Capitalism' in *Journal of Contemporary Asia*, 10, 4 (1980), 359–98; and Jairus Banaji, 'Capitalist Domination and the Small Peasantry' in *Economic and Political*

*Weekly*, 12, 33 and 34 (1977), 1375–404. The argument about the incorporation of India in an expanding Europe-based capitalist world economy is put forward in Immanuel Wallerstein, 'The Incorporation of the Indian Subcontinent into the Capitalist World-Economy', mimeograph, Delhi, 1985. For critiques of the 'incorporation' thesis see the contributions of C. A. Bayly, David Ludden and David Washbrook in Sugata Bose (ed.), *South Asia and World Capitalism*, Delhi, 1990.

Agrarian commerce, especially the nature of the grain market, in the late eighteenth century, is discussed in Rajat Datta, 'Merchants and Peasants: A Study of the Local Trade in Grain in Late Eighteenth Century Bengal' in *Indian Economic and Social History Review*, 23, 4 (1986) and D. L. Curley, 'Rulers and Merchants in Late Eighteenth-Century Bengal', unpublished Ph.D. dissertation, Chicago, 1978. Commercialization during the first half of the nineteenth century with particular reference to the indigo and opium economies forms the subject matter of Benoy Chowdhury, *The Growth of Commercial Agriculture in Bengal* (Calcutta, 1967); Amales Tripathi, *Trade and Finance in the Bengal Presidency, 1793–1833*, Calcutta, 1979 and K. N. Chaudhuri's chapter on 'Foreign Trade and Balance of Payments' in Dharma Kumar (ed.), *The Cambridge Economic History of India*, Vol. II, Cambridge, 1983. The early phase of the jute economy in late-nineteenth-century Bengal is described in Hem Chandra Kar, *Report on the Cultivation of and Trade in Jute*, Calcutta, 1877, and Binay Bhushan Chaudhuri, 'Growth of Commercial Agriculture in Bengal, 1859–1885' in *Indian Economic and Social History Review*, 7, 2 (1970). The structure of colonial domination of Bengal's commercialized agriculture in the late nineteenth and early twentieth centuries is ably delineated in Rajat Ray, 'The Crisis of Bengal Agriculture – Dynamics of Immobility' in *Indian Economic and Social History Review*, 10, 3 (1973), 244–79. The 'forced' or compulsive character of commercialization is suggested in Saugata Mukherji, 'Imperialism in Action through a Mercantilist Function' in Barun De (ed.), *Essays in Honour of Professor Susobhan Sarkar*, Calcutta, 1974, and 'Some Aspects of Commercialisation of Agriculture in Eastern India, 1891–1938' in Asok Sen *et al.*, *Perspectives in Social Sciences 2: Three Studies in the Agrarian Structure in Bengal 1850–1947*, Calcutta, 1982. The connection between subsistence and the market, as well as the structure and trends in the jute and rice markets, are elucidated in Sugata Bose, *Agrarian Bengal: Economy, Social Structure and Politics, 1919–1947*, Cambridge, 1986. Another acute analysis of the jute economy is to be found in Omkar Goswami, 'The Peasant Economy of East and North Bengal in the 1930s' in *Indian Economic and Social History Review*, 21, 3 (1984). The tea economy is discussed in Sharit Bhowmick, *Class Formation in the Plantation System*, Delhi, 1981. Several rustic poems and pamphlets reflect the vicissitudes of participation in a cash-cropping economy, including Abed Ali Mian, *Desh Shanti* [Country Peace], Gantipara, Rangpur, 1925, and Abdul Samed Mian, *Krishak Boka* [The Foolish Peasant], Ahara, Mymensingh, 1921.

## 3 Property and production

British land revenue systems in general and the zamindari systems of property relations in particular have been the topics of numerous books and articles. The ideological debates surrounding the making of the Permanent Settlement are explored in Ranajit Guha, *A Rule of Property for Bengal*, Paris, 1963. Other broad surveys of the zamindari system include N. K. Sinha, *Economic History of Bengal*, 3 vols., Calcutta, 1956; Amit Bhaduri, 'The Evolution of Land Relations in Eastern India under British Rule' in *Indian Economic and Social History Review*, 13, 1 (1976), 45–58; and Abu Ahmed Abdullah, 'Landlord and Rich Peasant under the Permanent Settlement' in *Calcutta Historical Journal*, 4, 2 (1980), 89–154. Two works dispel many popular misconceptions about the early operation of the Permanent Settlement, especially the nature and extent of the circulation of property rights in revenue collection: Sirajul Islam, *The Permanent Settlement in Bengal: a Study of its Operation*, Dhaka, 1979 and Ratnalekha Ray, *Change in Bengal Agrarian Society, c. 1760–1850*, Delhi, 1979.

The 'continuity' of agrarian social structures under colonial rule and the importance of rich peasants within them have been matters which have spawned much debate and disagreement in modern South Asian history. Descriptive approaches emphasizing the theme of 'continuity' can be seen in Rajat and Ratna Ray, 'The Dynamics of Continuity in Rural Bengal under the British Imperium' in *Indian Economic and Social History Review*, 10, 2 (1973), 103–28 and Dharma Kumar, 'Land Ownership and Inequality in Madras Presidency' in *Indian Economic and Social History Review*, 12 (1975). This volume tries to identify the elements of qualitative change in structures that appeared to display enduring characteristics. The key role of the 'jotedar' (big farmer/rich peasant) is strongly argued in Rajat and Ratna Ray, 'Zamindars and Jotedars: A Study of Rural Politics in Bengal' in *Modern Asian Studies*, 9, 1 (1975), 81–102. The Ray articles draw heavily on Francis Buchanan-Hamilton, *A Geographical, Statistical and Historical Description (1808) of the District, a Zila of Dinajpur in the Province or Soubah of Bengal*, Calcutta, 1883 and 'Account of Rongopur', Eur. Mss. D75 (IOR). A critique of the 'jotedar' thesis as well as a typology of agrarian social structure in the first half of the twentieth century can be found in Sugata Bose, *Agrarian Bengal: Economy, Social Structure and Politics, 1919–1947*, Cambridge, 1986; reference may be made to its bibliography for a full listing of survey and settlement reports as well as official and non-official enquiries for this period. For the late eighteenth and the early nineteenth centuries the power of the zamindars and merchants rather than the jotedars has been stressed in Rajat Datta, 'Agricultural Production, Social Participation and Domination in Late Eighteenth-Century Bengal' in *Journal of Peasant Studies*, 17, 1 (1989), 68–113. Zamindari influence in the late nineteenth and early twentieth centuries is also highlighted in Akinobu Kawai, *'Landlords' and Imperial Rule: Change in Bengal Agrarian Society, c. 1885–1940*, Tokyo, 1986. Rajat Ray's reconsideration of his earlier position in the light of various critiques is stated in 'The Retreat of the Jotedars?' in *Indian Economic and Social History Review*, 25, 2 (1988).

The relationship between landlords, planters and peasants in the mid nineteenth century is explored in Chittabrata Palit, *Tensions in Bengal Rural Society*, Calcutta, 1975. Labour relations on tea plantations are investigated in Sharit Bhowmick, *Class Formation in the Plantation System*, New Delhi, 1981. Gender relations form a sadly under-researched aspect in agrarian history but two fascinating articles on this theme are Mukul Mukherjee, 'Impact of Modernization on Women's Occupations: a Case Study of the Rice-Husking Industry of Bengal' in *Indian Economic and Social History Review*, 20, 1 (1983) and M. Aitchi Reddy, 'Female Agricultural Labourers of Nellore, 1881–1981' in *Indian Economic and Social History Review*, 20, 1 (1983). Gender roles are illuminated in Tarashankar Bandyopadhyay's novels set in early twentieth-century rural Bengal: *Dhatridebata, Ganadebata o Panchagram* and *Hansuli Banker Upakatha*. Other significant contributions to the study of agrarian social structure in colonial Bengal include J. C. Jack, *Economic Life of a Bengal District*, Oxford, 1916; Ramkrishna Mukherjee, *Six Villages of Bengal*, Bombay, 1971; André Beteille, *Studies in Agrarian Social Structure*, Delhi, 1974; Shinkichi Taniguchi, 'The Structure of Agrarian Society in Northern Bengal', unpublished Ph.D. dissertation, Calcutta, 1977; and Binay Bhushan Chaudhuri, 'The Process of Depeasantization in Bengal and Bihar, 1885–1947' in *Indian Historical Review*, 3, 1 (1975), 105–65. Students of the late colonial era may also wish to note the difference of emphasis on revenue and rent relations, and credit relations, respectively, as the major colonial context in Partha Chatterjee, *Bengal: the Land Question, 1920–1947*, Calcutta, 1984, and Sugata Bose, *Agrarian Bengal: Economy, Social Structure and Politics, 1919–1947*, Cambridge, 1986.

There is a growing empirical and theoretical literature on agrarian social structure and peasant differentiation in the post-colonial era: Willem van Schendel, *Peasant Mobility: the Odds of Life in Rural Bangladesh*, Assen, 1982; Shapan Adnan, 'Peasant Production and Capitalist Development', unpublished Ph.D. dissertation, Cambridge, 1984; Kirsten Westergaard, *State and Rural Society in Bangladesh*, Copenhagen, 1985; T. Jannuzi and J. Peach, *Agrarian Structure in Bangladesh*, Boulder, 1980; Peter Bertocci, 'Structural Fragmentation and Peasant Classes in Bangladesh' in *Journal of Social Studies*, 5 (1979), 34–60; Shapan Adnan and H. Zillur Rahman, 'Peasant Classes and Land Mobility: Structural Reproduction and Change in Bangladesh' in *Bangladesh Historical Studies*, 3 (1978), 161–215; John Wood, 'Class Differentiation and Power in Bondokgram: the Minifundist Case' in M. Ameerul Huq (ed.), *Exploitation and the Rural Poor*, Comilla, 1978; Abu Ahmed Abdullah et al., 'Agrarian Structure and the IRDP: Preliminary Considerations' in *Bangladesh Development Studies*, 4, 2 (1976); Amit Bhaduri, 'A Study in Agricultural Backwardness under Semi-Feudalism' in *Economic Journal*, 83 (1973), 120–37; Ashok Rudra, 'Sharecropping Arrangements in West Bengal' in *Economic and Political Weekly*, 10, 39, Review of Agriculture (September 1975); and N. Bandyopadhyay, 'Causes of Sharp Increase in

BIBLIOGRAPHICAL ESSAY

Agricultural Labourers, 1961–1971: a Case Study of Social Existence Forms of Labour in North Bengal' in *Economic and Political Weekly*, Review of Agriculture (December 1977), A11–A126.

## 4 Appropriation and exploitation

The level and burden of the colonial land revenue demand in the nineteenth century have now exercised and agitated four generations of scholars and polemicists. The argument about the link between a high land revenue demand and late-nineteenth-century famines in Romesh C. Dutt, *The Economic History of India*, Vol. II, *In the Victorian Age*, London, 1904, elicited a recent rejoinder in Michelle Burge McAlpin, *Subject to Famine: Food Crises and Economic Change in Western India, 1860–1920*, Princeton, 1983. In a permanently settled region such as Bengal, where the revenue demand was fixed in perpetuity, the colonial state nevertheless played a role in the rent offensive of the nineteenth century and its waning by the close of the century. The story of rent in Bengal has been interpreted in a large number of books and journals: Sirajul Islam, *The Permanent Settlement in Bengal: a Study of its Operation, 1790–1819*, Dhaka, 1979, and *Rent and Raiyat: Society and Economy of Eastern Bengal, 1859–1928*, Dhaka, 1989; Aditee Nag Chowdhury-Zilly, *The Vagrant Peasant: Agrarian Distress and Desertion in Bengal, 1770–1830*, Wiesbaden, 1984; J. H. Harrington, *Minute and Draft of Regulation on the Rights of Ryots in Bengal*, Calcutta, 1827; Rammohan Roy, *Exposition*, Calcutta, 1832; Chittabrata Palit, *Tensions in Bengal Rural Society: Landlords, Planters and Colonial Rule, 1830–1860*, Calcutta, 1975; Nariaki Nakazato, 'Agrarian Structure in the Dhaka Division of Eastern Bengal, 1870–1905', unpublished Ph.D. thesis, Calcutta, 1985; Shinkichi Taniguchi, 'The Structure of Agrarian Society in North Bengal', unpublished Ph.D. thesis, Calcutta, 1977; Akinobu Kawai, '*Landlords' and Imperial Rule: Change in Bengal Agrarian Society, c. 1885–1940*, Tokyo, 1986; and Asok Sen, 'Agrarian Structure and Tenancy Laws in Bengal, 1850–1900' in Asok Sen, Partha Chatterjee and Saugata Mukherji, *Perspectives in Social Sciences 2: Three Studies on the Agrarian Structure in Bengal, 1850–1947*, Delhi, 1982.

Appropriation through the mechanism of credit and debt and its collapse during the Depression of the 1930s is analysed in Sugata Bose, *Agrarian Bengal: Economy, Social Structure and Politics, 1919–1947*, Cambridge, 1986. Insightful considerations of the debt question in other agrarian regions of India include Malcolm Lyall Darling, *The Punjab Peasant in Prosperity and Debt*, London, 1925, 1947, reprinted Delhi, 1978; Neeladri Bhattacharya, 'Lenders and Debtors: Punjab Countryside, 1880–1940' in *Studies in History*, I, 2 (1985); and C. J. Baker, *An Indian Rural Economy: the Tamilnad Countryside, 1885–1955*, Oxford, 1984.

The problem of land alienation in Bengal in the late 1930s and the 1940s has been studied in P. C. Mahalanobis, R. Mukherjee and A. Ghosh, 'A Sample Survey of the After-Effects of the Bengal Famine' in *Sankhya*, 7, 4 (1946), 337–400; K. M. Mukerji, *The Problems of Land Transfer*, Santiniketan, 1957;

193

and A. Ghosh and K. Dutt, *Development of Capitalist Relations in Agriculture*, Delhi, 1977. Relations of appropriation in the post-colonial period are studied in Willem van Schendel and Aminul Haque Faraizi, *Rural Labourers in Bengal*, Rotterdam, 1984; N. Krishnaji, 'Wages of Agricultural Labour' in *Economic and Political Weekly*, Review of Agriculture (September 1971); A. V. Jose, 'Agricultural Wages in India' in *Economic and Political Weekly* (25 June 1988); Amit Bhaduri, 'A Study in Agricultural Backwardness under Semi-Feudalism' in *Economic Journal*, 83 (1973), 120–37; Pranab Bardhan and Ashok Rudra, 'Interlinkage of Land, Labour and Credit Relations: an Analysis of Village Survey Data in East India' in *Economic and Political Weekly*, 13 (February 1978); Khoda Newaj and Ashok Rudra, 'Agrarian Transformation in a District of West Bengal' in *Economic and Political Weekly*, Review of Agriculture (September 1980); Pranab Bardhan and Ashok Rudra, 'Types of Labour Attachment in Agriculture: Results of a Survey in West Bengal, 1979' in *Economic and Political Weekly* (20 August 1980); John Harriss, 'Making Out on Limited Resources: or, What Happened to Semi-Feudalism in a Bengal District' (University of East Anglia mimeograph, 1979); and Shapan Adnan, *Annotation of Village Studies in Bangladesh and West Bengal: a Review of Socio-economic Trends over 1942–88*, Dhaka, 1990.

## 5 *Resistance and consciousness*

Peasant resistance in colonial India in general and Bengal in particular has been the theme on which there has been the most prolific historical writing in the past twenty-five years. The voluminous literature on late-eighteenth-century peasant revolts and early nineteenth-century communitarian peasant and tribal movements includes Ranajit Guha, *Elementary Aspects of Peasant Insurgency in Colonial India*, Delhi, 1983; Jamini Mohan Ghose, *Sanyasi and Fakir Raiders of Bengal*, Calcutta, 1901; Nikhil Sur, *Chhiattarer Manwantar o Sannyasi–Fakir Bidroha* [The 1770 Famine and the Sannyasi–Fakir Rebellion], Calcutta, 1982; Narahari Kaviraj, *A Peasant Uprising in Bengal, 1783*, New Delhi, 1972; Suprakash Ray, *Bharater Krishak-Bidroha o Ganatantrik Sangram* [India's Peasant Revolts and Democratic Struggles], Calcutta, 1972; Biharilal Sarkar, *Titu Mir*, Calcutta, 1981; Muinuddin Ahmad Khan, *History of the Fara'idi Movement in Bengal, 1818–1906*, Karachi, 1965; K. K. Datta, *Anti-British Plots and Movements before 1857*, Meerut, 1970 and B. B. Chaudhuri, *The Transformation of Rural Protest in Eastern India*, Waltair, 1979.

The indigo revolt has been analysed in Blair B. Kling, *The Blue Mutiny: the Indigo Disturbances in Bengal, 1859–1862*, Philadelphia, 1966, and Ranajit Guha, 'Neel Darpan: the Image of a Peasant Revolt in a Liberal Mirror' in *Journal of Peasant Studies*, 2, 1 (1974), 1–46. Works on the anti-rent agitations of the late nineteenth century include K. K. Sen Gupta, *Pabna Disturbances and the Politics of Rent, 1873–1885*, Calcutta, 1974; 'Agrarian Disturbances in 19th Century Bengal' in *Indian Economic and Social History Review*, 8, 192–212; B. B. Chaudhuri, 'Peasant Movements in Bengal, 1850–1900' in

*Nineteenth Century Studies*, Calcutta, 1973; 'The Story of a Peasant Revolt in a Bengal District' in *Bengal Past and Present* (July–December 1973), 220–78.

Caste and religious reform movements with a bearing on peasant consciousness are studied in Shekhar Bandyopadhyay, *Caste and Community in Nineteenth Century Bengal*, Calcutta, 1991; Rafiuddin Ahmed, *Bengal Muslims: the Redefinition of Identity, 1876–1906*, Delhi, 1982, and Asim Roy, *The Islamic Syncretistic Tradition in Bengal*, Princeton, 1983. On comparisons with Punjab see David Gilmartin, *Empire and Islam: Punjab and the Making of Pakistan*, Berkeley, 1989 and Ayesha Jalal, 'Post-Orientalist Blues: Cultural Fusions and Confusions' in *Indian Economic and Social History Review*, 27, 1 (1990), 111–18.

The nature of the links of peasant resistance to the broad currents of nationalism and communalism is addressed in Sugata Bose, *Agrarian Bengal: Economy, Social Structure and Politics, 1919–1947*, Cambridge, 1986; 'The Roots of Communal Violence in Rural Bengal: the Kishoreganj Disturbances of 1930' in *Modern Asian Studies*, 16, 3 (1982), 463–91; Partha Chatterjee, 'Agrarian Relations and Communalism in Bengal' in Ranajit Guha (ed.), *Subaltern Studies* 1, Delhi, 1982; 'More on Modes of Power and the Peasantry' in Ranajit Guha (ed.), *Subaltern Studies* 2, Delhi, 1983; 'The Colonial State and Peasant Resistance in Bengal, 1920–1947' in *Past and Present* (1984); Sumit Sarkar, *The Swadeshi Movement in Bengal, 1903–1908*, Calcutta, 1974; Rajat Ray, 'Masses in Politics: the Non-Co-operation Movement in Bengal 1920–22' in *Indian Economic and Social History Review*, 11, 4 (1974), 343–410; Hitesranjan Sanyal, 'Dakshin-Paschim Banglay Jatiyatabadi Andolan II' ['Nationalist Movement in Southwest Bengal'] in *Chaturanga*, 38, 3 (October–December 1976); 'Congress Movements in the Villages of Eastern Midnapore, 1921–1931' in Marc Gaborieu and Alice Thorner (eds.), *Asie du Sud: Traditions et Changements*, Paris, 1979. Sharecroppers' agitations have received special attention in Sunil Sen, *Agrarian Struggle in Bengal 1946–7*, Calcutta, 1972; Jnanabrata Bhattacharya, 'An Examination of Leadership Entry in Bengal Peasant Revolts, 1937–1947' in *Journal of Asian Studies*, 37, 4 (1978); and Adrienne Cooper, *Sharecropping and Sharecroppers' Struggles in Bengal 1930–1950*, Calcutta, 1988. Studies of agrarian resistance in postcolonial Bengal include A. H. Ahmed Kamal, 'Decline of the Muslim League in East Pakistan, 1947–54', unpublished Ph.D. dissertation, Australian National University, Canberra, 1989; Samar Sen et al. (eds.), *Naxalbari and After*, Calcutta, 1978; Sumanta Banerjee, *India's Simmering Revolution: the Naxalite Uprising*, London, 1984; Sankar Ghose, *The Naxalite Movement*, Calcutta, 1981; Swasti Mitter, *Peasant Movement in West Bengal*, Cambridge, 1977; and Amrita Basu, 'Democratic Centralism and Decentered Democracy: Dilemmas of Women's Resistance in Contemporary India', paper presented at a conference on Democracy and Development in South Asia, Tufts University, 1990.

Important general interpretations and case studies of peasant resistance and consciousness in other regions of colonial India include Eric Stokes, *The Peasant and the Raj*, Cambridge, 1978; *The Peasant Armed*, Oxford, 1985;

A. R. Desai (ed.), *Peasant Struggles in India*, Bombay, 1979; D. N. Dhana-gare, *Peasant Movements in India*, Delhi, 1983; David Hardiman, *Peasant Nationalists of Gujarat Kheda District 1917–1934*, Delhi, 1981; Jan Breman, *Of Peasants, Migrants and Paupers*, Delhi, 1985; Gyanendra Pandey, *The Ascendancy of the Congress in Uttar Pradesh, 1926–1934*, Delhi, 1978; and Ranajit Guha and Gayatri Chakravarty Spivak (eds.), *Selected Subaltern Studies*, New York, 1987.

# INDEX

# THE NEW CAMBRIDGE HISTORY OF INDIA

## I The Mughals and their Contemporaries

## II Indian States and the Transition to Colonialism

## III The Indian Empire and the Beginnings of Modern Society

## IV The Evolution of Contemporary India

* Already published
† Available in paperback